PRAISE FOR *Joy at Work*

"*Joy at Work* is a remarkable book about a remarkable company told by a remarkable man. For almost 20 years, AES defied most conventional management wisdom as it built a culture in which people were treated as adults, leaders were truly servant leaders, and fun was a core value that became actualized in the day-to-day lives of AES people, not something just hung on the wall to be talked about. The lessons of this journey are captured by Dennis Bakke in a brilliantly written, frank, and honest account of the ups and the downs. In a world in which fear often seems to have replaced fun, the search for profits has replaced the pursuit of purpose; conformity and following the crowd have replaced the courage to do the right thing and live by principles; and widespread corruption has replaced the conviction of ideals, this book offers both the recipe for a better way of organizing and being in an organization and the inspiration to try. Never has a book such as this been more needed, more important, or more welcome."

— **Jeffrey Pfeffer, professor of organizational behavior, Stanford Graduate School of Business**

"The idea of creating a workplace in which everyone maximizes his or her God-given potential and serves the community is a strong biblical principle. This book provides valuable ideas for leaders who wish to build or strengthen organizations using sound spiritual principles: service, integrity, and social responsibility. Dennis Bakke knows firsthand what it is to put these truths to work."

— **Chuck Colson, founder, Prison Fellowship Ministries**

"All leaders—and aspiring leaders—should read this provocative book. Writing from his own experience, Dennis Bakke turns conventional management thinking on its head. He's big on accountability, but his unorthodox views will shock most of today's corporate-governance gurus. And when did you last hear a CEO give himself less than straight A's on his published report card? Bakke is a committed Christian, but you don't have to share his religious views to appreciate his vision of leadership. *Joy at Work* is a joy to read."

> **— Lynn Sharp Paine, John G. McLean Professor,**
> **Harvard Business School**

"Dennis Bakke is one of the best examples of postmodern management, illustrating that the best way to do business is to create an organization in which both labor and management become joyfully self-actualized human beings. In this book he proves that it works. If you're looking for a model in which labor and management reach a respect and make work a fulfilling experience, look no further."

> **— Tony Campolo, professor emeritus of sociology,**
> **Eastern University**

"Dennis Bakke is widely known as an innovator in business and in the development of the people who make up the firm. In this book, he shares both the joys and some of the difficulties of walking the talk in the real world of the marketplace. It's a book that every leader in business should read."

> **— C. William Pollard, chairman emeritus,**
> **ServiceMaster**

"Dennis Bakke gives a riveting account, warts and all, of how he tried to practice what he preached. Anyone who believes that values are relevant to a publicly traded company will find this book provocative, challenging, and stimulating."

> **—Lord Brian Griffiths of Fforestfach, vice chairman,**
> **Goldman Sachs International**

"Finally! Here's a truth-telling CEO, with years of in-the-trenches experience, who practices what he preaches. Dennis Bakke thoughtfully dispels popular business myths, and he'll persuade you to think differently about your workplace. People are not "our most important asset." (People are people, not assets.) Customers are not always No. 1. (It's not that simple.) Gutsy CEOs will buy *Joy at Work* for every co-worker—and feed a revolution of joy in the workplace. Managers who thrive on power, prestige, and phony empowerment will hate this book. I hope *Joy at Work* becomes a movement."

— **John Pearson, president and CEO,**
Christian Management Association

"Dennis Bakke's exciting and provocative approach may be the answer. Getting extraordinary performance from 'ordinary' people has the potential to change organizations and even, perhaps, our society. It is worth pondering."

— **Walter Scott, professor of management,**
Kellogg School of Business

"I have espoused for many years that you should 'love your job,' but *Joy at Work* takes this concept much deeper. This book challenges the traditional organizational structure and the purpose of the organization. It's a must-read and will also challenge your thinking about better ways to run a business."

— **Roger Eigsti, former CEO and chairman,**
Safeco Corporation

"Not surprisingly, Dennis Bakke vaporizes the wall between 'secular' and sacred. His vision of leadership, hammered on the anvil of the highest level of corporate experience, is radically right for the church and the nonprofit world as well."

— **John Yates, rector,**
The Falls Church

"The beauty of Dennis Bakke's philosophy and approach is its humane simplicity. Dennis's fun and practical insights into creating and sustaining a joy-filled workplace come from his personal and shared journey of more than 20 years of hard-fought incubation and nurturing, trial and error, frustration and exhilaration, and ultimately failure and success at AES—in short, life. By sharing some of that journey, I felt the power and excitement of *Joy at Work*."

— **Barry Sharp, chief financial officer, AES**

"In *Joy at Work*, Dennis Bakke walks us through the tough, real-time dilemmas of a large, complex international business. It should be required reading for younger executives striving to balance success and significance."

— **J. McDonald Williams, chairman emeritus, Trammell Crow Company**

"Dennis Bakke's *Joy at Work* presents us the high vision of our daily work as a joyous, sacred calling. You will find his remarkable story inspiring and fascinating."

— **Howard E. Butt, Jr., vice chairman, HE Butt Grocery Company**

"Dennis Bakke has written a totally helpful book, and not only for business types. As a pastor, I was deeply challenged by the holy realism and enduring hope in spite of human setbacks. The principles approach is as wise as it is concrete. I recommend this book."

— **Earl F. Palmer, senior pastor, University Presbyterian Church**

"Dennis Bakke reminds us that no matter the role, whether it be manager or employee, coach, star, or backup, it is getting to make decisions that makes work fun! Out of all the books I've read on leadership, few have been as powerful as *Joy at Work*."

— **Trent Dilfer, Super Bowl champion quarterback**

Joy at Work

JOY
AT
WORK

A Revolutionary Approach
to Fun on the Job

DENNIS W. BAKKE

PVG

www.dennisbakke.com

P V G
P.O. Box 70525
Seattle, WA 98127-0525
U.S.A.

This book may be purchased for educational, business,
or sales promotional use. For more information, please visit
www.DennisBakke.com

Project editor	Stephen Smith
Cover design & graphics	Greg Pearson
Page layout	Tracy Cutchlow
Back cover photograph	Margaret Bakke
Flap photograph	Cade Martin
Copy editing	James Bock

Library of Congress Cataloging-in-Publication Data
Bakke, Dennis W. (Dennis W), 1945-
Joy at work: a revolutionary approach to fun on the job/Dennis Bakke. – 1st ed.
p. cm.
Includes bibliographical references and index.
ISBN: 0-9762686-0-4 (hc)
1. Leadership. 2. Organizational change. 3. Strategic planning. 1. Title
Library of Congress Control Number: 2004116572

To my mother, Ruth Hawkinson Bakke,
who taught me how to work

To Eileen Harvey Bakke, who walked with me
every step of the journey

To Dave McMillen, who used my theories
to help build a workplace filled with joy

CONTENTS

A NOTE ABOUT THE COVER

"THIS IS JUST LIKE AES!" exclaimed my then-12-year-old son, Peter, as I arrived home. He had presented me with a rubber-band ball that he and his sister, Margaret, had proudly created. "See all the different colors and sizes of rubber bands; they represent all the different abilities and cultures of AES people." (He had visited AES businesses in Argentina, Brazil, England, Hungary, Pakistan, Uganda, and the United States).

He then bounced the ball off the kitchen floor. "Dad, it does what it's supposed to do. It bounces." Peter took one of the rubber bands off the ball and threw it on the floor. "You see, it doesn't bounce by itself. It only works when the rubber band is stretched around all the other rubber bands. That makes it bounce."

I was amazed by and proud of his insight. He had captured much of the essence of what I was trying to create at AES: a group of people from different cultural backgrounds, with unique talents, skills, and aspirations, stretched and bound together to serve the world.

Principles are the bottom line.

———————— ✦ ————————

PREFACE

My passion is to make work exciting, rewarding, stimulating, and enjoyable. Most books on organizational life and work focus on top executives and the strategies they use to guide their organizations to success, which is usually defined by financial results. This book is aimed primarily at the working life of the other 90 to 95 percent of people in large organizations. While economic success is also an important goal for them and their companies, the meaning of success goes far beyond the bottom line. For them, the crucial measure of success is the quality of their work lives.

I have had the good fortune to help thousands of people find joy at work. My dream, perhaps quixotic but worth every last ounce of my energy, is to spread this joy to businesses and other organizations large and small. (See Appendix A for an overview of my approach.)

This is a book that celebrates the feelings of fulfillment that can be found in a humane and enlightened workplace. This sort of workplace does not preclude economic success. Indeed, there is ample evidence that a joy-filled workplace improves financial performance. But this is *not* a how-to book for executives looking to improve their stock price or beat the competition. This is a book for people who want more from their jobs than a paycheck and a benefits package.

This book is for you if you are:

Stuck in a miserable job but motivated to do something about it. You are creative, capable, and responsible, and you desire a greater opportunity to use your talents and skills. A place just to make money is not good enough for you.

A student in a management or leadership program who is not yet intoxicated by the exercise of power over people in the workplace. You are open to an alternative view of leadership, a different sort of workplace, and a new definition of success for the organizations that you will one day lead.

A high school or college student who wants to earn a living and have fun at the same time, in a way that is compatible with your values and beliefs.

A mid-level manager who feels trapped by a top-down, highly centralized organization. You know that your company is inhospitable to a values-based approach, but you are willing to suggest radical changes, even though you may be putting your job on the line.

A government, business, nonprofit, or educational leader who appreciates the personal qualities of your colleagues and sees them as more than robots performing designated tasks. You seek a workplace that honors their talents and encourages them to strive.

A president, director, or CEO who would be open to a different organizational model if it would bring joy to workers while still allowing your organization to achieve important business goals.

A scholar, researcher, or writer who understands, in your heart, the values and virtues of a joy-filled workplace. You need the courage to resist the blandishments—book contracts, consulting work, high-paying jobs—that are routinely offered to people who preach ruthless efficiency and unstinting pursuit of profits.

A priest, pastor, imam, or rabbi who is looking for a better way to understand and explain the relationship between faith and the jobs where congregants spend much of their time.

The idea of writing about the philosophy described in *Joy at Work* originated in the mid-1990s. I was CEO of AES, an energy company that by 2002 had plants in 31 countries, $8.6 billion in revenue, $33.7 billion in assets, and 40,000 AES people. In a dozen years of operations, we had developed a highly unconventional workplace culture and also achieved enviable financial results.

Several family members, some close friends, a few business associates, and numerous students who persevered through my lectures suggested that I start putting what I was learning at AES in some publishable form. Joel Fleishman, distinguished professor of public policy at Duke University, was the most persistent, even offering to hire someone to follow me around to my lectures and write the book for me.

I kept putting people off. "Maybe someday," I would say, or "I'm too busy being a CEO, husband, and father," or "I'm not sure there is enough here for a book."

While these excuses were at least partially true, fear of failure was probably the biggest roadblock. I knew that writing was difficult for me, especially writing something that was fresh and interesting—and perhaps even transforming, if I could put my thoughts and beliefs on paper in a clear and convincing way. Most authors writing about business topics say, in effect, "I did it, and here's how you can, too." This is not my purpose. I feel confident that I am on the right path, but I know I am still far from my destination. This book is an extended argument for a simple proposition: The workplace should be fun and fulfilling.

The case I make lacks the precision of science and the airtight logic of law. Instead, it is built on passion, experience, and common sense. These are the emotional and mental tools that guide us in our everyday lives.

Many people have been on this journey with me. My brilliant and loving wife, my children, other family members, AES colleagues, and friends have provided insights, wisdom, and encouragement.

Despite their support and guidance, I still make mistakes in plotting my route and staying on course. Undoubtedly, some of these errors have crept into this book.

I am not a master of philosophy, theology, psychology, or sociology, but my wanderings have taken me into the territory of each. My lack of a thorough grounding in these disciplines made it necessary to lead the AES Corporation in a way that was best described by my colleague Tom Tribone (one of our most creative developers of new business): "We try it out in practice and then see if it works in theory." Much of what might sound like theory or philosophy in this book is the product of trial and error.

I plan to write only one book, and I'm going to lay out everything I know. This is it. As my college football coach always said before each game, "Leave everything on the field."

My brother Ray, author of several books on the urban church, often reminds folks in his writings and sermons that "a point of view" is really "a view from a point." I have tried to write this book from the perspective of a God-centered world rather than a human-centered world, which is the vantage point of many of our nation's leaders in business, government, and academia. (See "Enter Into the Master's Joy," the postscript of this book, for a discussion of my faith journey and its effect on my views of the workplace.)

My understanding of work, business, and life is colored by my early years in the picturesque, isolated Nooksack Valley at the foot of Mount Baker in Washington state. The nearest small town was 30 miles away. All four of my grandparents had immigrated to Washington from Norway early in the 20th century. My dad never went to college. He went from job to job as a day laborer in construction or logging. He was a lifetime union member, a source of great pride to him. During most of my formative years, he was forced to leave home for six to seven months each year to find work in Alaska.

Seldom was he able to take home more than a few thousand dollars a year during the 1950s and early 1960s. My mom ended her formal schooling in 10th grade after her father died. Like my parents, none of my aunts and uncles went to college.

In the spring of my senior year at the University of Puget Sound in Tacoma, Washington, I phoned my dad to get his blessing on my choice of graduate schools. I had gone to UPS primarily because the school gave me a bigger scholarship to play football and basketball than others did for academics. I am sure he thought that four years of college was enough—and that it was time to get to work. But he was gracious enough not to raise that issue.

"Where are you thinking about going?" he asked.

"The Harvard Business School," I answered.

There was a pause on the phone.

"Where's that?" he asked.

"In Boston," I replied.

After another extended pause, he said, "I don't recommend you do it, Denny. It's very far away, and I have never heard of it. It can't be a very good school." Needless to say, this story has been well received at my lectures over the years at places like Stanford, Michigan, Georgetown, and the Kellogg School at Northwestern. It is also strong evidence of my early isolation from the centers of higher education that have had such a powerful influence on the philosophy of business, organizations, and marketplaces. In intellectual terms, I entered graduate school as a blank slate, open to new ideas and unencumbered by the intellectual complacency that afflicts many undergraduates at Ivy League schools.

There is a disturbing preoccupation with economics in our world. We often calculate our worth as individuals by the salary we receive or our net worth. "It's the economy, stupid!" reminds us that our government and its leaders are judged more on economics than on principles. Not surprisingly, the same belief that "economics is king" also drives most business organizations. I believe that economics is important for individuals, organizations, and nations.

However, it is only one element of a healthy life and far from the most important one. On my bookshelves are more than 100 volumes about businesses and organizations. Most of them attempt to make a case for a particular set of values, principles, and strategies that will help organizations achieve financial success, grow, and sustain themselves over a long period of time. They contain mountains of useful information about how to lead organizations. But most are deficient in one major respect: They don't define the ultimate purpose of an enterprise.

The principles and purposes that I espouse are meant to be ends in and of themselves, not techniques to create value for shareholders or to reach other financial goals. Some critics may discount my views because the AES stock price has fallen precipitously from its heights of 1999 and 2000. To dismiss my views on these grounds ignores three fundamental points: First, the workplace values that I advocate took AES to a lofty share price in the first place. Second, external factors—notably the Enron scandal and the California blackouts—clobbered the stock price of most energy companies, regardless of whether they were involved in the difficulties that beset the industry (AES was not). Third, and by far most important, the principles embraced by AES stand on their own merits whatever the company's share price.

Winning, especially winning financially, is a second-order goal at best. Working according to certain timeless, true, and transcendent values and principles should be our ambition. A major point of this book is to suggest a broader definition of organizational performance and success, one that gives high priority to a workplace that is filled with joy for ordinary working people. Such a place gives all workers an opportunity to make important decisions and take significant actions using their gifts and skills to the utmost. Our experience at AES showed that this kind of workplace can be the cornerstone of an organization that is vibrant and economically robust.

*A joy-filled workplace gives people the freedom
to use their talents and skills for the benefit of society,
without being crushed or controlled by autocratic supervisors.*

CHAPTER 1

My Introduction to Work

KENNY WAS A bright-eyed, smallish 2-year-old with an ugly scar and
a slightly deformed face. He and his two older sisters had come to
live as foster children at the Bakke home in Saxon, Washington, a
few months earlier. They had been "temporarily" taken away from
their parents by the county welfare department and placed in our
family's care for an indefinite period of time.

On this particular day, my mother had organized the evening
work in her usual style. The kitchen was abuzz with activity. I was
16 years old and charged with cooking creamed peas for supper. My
younger brother was carrying wood from the shed to the storage
area next to the kitchen. Kenny's older sisters were clearing dirty
cooking dishes and setting the table with dinnerware. Mom was
overseeing all of this as she swept the floor and kept an eye on the
homemade ice cream being churned. No one was paying attention
to Kenny, who watched the work scene in front of him while running his matchbox car back and forth across his highchair tray. Suddenly, the 2-year-old threw his car on the floor and picked up the
spoon on his tray. "I want jobs, I want jobs, I want jobs," he chanted
as he pounded his spoon.

I think this little guy with a crooked smile and troubled past
was saying, "I want to contribute. I can make a difference. I want

to be a part of the team. I'm somebody. I want to have fun working, too!" Over the years, I have reflected on this moment and come to believe that it captures the early and substantial influence Mom had on my concept of fun in the workplace. Somehow, she created an environment in which everyone was energized, not from fear of punishment or promise of rewards but from a desire to accomplish something positive. She had unbridled confidence in our ability to accomplish the tasks at hand. I can think of few things she didn't believe we could achieve, even at an early age. She gave us enormous freedom to work and make decisions. Somehow she made work so attractive that even an abused 2-year-old wanted desperately to pitch in for the sheer joy and excitement of it.

Like a lot of rural families with immigrant roots, we knew about work. My first regular job outside the home was as a 5-year-old when my grandfather hired me to chase the cows home to the barn each evening for milking. Looking back, I marvel at the skills I acquired while performing this job. I learned the importance of time, because I had to leave my house precisely at 5 p.m. to scour more than 180 acres of fields and woodlands and a mile of riverfront to round up the cows. I learned that they would gather in different places during rain, cold, or summer heat. I learned how to cope with darkness because it arrived at 4:30 p.m. during winter on the 49th parallel. I gained my initial understanding of stewardship—a concept that would become central to my life and that I will explain later in this book—when I was required to put 5 cents of the 50 cents a week I earned into the offering at church on Sunday. I voluntarily put the rest in my piggy bank. When the bank was full, I used the contents to buy government savings bonds.

When I was 7, I drove the tractor that lifted hay bales from the loaded wagons coming from my grandfather's fields into the barn mow. This was exciting because of the pressure involved in stopping the tractor at precisely the right moment so that the bales would fall in the part of the barn where they were to be stacked.

For 10 years after I turned 6, I also picked strawberries for 25 to

30 consecutive days every June and July. When that season came to an end, my family and I would harvest raspberries, blueberries, and hay at local farms. In all of these endeavors, I had significant control of how fast I worked and how much time I spent on the job. I knew at the end of each day how good or bad my performance was.

The first "manufactured" goods I produced were bundles of kindling that my brother Lowell and I cut from old cedar logs. We sold them to relatives and their neighbors who lived in faraway Seattle. This experience taught me not only how to use an ax and a power saw but also how to package a product and how to price it for the marketplace.

When I was 13, my Uncle Aadne, who lived on the farm next door, gave me a young steer to raise. I sold it back to him 18 months later and used the money to start my own cattle business. Uncle Ralph from San Francisco invested over $800 in my purchase of eight Hereford heifers, the beginning of a herd that would reach 29 head of cattle by the time I left home for college. Unfortunately, this financially successful business ended abruptly when my mom phoned me at college to say that the cows had broken through the fences into the neighbors' property "one too many times." She had sent the entire herd to be sold at the regional auction barn.

These early work experiences were more important to my later understanding of the workplace and business than my formal schooling, including the two wonderful years I spent at Harvard Business School. In fact, I don't recall the words "fun" and "work" being mentioned in the same breath during my time at Harvard.

Also crucial to my sense of what makes a workplace fun (or not so fun) were the six years (1970–76) I spent in the federal government—first at the Department of Health, Education, and Welfare, then in the Office of Management and Budget, and later at the newly formed Federal Energy Administration. It was during those years that I learned that having a purpose made work meaningful. I also came to understand the destructive tyranny of most central staff operations. For people who did not have the privilege of working in those central offices, the workplace was seldom rewarding or fun.

One of the most productive and exciting hours of my life was a car trip from Annapolis, Maryland, to Washington, D.C., in 1980 with Roger Sant, AES co-founder and my extraordinary business partner for over 20 years. Roger is the finest business strategist I have ever known. Without him, AES would never have come into existence or survived past the first few years. My gratitude to this remarkable person cannot be exaggerated. His great gift to me was providing the freedom to develop and implement the ideas in this book. He also graciously granted me the title of co-founder, although I was not deserving of the equal status this designation implied. Roger started the company; I helped. Few board members, even those who joined long after the company began, believed the co-founder premise. "Roger and the kids" was the way one board member put it.

We were returning from a conference where we had just decided to end the work of the Energy Productivity Center at Carnegie Mellon Institute (a research arm of Carnegie Mellon University), where I worked from 1977 to 1981. During the drive, we outlined our dream for a new company that would become Applied Energy Services, Inc. (later the AES Corporation and finally AES, The Global Power Company). As I recall, the only reference to the eventual values and principles of AES during that conversation was Roger's comment as he dropped me off at my house: "And let's make it fun."

The business logic of the company was outlined in a study that grew out of the work Roger and I did at the Mellon Institute. (In 1984, the study was published as a book, *Creating Abundance: The Least Cost Energy Strategy*.) Our premise was that if the generation of electricity was not owned or regulated by the government, the competition among private owners would reduce prices to consumers and improve efficiencies and service. We launched the company in January 1982 with a bank loan of $60,000, which we personally guaranteed, and a million dollars from investors, including a few family members. (For a thumbnail history of the company, see Appendix A.)

A year after starting AES, Roger and I were returning from a frustrating visit in Los Angeles with the ARCO Corporation (later BP/Amoco). AES had an agreement with one of ARCO's largest operating divisions to build and finance a new electricity-producing cogeneration facility at its Houston refinery. Our approach was fairly new at the time. We proposed to obtain financing for the facility without making ARCO responsible for any of the $181 million required. The ARCO treasury department (a typical staff department found in most large organizations) did not agree and would not allow the ARCO operating group to proceed with the project. "You can never do what you are proposing. It will never work," was the response of some of the junior and senior treasury staffers at ARCO headquarters. They seemed to be saying, "We know all there is to know about financing and we are in charge here."

At the time, ARCO was widely respected both inside and outside the oil industry as one of the most progressive and well-managed companies in the world. To me, however, ARCO seemed no different than the bureaucracy I had seen in the federal government. It had layers of hierarchy, and important decision making was the purview of a few senior people. Young, smart people in staff offices ran roughshod over executives with line responsibility for creating and running the businesses. It took over a year to persuade them to change their minds and get on with the project. The plant was eventually financed as we had proposed.

I asked Roger a rhetorical question: "Are ARCO and other large organizations the way they are because (1) they are large, (2) because of the age of the organization, or (3) because of their values, principles, and philosophy? I hope it is No. 3, because someday AES could be old and maybe large as well."

I desperately wanted AES to be a different kind of organization. Our only hope of creating a radically different kind of company was if a particular set of principles could drive and shape the business regardless of its size, complexity, or age.

Our first attempt to write down the principles that would define

AES did not take place until several years after the company started. Approximately 20 of the company's 50 employees gathered for a two-day retreat at a conference center outside Washington, D.C. One of the sessions focused on completing the Seven-S framework made famous in the bestselling book *In Search of Excellence*, which was coauthored by Bob Waterman, an original member of the AES board. As the term suggested, Seven-S entailed organizing a business around seven qualities beginning with the letter "S"—strategy, skills, staff, and so forth. At the center of the Seven-S framework was "shared values." Most of that day's discussion focused on the central values we hoped would drive the company. We also dutifully described how we saw the other parts of the framework, but they seemed less important to us. After a few years, only the shared values remained an integral part of AES's corporate discussions.

The shared values we wrote in the circle of the diagram that day were *Integrity, Fairness, Social Responsibility*, and *Fun*. Other important words were used from time to time to describe our aspirations, but they never made it to the center circle. Concepts like ownership, trust, and accountability were subsumed in the four overarching values we chose. No purpose or goal was defined at that time because the Seven-S framework curiously did not have a place to describe the primary reason that an organization existed. AES's purpose was articulated a couple of years later, and in the ensuing years it gradually became an integral part of our shared values and principles.

When Roger Sant first used the word "fun" to capture the kind of working environment we wanted to create, neither of us could have guessed at its layers of meaning. It forced us to think through exactly what was meant by "fun" and the best ways to explain it. We defined fun to mean rewarding, exciting, creative, and successful. The idea that a company could be fun kept AES fresh and vibrant for years.

At the time, Apple Computer was the darling of the fledgling high-tech industry. One thing that set it apart was the beer parties it held every Friday afternoon. We were very clear that this was *not* what we meant by fun. Nor did we believe that business success or "winning" made work fun. Nor was fun related to the type of tasks an individual performed. What we meant by fun was captured many years later, in slightly broken English, by an AES employee writing from Kazakhstan: "The common principles of integrity, fairness, fun represent AES culture which are mostly convincing. They are also the basic spirits. I work on the site whether day or night, whether weekend or working days, whether with pay or without. In this kind of working environment, my talent was fully exerted. I felt a lot of fun to use my talent and experiences accumulated throughout years of hard work. I feel I am standing on the shoulder of a giant fulfilling the social responsibilities."

People I have met—regardless of class, income, nationality, and education level—want a chance to meet the needs of their families while doing something useful for society.

Joy at work gives people the freedom to use their talents and skills for the benefit of society, without being crushed or controlled by autocratic supervisors or staff offices. The World Bank recently conducted a study of 70,000 poor people around the world. One of the questions asked of respondents was this: "What is your most pressing need?" The answer was not social services or homes or other material things. What these people wanted most was the freedom and wherewithal to be entrepreneurs. This was not surprising to me. People I have met—regardless of class, income, nationality, and education level—want a chance to make the most of their abilities to meet the needs of their families while doing something useful for society.

When we made "integrity" one of our shared values, we defined it in the classical tradition. The word is derived from the Latin *integra*, meaning wholeness or completeness. It is the same root word from which we get integer (whole numbers) and integration. It has to do with how things fit together in some cohesive and appropriate way. Being truthful is part of what it means to have integrity; living up to commitments is another.

I believe that integrity requires an organization to communicate the same message to the general public that it does to its own employees. That means openly admitting mistakes to shareholders, bankers, and governments. Readers of my letters in AES annual reports may have noticed that I took pains to discuss our mistakes and problems during the year. The letter was meant for all stakeholders who helped us achieve our purpose, not just shareholders. I believe they all deserve the same basic information, both positive and negative. Integrity also means fully explaining values and corporate purpose to all stakeholders, especially when these principles are unconventional, potentially controversial, or hard to understand.

Business executives don't spend much time talking about values, so misunderstandings and disagreements are bound to occur. Once, when we were in Minneapolis to raise equity for AES, a potential investor left the breakfast early. On the way out the door, he laughingly told one of the investment bankers: "They can have all the fun they want, but not with my money." Another humorous incident—there were many others that were not so funny—occurred when we prepared a slide presentation before a public offering of AES stock. We designed a chart to try to explain what we meant by "fun." We gave it to our investment bankers to review:

The investment bankers reviewed the chart, added one circle, and sent back the revised version:

Several years later, when a consultant from McKinsey was giving a presentation about AES, one of our executives asked why he hadn't mentioned our shared values. It turned out that the consultant was enthusiastic about our values—for all the wrong reasons. "They really reduce labor costs," he said. "Employees love these values, and they work harder and more productively because of them." This is the pragmatic line of thinking about values that I had fought since the early days of the company. It ignores the moral dimension of values and regards them as nothing more than a means to make money. The distinction was articulated by an Oxford professor named John Kay: "There is a real difference between saying to your workers, 'We care about your welfare because we do,' and saying, 'We care about your welfare because that will make you work harder for us.'" Employees can tell when values are genuine and when they're adopted for ulterior purposes.

I feel strongly that people should be able to bring many of their basic beliefs about life into an organization. AES people were encouraged to live their beliefs inside the business just as they would at home, in their places of worship, and in their communities. This was very popular with most AES people and somewhat novel. Most of us have heard the phrase "Business is business." The phrase implies that business has its own set of rules. When we go to work, we're supposed to leave our "Sunday school" or "homespun" values at the door. My view is just the opposite. Because our central values and principles were derived from mainstream values practiced by billions of people around the world, we hoped that most of our people could bring the key elements of their personal philosophies into the workplace.

Less popular was the idea that we should practice AES values both at work and in other areas of our lives. For example, integrity at AES meant that we did not cheat, steal, or lie on the job. It seemed logical that we should also adhere to those strictures in our private lives. "It's personal" or "I'm on my own time" are no more appropriate excuses than "business is business" for not acting according to basic shared values whether we're at work or not. Cheating on your income tax returns is not consistent with AES's concept of integrity. If we became aware of such behavior away from the workplace, we would ask the employee to act in a more upstanding way—or to leave the company. My colleague Stu Ryan, an excellent strategist and an even better person, continually pressed me and other company leaders to deal aggressively with discrepancies between professional and personal behavior. I do not think we did a very good job living our values outside work. Many of our top people felt uncomfortable about becoming involved in the personal lives of other AES employees. I understood that doing so was delicate and difficult, but I thought we should at least struggle to achieve moral consistency.

When it comes to "fairness," I often think we chose the right value but the wrong word. In my lectures, I often ask people to complete the sentence. "Fairness means treating everyone _____." Ninety-five percent of the people I ask respond, "the same." I usually respond, "I mean just the opposite." The word "justice" better describes the standard we set for ourselves and AES.

I like the traditional Jewish definition of justice: "To each person what he deserves, to each one what is appropriate." If I combine this definition with an assumption that each person is unique, I logically complete the sentence this way: "Fairness or justice means treating everyone *differently*." We've all heard the story of the sergeant who stands before his troops and announces, "Nobody gets special treatment around here!" What fairness meant at AES was that *everyone* got special treatment. The interpretation of these concepts gets confused because of another concept we hold dear: equality. The logic of equality goes something like this: "I'm the same person or do the same job as another per-son, so I should be treated the same as that person." Equality and fairness are not synonyms, however, and neither captures organizational justice the way I use it.

Leaders of organizations (including unions and corporations) consistently ignore the fact that employees are unique.

I can best illustrate my point using an example from my home. Even at an early age, my son, Dennis Jr., loved to spend hours of his time alone in his bedroom reading, designing games, and pursuing other solitary interests. His younger sister, Margaret, loved to spend much of her spare time in the kitchen or den with family members and friends. Whenever we had a party she was in the middle of the festivities, engaging older and younger people in conversation. When Dennis Jr. and Margaret misbehaved, my wife and I attempted to discipline them in ways consistent with their different personalities, even if both had committed the same transgression. It would have been easier and more conventional to punish them the same way, perhaps by sending them to their bedrooms alone for the evening with no TV or telephone privileges. But Dennis Jr. would have thought this was great, and Margaret would have felt she had been exiled from her family and cut off from her friends. We love them equally, but they are unique individuals, and we had to treat them differently in order to be fair or just.

While parents often understand that children need to be treated differently to get a fair result, leaders of organizations (including unions and corporations) consistently ignore the fact that employees are unique. Most managers prefer not to get enmeshed in the personal lives of the employees who report to them. This often makes it impossible to make judgments about individuals and their performance consistent with their personal differences. Furthermore, employees and their union leaders generally don't trust managers to make fair judgments about individuals. As a result, businesses are forced to pigeonhole their employees according to artificial classifications such as years of service, union membership, level of education, and job title. If real justice or fairness were applied in organizations, it would radically change most of them, sometimes in very surprising ways—and almost always for the better.

In making "social responsibility" one of our core values, we recognized that every corporation is given certain rights and privileges by the state. In return, the company should operate in ways that benefit society and mitigate the potential negative consequences of its activities. Improving the environment is an obvious way to be socially responsible. For example, AES was widely praised for its programs to offset CO_2 emissions from our U.S. and U.K. facilities by helping to plant 52 million trees in Guatemala and by preserving hundreds of thousands of acres of forest land in the Amazon region and in Paraguay. Charitable activities to help the disadvantaged and safety programs for employees and the public constitute other socially responsible corporate activities.

While these undertakings are important, I gradually concluded that we could serve society best simply by fulfilling the company's mission. The primary social responsibility of AES was to be the best it could be at meeting the world's need for safe, clean, reliable, and economically priced electricity. That took 90 to 95 percent of our resources and of our people's skills and efforts.

For example, in Leflore County, Oklahoma, unemployment fell from 13.6 percent to 4 percent after AES built a 320-megawatt plant there. But that was minor compared with what happened after AES acquired a distribution company in the Dominican Republic in 1997. The year before we bought it, 385 Dominicans had died in electricity-related accidents within our utility service area—a fairly typical toll at the time. By 2000, the number of fatalities had dropped to 29. In other words, we saved hundreds of lives because AES took seriously its primary mission "to serve society in an economically sustainable manner with *safe*, clean, reliable electricity." I can think of no other "project" AES has undertaken that was as socially beneficial.

The selection and identification of our shared values were just the first step in creating an ethos for AES. The role of these values and principles in the life of our organization became more important each year. After that first strategy session, I kept working to define what our values meant in a practical sense, both to me and to others in the organization. We then integrated the values into all aspects of AES life. As a result, we never needed special values or ethics initiatives or programs to encourage diversity or community involvement. These things were part of our everyday working lives. They were perfectly compatible with the way we did business. As Lynn Sharp Paine, a professor at the Harvard Business School, put it, "Values are not a 'management tool' or a special type of management system that runs parallel to a company's audit or compensation system. Nor are they bits of ethereal matter ... [they are] beliefs, aims, and assumptions that undergird the enterprise and guide its management in developing strategies, structures, processes, and policies. They constitute an organizational 'infrastructure' that gives a company its distinctive character and ethos—its moral personality."

When we first defined our values, two of the AES senior leaders who had participated in the conference were skeptical. They had a hard-nosed, no-nonsense approach to business and took a dim view of the "soft, touchy-feely stuff" that they believed was on the table. Economics was "hard" and important; other things were not. Knowing the belief system and personalities of the two, I was not particularly surprised by their lukewarm response.

The surprise came the following year when we gathered for another strategy meeting. We decided to raise the Seven-S framework we had drafted a year earlier and asked for evaluations, including suggested changes. Almost immediately, the two skeptical leaders jumped into the conversation. "Don't change anything," one of them said. "We love these values. They really work! People like doing business with us. I think it's because they trust us." They were nonplused when I responded with a downcast face and silence. "What's wrong, Dennis? We think this stuff is great. People like to do business with us because of fairness and integrity."

"I think you have missed a most important point," I said. "We are trying to live these values because they are *right*, not because they *work*." High ethical values rarely conflict with pragmatic economic behavior. However, this does not mean that economics should be the reason or motive the organization undertakes to live the shared values. Amar V. Bhide and Howard H. Stevenson explained why in a *Harvard Business Review* article titled "Why Be Honest if Honesty Doesn't Pay?" They wrote: "There is no compelling economic reason to tell the truth or keep one's word—punishment for the treacherous in the real world is neither swift nor sure. Honesty is, in fact, primarily a moral choice. Business people tell themselves that in the long run they do well by doing good. But there is little factual or logical basis for this conviction. Without values, without basic preference for right over wrong, trust based on such self-delusion would crumble in the face of temptation. ... And for this, we should be happy. We can be proud of a system in which people are honest because they want to be, not because they have to be."

Why it's important to *live* values and how we judge their efficacy were recurring questions inside and outside the company for 20 years. They were also the source of many disagreements between me and some AES board members and managers, not to mention students of management outside the company.

Related to the question of whether we should adhere to values simply because they are *right* is whether values should change when circumstances change. Should we adjust our interpretations of principles when the stock price goes down or our product doesn't sell well or we make a mistake on an acquisition? My answer has been no, but it is a no that remains open to further examination and new insights.

I believe there is a transcendent truth behind principles like integrity and justice that does not and should not change over time and should certainly not be adjusted because of economic setbacks. Adjustments in definition and interpretation should take place only when we gain new understanding of the truth. Our *understanding* of the values may change with time, but the

> *"Methods are many, principles are few. Methods change often, principles never do."*

values and principles themselves are timeless. As an old rhyme puts it, "Methods are many, principles are few. Methods change often, principles never do."

There is little disagreement that the corporate values at AES arose out of the personal values of the co-founders. The transformation of personal values to organizational values is accomplished with the word "shared." Shared implies that members of an organization agree on the definition and importance of a value. Sharing values, especially in a secular company, can run afoul of the popular view in our society that people should decide for themselves how values are to be interpreted. If individuals, whether they are vice presidents or board members, interpret values individually, the values are not shared.

We attempted to mitigate this problem through an extensive written and oral orientation for prospective employees before they joined AES. We discussed and defined our values so people could decide whether they wanted to be a part of the AES community. Discussions of our values continued at monthly and quarterly business review meetings. The company's insistence on articulating its values in all types of settings mystified outsiders. A banker who worked with us expressed amazement at his visit to AES headquarters. "I went by an office and two VPs were arguing about whether something was fair or not. Can you believe that?"

At AES, revising the interpretation of a shared value required a leader who spoke for the entire organization to listen to the reasons for the proposed change, get advice from colleagues, and then decide if a change was appropriate.

I suspect that in most companies, especially ones that put a premium on individual freedom and diverse views, values are not really shared by the majority of the employees. The values either are adjusted frequently to suit changing situations, or they are defined so ambiguously that everyone can agree with them. As a result, they have very little effect on the behavior of the organization or the individuals who work there. They become especially irrelevant in times of trouble.

"Hey, Dennis, our organization has values too," was a comment I sometimes heard from people outside our company. It was a helpful reminder that we were sometimes perceived as arrogant or even sanctimonious. Every person and every organization have values. But in this age of "tolerance," it is politically incorrect to say that any of these values is more appropriate than others. The truth, however, is that some values *are* better than others. Truthfulness and selflessness, for example, are preferable to deception and selfishness.

Several articles I have read recently suggest that it doesn't matter what purpose or set of principles you follow as long as you establish some set of standards for everyone to get behind. A friend of mine from California put this "all values are equal" philosophy in perspective when he recalled a conversation he had with a person he met on the beach. It concluded with, "Hey, that's great. You're into Jesus and I'm into surfing." After hearing that story, I began to use the word "principles" along with the word "values" to describe the key concepts that guide organizational life. Principles connote less ethical relativism than values and more of the unchanging truths by which I believe we should live. The question is not whether we have values, but which values and principles really guide our behavior.

Since the early 1980s, many corporations have adopted values statements. Companies hang them on office and factory walls, post them on their Websites, and include them in their annual reports. The proliferation of values statements prompted one journalist to call them "a deodorant for self-interest." There is often basis for cynicism. The values articulated by many companies have only a minimal effect on how they conduct their businesses. CEOs rarely talk about them at investor meetings. Try to think of a company that makes ethics one of its most important criteria for evaluating individual performance, calculating raises and bonuses, or awarding stock options. How often do principles drive the financial invest-ments and operating strategy of a company? Paying lip service to values may be good public relations, but it is a hollow and cynical exercise. Values and principles mean something only when they af-fect everything we do, every day of the week.

My strong belief in shared values and principles does not mean that either AES or I consistently met the standards we set for our-selves. They were our aspirations, and they were deeply felt, but we were fallible like anyone else. At the same time, I resisted all efforts to lower our standards or to ease the burden of accountability that we imposed on ourselves. It was better to try our best, I felt, and be willing to come clean when we fell short of our goals.

In the early 1980s there was a small start-up company that shared office space with AES in Arlington, Virginia. The founders had designed clip-on neckwear for women to wear as an accessory to their outfits. After several false starts, the company leaders at-tended an industry trade show to see if they could market their bows. Somewhat to their surprise, they got orders for several thou-sand. When the president got back from the trade show, he came running into my office to tell me the good news. Then he paused and asked, "Dennis, how are we going to make all them bows?"

A year or so later, we were in much the same position at AES.

Our power plant in Houston was under construction, and we were beginning to think about how to operate the plant. Most of us in the company had hardly seen the inside of a power plant, let alone worked in one. Board members who had significant industrial operating experience said, "You don't know anything about operating a power plant. Get somebody who does."

I followed their advice. Several advisers also suggested that we would need a whole different approach with our employees in the power plant than we had with the M.B.A.'s, engineers, and other college graduates who filled the home office at the time. "These people are different," one board member said. "They want to be paid weekly, preferably in cash. They don't care about your soft-headed stuff like values. Fun will be a totally foreign concept that is just not applicable to industrial operations."

"These people are different" was the statement that troubled me the most. I remembered hearing the same kind of language used to belittle African-Americans in the '60s. It turned out to be dead wrong. Would it be true of people hired to work at our new cogeneration facility in Houston? I wasn't sure, and it took me over two years to confirm my original misgivings.

Once I did, I set in motion a revolution in that plant that dramatically changed the AES workplace and the way we operated our facilities. The shared values of the home office eventually would be used to guide every aspect of life at the plants—from hiring and compensation to organization and decision making. It was the beginning of an audacious effort to create the most fun workplace ever.

At another strategy conference in the late 1980s, an AES vice president asked the 30 people in attendance to close their eyes and make a "movie" of their lives. A number of people then shared the outlines of their movies with the group. The plots differed widely, of course, but the same theme cropped up again and again. In almost all the movies, people used their talents and skills to make a positive contribution in the world. Although it was hardly a scientific sampling of working Americans, the consistency of their goals was striking. We used the result of this exercise to start the process of defining the purpose of our company. If the goal of our individual lives was to make a positive difference in the world, shouldn't we try to do the same thing as a corporation? During that conference we wrote the first draft of our company's purpose—to meet the electricity needs of people and organizations. Over time this statement of purpose would be refined and become an important part of the shared values and principles of the company.

During the 1980s and early 1990s, my wife, Eileen, and I met weekly with five or six other couples for Bible study, prayer, and a discussion of our joys and problems. One of the key areas of learning from my time with this group was a deeper understanding of "stewardship"—the idea that we have a larger purpose than simply satisfying our own needs. I came to realize that what I had learned as a 5-year-old was incomplete at best. Stewardship was more than giving money to the church or contributing to other good causes. I learned that it was more about what I did with the money I kept and spent than the money I gave away. It was more about how I lived my daily life. It was about how I used my abilities and skills to make a positive contribution to society and to serve others.

About this time, I read a book by Peter Block (an author unknown to me at the time) entitled *Stewardship–Choosing Service Over Self-Interest*. It had an enormous influence on me. It showed me how my biblical understanding of stewardship could be applied to a major business. Stewardship is a concept that assumes the resources we are using belong to someone else. We are protecting them, taking care of them, making them useful—all for the rightful owner. For those operating within an organization, Block wrote, it is "the willingness to be accountable for the well-being of the larger organization by operating in service, rather than in control, of those around us. Stated simply, it is accountability without control or compliance." My response was to make serving the needs of society the cornerstone of our corporate purpose.

Early in 1990, we began exploring the possibility of going public.

Our privately held shareholder base was rapidly approaching 500 stockholders. Unless we took extraordinary measures to reduce the number of people who owned AES stock, we would be deemed a public company by law. One of our major concerns about going public was that serving shareholders might be incompatible with serving society. Could we maintain our values while striving to meet ambitious economic goals?

We consulted investment banking firms about our concerns. They were quite positive about our ability to live in the "public" world in a way that was consistent with our principles. I realized later that like many of us trained in sales, the bankers emphasized the positive aspects of our "strange" set of values and minimized the problems. One particularly persuasive banker even suggested that I owed it to the world to go public so that I could better spread the ideas of the company's radical approach to organizational life.

There are four major shared values (at AES): to act with integrity, to be fair, to have fun, and to be socially responsible.

Our board members were supportive of going public. I should have been more skeptical of their advice. I was already aware that some of them were very excited about the business prospects of the company but were less committed to our values than I was, or simply viewed them as a way to improve economic performance. I was convinced, however, that in spite of all the red flags, we could become a public company without losing our special qualities.

But a number of shareholders, many of them AES employees, were concerned that going public would change the company for the worse. Roger and I addressed some of their concerns with a letter to AES employees and shareholders in March 1991:

> We have contemplated the pros and cons of being public since the beginning of AES. We have until now concluded

that staying private made the most sense. However, we now believe that registration as a public company may ultimately be inevitable. ... We continue to be committed to the purpose and values of AES. ... To that end, we have established 'Going Public Principles' for ourselves. ... These principles are: Make the process fun; if it stops being fun, we should change the way we are doing it or quit. ... *If we find ourselves tempted to change any significant elements of the way we do business, we must consider the change to be a major red flag and we should make the change only if our current rationale for acting as we do doesn't make sense—independent of the public offering process. ... We will do our best to uphold these principles* [emphasis added].

True to our promise, we prepared the draft of our public-offering memo with a forthright paragraph under the "Business of the Company" section. It read as follows:

Adherence to AES's Values—Possible Impact on Results of Operations. An important element of AES is its commitment to four major 'shared' values: to act with integrity, to be fair, to have fun, and to be socially responsible. See 'Business—Values and Practices.' AES believes that earning a fair profit is an important result of providing a quality product to its customers. However, if the Company perceives a conflict between these values and profits, the Company will try to adhere to its values—even though doing so might result in diminished profits or forgone opportunities. Moreover, the Company seeks to adhere to these values not as a means to achieve economic success, but because adherence is a worthwhile goal in and of itself. The Company intends to continue these policies after this offering.

When the draft document was reviewed by staffers at the

Securities and Exchange Commission, they offered a number of helpful suggestions. The most intriguing was advising us to move the above paragraph to the first section of the document called "Special Risk Factors" with the additional title "Possible Impact on Results of Operations." This is the equivalent of a warning label on a medicine bottle. Investors might be told that a company has very little existing business, that it is essentially controlled by two principals who might die tomorrow, that there's no guarantee it will be able to attract any new business. In our case, the SEC officials thought our values were a hazard.

> *We should attempt to live according to a set of unchanging shared ethical principles, because it is the right way to live.*

Some of our people were upset by the SEC's reaction. I loved it. I could now say that the U.S. government thought it was *very risky* to attempt to operate a business with integrity, fairness, social responsibility, and a sense of fun. AES has continued in all of its public offerings to carry the original statement, with only minor changes, describing its shared principles.

We should attempt to live according to a set of unchanging shared ethical principles, because it is the right way to live. Our efforts to do so need not be sweetened with additional benefits, such as better financial results, more successful recruiting, happier employees, or even improved productivity. These goals are worth pursuing irrespective of the bottom line. It is not only whether I live a certain way that is important. It is whether the way I attempt to live is based on true and moral principles.

We have made the workplace a frustrating and joyless place
where people do what they're told and have few ways
to participate in decisions or fully use their talents.

CHAPTER 2

A Miserable Workplace

COLLIN DOHERTY ARRIVED a full hour before 6 a.m., the time he had been told to report to his new job at the textile mill. "Be here on time or I will give the job to another man," were the parting words of the assistant mill supervisor who had offered him the job. Collin had awakened extra early that morning to walk the 3 miles from his farm to the new steam-powered textile mill in the village. He had been trying since before the plant opened to get hired. He did not want to be late.

Collin was 31 years old. He and Rowena had been married for 14 years. Ten children had been born to them, although only six were still living. The drought of the previous year and the particularly harsh winter that followed had been the last straw. The family had nearly starved that winter and did not have sufficient money to buy seed and replacement animals. Surviving another winter in Wales was not assured. Collin decided to quit farming and look for work in one of the new factories built in the region.

The family had planted crops and raised sheep and goats on the 5-hectare farm for at least the six generations recorded in the family Bible. Collin knew nothing else but dawn-to-dusk work to provide food and clothing for his family, just as his father, grandfather, and great-grandfather had done before him.

The mill employed upwards of 100 workers. In addition, there were supervisors for each of the functions performed at the mill. The employees were divided into groups, each with a specialty. For example, one group prepared the wood for the steam engine, another operated the weaving machines, and still another rolled the cloth before sending it to the shipping department. The workers who maintained the steam engine and the weaving machines were paid more than the others because their jobs required the most skill. Each group of workers had a supervisor who gave instructions, set work schedules, and made sure every man and woman did his or her job in a specified manner.

Collin checked in at the plant gate and was shown to a little room off to the side, where he was met by a supervisor. "You are assigned to the clean-up crew in the weaving area," the supervisor said. "You will be paid 1 shilling per week. Hours are 6 a.m. to 6:30 p.m. Monday through Saturday with 30 minutes off for lunch, as long as you have completed all your morning assignments. The mill will be closed Sundays and Christmas Day." Collin was relieved that his family would have sufficient money to feed themselves. He also noted that he was expected to put in fewer hours at the mill than the average he spent working on the farm. He also looked forward to a new kind of work, although he wondered what his deceased father would have thought about his decision to leave the farm.

His supervisor showed him the tasks for which he was responsible and made it clear that Collin should look to him for guidance or assistance. Collin noticed an office overlooking the weaving department floor. He was told later that it was where the plant superintendent and the assistant superintendent worked, as well as the bookkeepers, timekeepers, payroll staff, and salesmen. In his first two years of working at the mill, he never met the plant superintendent, nor did he ever see the "big boss," the owner of the mill who lived in a distant city and seldom visited the site.

Collin didn't miss a day of work in his first year at the new workplace. He moved up from the cleaning crew to a position in the weaving department and became quite skilled at the task to which he was assigned. Rowena observed a different Collin, however.

"I work hard and I get paid enough to keep food on the table and clothes on our backs. Not much else matters, does it?" he replied in response to his wife's questioning.

"You don't seem to care about the work the way you did when you worked here on the farm," Rowena said. "It seems like you are going through the motions. You never tell me about the problems you are struggling with and the dreams you have for the future like you did here on the farm."

"It's like being one of the oxen on our farm," Collin replied. "I get fed regularly, but at work time I'm put in a yoke that doesn't give me much freedom. I don't have to think much about what I'm doing, let alone dream about my future."

"Maybe it will be different if I can become a supervisor at the mill someday. Then I will be somebody. I will have some control. I bet I could improve that place if I were in a position to have some say in things."

Collin Doherty is a character of my creation. He was born of my reading about the Industrial Revolution and is a composite of the ordinary people who pop up in the histories of the period. So while he may be fictional, he is *true*.

Most historians mark the Industrial Revolution as a pivotal moment in our economic and social history. The nature of work changed in fundamental ways. Until Thomas Newcomen's invention of the first practical steam engine in 1711, most people worked the land as farmers and before that as hunters and gatherers. Large organizations of working people were mostly limited to soldiers, servants, or slaves. During the Middle Ages craft shops sprung up in the cities, but each shop typically provided work for only a small number of people. When building the great cathedrals of Europe, men banded together to work for years on a single project, an organizational structure that had some elements of the Industrial Revolution workplace. However, it was not until industrialization began that the workplace changed rapidly for millions of people like Collin Doherty.

Many of the attitudes that took hold during the Industrial Revolution linger on today, a circumstance brought to my attention by author Bob Waterman, who in our early days at AES had walked us through his Seven-S framework. "Based on what you know about the workplace and organizational arrangements of those businesses operating several hundred years ago, what were the assumptions made by the owner/managers about the workers who labored in their factories?" he asked.

I have asked that same question hundreds of times of people in my company, students in colleges and graduate schools, government employees, and leaders in many other organizations. Here is a summary of their responses:

- Workers are lazy. If they are not watched, they will not work diligently.
- Workers work primarily for money. They will do what it takes to make as much money as possible.
- Workers put their own interests ahead of what is best for the organization. They are selfish.
- Workers perform best and are most effective if they have one simple, repeatable task to accomplish.
- Workers are not capable of making good decisions about important matters that affect the economic performance of the company. Bosses are good at making these decisions.
- Workers do not want to be responsible for their actions or for decisions that affect the performance of the organization.
- Workers need care and protection just as children need the care of their parents.
- Workers should be compensated by the hour or by the number of "pieces" produced. Bosses should be paid a salary and possibly receive bonuses and stock.
- Workers are like interchangeable parts of machines. One

"good" worker is pretty much the same as any other "good" worker.

- Workers need to be told what to do, when to do it, and how to do it. Bosses need to hold them accountable.

These assumptions have had a profound effect on personnel arrangements and decision-making structures in large businesses, governments, schools, and other large organizations. Specialization became the rule. Lines of authority were clear. Workers were told exactly what was expected of them. A curious arrangement of staff and line positions emerged (experts suggest that the Prussian Army was the first to use this approach, late in the 19th century). The paternalistic impulse led to the creation of "benefits" that were provided in lieu of cash (free or cut-rate housing, schooling, and medical care). Most of the systems, controls, compensation criteria, and decision-making and leadership styles that we find in organizations today can be traced to these beliefs about workers.

When I ask people whether they believe the assumptions listed above still apply to modern-day working people, especially in the Western world, almost everyone says no. Most would agree with Max De Pree, a manufacturing executive who was a pioneer in participatory management, that advanced countries are entering a period in which 80 percent of workers will make their living by brainpower.

However, based on my own observations, I suspect that many corporate leaders still hold some Industrial Revolution views. What's more, many of the approaches and practices in modern workplaces are nearly as demeaning as those used during the Industrial Revolution. Executives are either oblivious to the similarities—or won't admit them. These are the only plausible explanations for the relative lack of change in the structure of work in modern corporations, government agencies, and nonprofit organizations.

A newborn shark, 6 or 7 inches long, can survive in the sort of fish tank seen in homes, but its growth is seriously stunted and its body deformed. It becomes extremely aggressive and can be kept from escaping only if the tank has a heavy cover.

Have new assumptions about working people eliminated work environments that resemble this cramped aquarium—and that prevent them from reaching their potential? Obviously, much has changed. The hours are shorter. The workplace is physically more pleasant. Compensation is usually higher. Workers have more legal rights and protections.

Fundamentally, however, working conditions in large organizations today are no more exciting, rewarding, or fun than they were 250 years ago. Most working people are boxed in by job descriptions and corporate hierarchies and have little opportunity to make decisions on their own. I was struck by this lack of freedom during visits to Japan in the 1980s. Several bestselling books had been written in the previous decade analyzing and to some extent glorifying Japanese business prowess. I got a very different impression. What struck me was that work in Japan lacked passion and joy. Fun was something that happened away from the workplace. Work was work and play was play, and the two never overlapped. Japanese "salary-men" didn't leave work as much as escape it, often during hard-drinking nights with the "boys."

In the modern workplace, an employee's full talents are rarely used and often go unnoticed. Damian Obiglio, who led an AES distribution company that won the award for the finest utility in Brazil several years running, tells the story of a young man who worked in a city library in Argentina for a decade. His job was to put the books that had been returned to the library back on the shelves where they belonged. Each day he faithfully put in his eight hours and left the library immediately. He showed no interest in taking on greater responsibilities at the library, and none of his colleagues ever engaged him in conversation about his interests or hopes for the future. He caused no problems. He did his job as instructed, nothing more, nothing less. One day the national paper in Argentina ran a story celebrating the person who had won a contest for his design of a gas-powered model airplane. It turned out that the young man in the library was one of the most brilliant aeronautical designers in the entire country.

Why do so many people work so hard so they can escape to Disneyland? Why are video games more popular than work? Why is driving an automobile more exciting and enjoyable to many people than their work? Why do rank-and-file employees generally spend less time at work than top executives? Why do many workers spend years dreaming about and planning for retirement? The reason is simple and dispiriting. We have made the workplace a frustrating and joyless place where people do what they're told and have few ways to participate in decisions or fully use their talents. As a result, they naturally gravitate to pursuits in which they can exercise a measure of control over their lives.

In most organizations I have been exposed to around the world, bosses and supervisors still make all important decisions. The more important the decision, the more important the boss assigned to make the call. This is especially true of decisions that have financial implications. We still have the offices "above" the working people, filled with staff (some with "green eyeshades") and supervisors who, without consulting workers, make decisions that dramatically affect their lives. Many layers of bosses and assistant bosses control the behavior and performance of the people below them.

In the past three decades, there has been a proliferation of staff specialists who oversee almost every aspect of corporate life. Many of their names and missions have an Orwellian ring: engineering services, human resources, training, environmental control, strategic planning, legal affairs, finance, risk management, accounting, internal auditing, internal communications, public affairs, investor relations, community relations, production control, quality control.

As a line executive responsible for the Energy Conservation Program in the federal government during the early 1970s, I experienced the debilitating effects of these "serving" central staff groups. It seemed as if I had 15 bosses. Each one of the offices was responsible for something I thought was essential to operating my program. My budget was the responsibility of the budget department. When an issue regarding energy conservation legislation or inquiries concerning my program came from Capitol Hill, the staff of the assistant secretary for legislation took the lead. People like me couldn't even testify before a congressional committee without an entourage of people concerned that I might say something related to their areas of responsibility. As the executive in charge of the program, I was not really trusted to operate it or to speak freely about it. It was almost as if I didn't have a job. At best, my "line" job was about coordinating all the "staff" people who drifted in and out of my program. It is easy to understand why a Collin Doherty could become disenchanted with his workplace.

Workers get paid for the hours they work and, curiously, get extra pay if it takes them longer than a colleague to complete a job.

Basic compensation schemes have not changed significantly either. Workers get paid for the hours they work and, curiously, get extra pay if it takes them longer than a colleague to complete a job. Supervisors and other leaders get paid a basic salary according to their responsibilities, regardless of the time spent performing them. They are usually eligible for bonuses and increasingly participate in ownership benefits as well. As has been the case for nearly three centuries, most organizations employ only two significant "classes" of people—management (variously called executives, leaders, supervisors, directors, and officers) and labor. Discrimination against labor by management is more subtle today than it was during the Industrial Revolution, but it remains demeaning and destructive.

Workers are still "trained" in the narrow function they are expected to perform. Most bosses, however, acquire broader expertise through schooling or doing stints in a variety of jobs. Most organizational leaders still believe a detailed job description for every employee is essential to a smoothly performing operation. In most firms, "control" systems pushed by auditors and managers limit each person's ability to make decisions on spending the company's money. The amount is set at zero or near zero for the lowest employees on the organizational ladder. This number usually climbs with each layer of supervision. At the top, the executive director, president, or CEO can often make a decision to spend millions of dollars, and the board of directors or trustees have leeway to spend even more. When it comes to financial matters, average employees and lower-level supervisors enjoy the same level of trust as they did in the 19ᵗʰ century.

> *"Human resources" has a dehumanizing connotation.*

The nomenclature of business also remains largely the same. Labor or labor costs, personnel or personnel departments, are all in common use. Economists still put people in an economic formula (labor plus material plus capital equals production). In effect, people (labor) are simply variables like money and material. Similarly, the label "human resources" has a dehumanizing connotation. We have financial resources, fuel resources, and *human* resources.

In reading annual letters by CEOs, I have noticed that when an organization wants to make a positive statement about its employees, the letter often says something like, "Our people are our best assets." After I used similar language in one of my annual letters, I had second thoughts about using the word "assets" to describe people in my company. What do we do with assets? We use them. We buy and sell them. We depreciate them. When they are used up, we dispose of them. I vowed that I would never again use that word to describe the people in my organization. I don't even like the word "employee" because it has a lingering association with the demeaning workplaces of the Industrial Revolution. (I reluctantly use the word "employee" in this book because it is familiar to readers—so familiar, in fact, that most have never given its connotation a second thought.)

Earlier, I noted that most of the recent books written on organizational success treat uniquely human factors—principles and values, for instance—as nothing more than techniques to achieve wealth and success. The behavior of people is equated with the cost of raw materials and plant equipment. One bestselling book a few years ago was *Re-Inventing the Corporation*. Invention is a word usually associated with machines or processes, yet much of the book is about the people who work in corporations. How do you reinvent them? Even more problematic from my perspective was the title of another bestselling book, *Re-engineering the Corporation*. Engineering is a word almost exclusively related to machines, but here again the book was primarily about people and the structure in which they work.

Many business leaders are far more concerned with the tasks people perform than with the people themselves. As Henry Ford famously quipped, "Why is it I get a whole person when all I want is a good pair of hands?"

Several years ago in China, I was visiting with three young women employed by AES. All three had returned to their homeland after attending Ivy League schools in the United States. They told me how in each case their parents had made the decision for them about which school to attend and what classes to take, even though none of their parents had ever attended a college or even traveled outside of China. The parents had treated their grown daughters as small children.

We turn things upside down in the United States. When our children are young, we (wrongly, I believe) let them pick their friends, their schools, their clothes, their movies and music, even their religion, assuming they choose any faith at all. By contrast, when they go to work, their bosses tell them what to do, how to do it, and when.

When I attended business school in the late '60s, a good deal of pioneering research had been done on how employees respond to different conditions in the workplace. In cynical moments I characterized most of this research with the phrase, "Be nice to the 'machines' and they will produce more for you." That said, many experts over the past 50 years have argued that we should replace outmoded assumptions about workers and fundamentally change the workplace.

Indeed, most thoughtful people today reject the assumptions about working people that guided business leaders at the time of the Industrial Revolution. We understand more about what makes people grow and learn and enjoy work. We have experienced political and individual freedom and love it. Most of us believe that every individual is unique and valuable.

Why, then, has there been so little real change in our large organizations? If we have different assumptions about the nature of people today, why do our workplaces have so many characteristics that their forerunners had two centuries ago? Why are compensation arrangements still designed as if people work primarily for money? Why do managers exercise most of the power? Why do staff officers still hold so many of the levers that control organizational behavior? If we believe that the workplace of Collin Doherty leads to drudgery, emptiness, and dissatisfaction, why hasn't there been an Information Age "revolution" to correct the problems?

I believe there are three reasons for this resistance to change. The first is inertia. Anytime something is moving in one direction, it takes extraordinary forces to change its course. Restructuring the working environment shaped by the Industrial Revolution is like trying to stop a powerful locomotive heading down a mountain pass. Nothing in the contemporary workplace has matched the power of the innovations that occurred during the 18th century.

Second, the Industrial Revolution produced so much good that no one wants to risk tampering with its successful workplace formula. In a few hundred years, the gains in health care have extended life expectancy by roughly 40 years around the world. Average family income is up, and, even with the large disparity between rich and poor, poverty has been reduced substantially. The green revolution has made it technically possible to eliminate hunger and famine, as long as corrupt governments and civil wars don't intervene. Few would question that our corporate system has produced social progress and an enormous amount of wealth. Even if a side effect has been to create a workplace that is stifling and joyless, most business leaders consider it a price worth paying.

Third, to change the workplace in a positive way would require executives to give up a large measure of their power and control. This is the chief impediment to a radical overhaul of our working environment. Even if a corporate leader were convinced that surrendering these prerogatives would improve the lives of millions without hurting economic performance, the rewards of power are usually too strong to give up. The result is that few leaders have been willing to take the bold steps necessary to junk a workplace model that reduces employees to little more than gerbils on a treadmill.

Not all workplaces are miserable, of course. Exceptions can be found in all types of institutions—businesses, nonprofits, and governments. But these exceptions usually are not as progressive as their leaders think. Small organizations, especially those where most of the workforce is homogeneous, with similar educational and socioeconomic backgrounds, will often have a more collegial feel than organizations of the industrial age. Law partnerships and consulting groups often operate in ways that make the work enjoyable—at least for the partners. Associates, clerical people, and others in the firms may have a work experience as unhappy as Collin Doherty's.

Many forces conspire to return organizational structures to the "tried and true" model of the past. Rapid growth diverts the energy needed for organizational innovation. Pressure from aggressive investors or lackluster economic performance can prompt executives to play it safe and organize their enterprises along conventional lines. Finally, no change can be sustained unless leaders have an unwavering conviction that change in the workplace is both right and necessary. This requires leaders with courage, stamina, and a high degree of moral clarity.

These are extremely difficult barriers to overcome. The qualities needed to bring about radical change are rare, even among leaders who share my philosophy and recognize that the results are compelling. It does not surprise me that so few large organizations have instituted workplace reforms and that fewer still have managed to sustain them. And it should not come as a surprise that the culture of drudgery seems as pervasive as it did 200 years ago.

Most of today's start-up companies begin with a flexible, human-centered approach. This often includes many decision makers, a flat organizational structure, and a collegial environment. Information is shared, relationships are trusting, and management systems are almost nonexistent. In the early days of AES, I was lulled into feeling that living our shared values and principles was going to be easy. "Wait until you grow up," warned more experienced leaders. "This will not work when you are bigger and substantial changes are inevitable." They understood that most new workplaces soon become more concerned about improving efficiency and making profits than about creating a more fun and humane environment.

Bureaucratic behavior remains the heart and soul of most work environments. Important decisions are still made at the top. The rest of the leaders and employees are left out of the process or, at best, are asked only for their suggestions. President Clinton once told me about a relatively minor matter that was neatly summed up on a single piece of paper. It contained 22 signatures of people "signing off" on the issue before the president made the final decision.

Most employees in large organizations seldom see, meet, or know the CEO or other senior managers. Countless AES people approached me over the years to say that they were grateful to have spent time talking with me. "I never met the plant manager of the company I used to work for," was a refrain I heard on almost every trip I took around the company. In effect, they were telling me, "in the other company I wasn't important, and in this company I am important." Most employees in large organizations have about as much contact with senior leaders as Collin Doherty did.

Frederick Taylor is given credit for the new era of "scientific management." He disappointed his wealthy Philadelphia family by going to work in a steelworks, which he found shockingly inefficient. Taylor then became an early version of a management consultant. He timed how long it took workers to perform tasks and rearranged factory equipment to speed the production process. His ideas about improving efficiency swept the country in the first 30 years of the 20th century. While his research led to some useful innovations, his approach reinforced the idea that people are like machines in a manufacturing process. Unfortunately, this view of workers has not changed much in the intervening years. Just listen to the cold, quantitative analyses of people in the workplace articulated by organizational and strategic gurus today.

Even the current emphasis on "training" is demeaning. "Let's see. I train horses and dogs, and I toilet-train children." There are, of course, cases in which people need training to master higher specialized functions. But the main image that comes to mind is opening the top of a person's head and pouring data inside it, much as you would pour oil in a machine or install software in a computer.

Education broadens our experience and understanding. Training confines a person by teaching narrow skills. But you would never know it's a blind alley from the way it's described by management and HR departments. They sell employees on the idea that training is a way to advance their careers. It would be better, I believe, to substitute education for training. Education allows people to seek out information that they consider important—and that has the potential to transform their working lives.

Two centuries after Collin Doherty, company finances remain a mystery to all but a few. In companies with thousands of employees, fewer than 50 to 100 people may have access to important financial information, and even fewer have a substantial say over how funds are used. This is true in most governments, corporations, not-for-profit groups, and educational institutions.

While time clocks aren't found as frequently as they were in the past, most lower-level employees still punch in, metaphorically at least. One of my associates used to work at a law firm where she was made to "understand" that she should be in by 8:30 a.m., even though her boss did not have such a rule for himself and her work was only marginally related to the time of day. In most organizations there might as well be a sign on the wall that says, THE MACHINES START AT 8 A.M., AND YOU ARE ONE OF THEM.

The ever proliferating staff offices do not have direct responsibility for producing a product or offering a service. As one cynical line person once said to me, "staff offices do nothing but keep me from producing what I am supposed to produce." In their "support" and "coordination" roles, these staff offices often take power and control from people with line responsibilities. Their control of vital information and their usurpation of functions once performed across organizations have made staff offices a major contributor to the humdrum routines of so many working people today.

As noted earlier, the greatest obstacle to worker satisfaction is management's craving for status and power. But there are other powerful forces within most organizations that push them toward centralization, putting almost all important decisions in the hands of managers, supervisors, officers, and owners. These forces include:

Information and data-gathering technology: John Naisbitt's book *Megatrends* suggested that technologies like the Internet would help decentralize organizations, make them more democratic, and give power to more employees. Is this true? Is the Internet making the workplace more fun? It is too early to give a definitive answer. It is clear, however, that the same technology that can allow people to make decisions in a decentralized manner also can be used in the opposite way—to centralize everything.

One of my vice presidents invited me into his office not long after we started operating our first power plant in Houston. On his desk he had a computer that had the control panel for the plant. "Dennis, I can essentially watch and control the operations from here. I can get one for you as well, and we can add all the new plants as they go commercial." I told him not to bother and suggested he get rid of his as well. This kind of centralization can have a major negative effect on the workplace. It reinforces the idea that plant employees are automatons who have little or no control over the way they work or how their plant is organized and operated. It seems straight out of Orwell's 1984.

More often than not, lower-ranking people are closer to the problem and better positioned to come up with a solution.

Top-down responses to mistakes and problems: Ken Woodcock was AES's first full-time business development person and probably our most effective one. Early in the company's history he came to the monthly business review meeting with a problem. A competitor seemed to be following him from place to place making pitches to potential customers within two weeks of Ken's visit. Someone suggested that the problem was the internal newsletter that we published monthly to keep everyone at AES informed about what we were doing and what companies we might be interested in acquiring. It was showing up on a competitor's bulletin board. The obvious solution was to have Ken be a little less specific. One senior person, however, was adamant that the entire letter be reviewed by me before it went out. No one objected to the new policy. Within minutes of leaving the meeting, I realized that we had taken a decision away from the people responsible for our newsletter.

It was a minor issue, but it alerted me to the inadvertent ways we undermine decentralization when someone makes a mistake or a problem arises. There is an intrinsic organizational assumption that mistakes or problems could be avoided if high-ranking people made all the decisions. But more often than not, lower-ranking people are closer to the problem and better positioned to come up with a solution, especially if they seek advice from their colleagues. The tendency to turn to top executives was most pronounced when our stock plummeted in 1992 and again in 2001–02. When the share price turned south, many board members pushed for centralization, which seemed to provide reassurance that the business was being run in a conventional and "safe" way.

Government regulation: The Sarbanes-Oxley Act of 2002, which requires CEOs and CFOs to certify financial results, will have a similar effect of centralizing decisions and making the consequences of work less important and meaningful to the people who actually do the work. Government agencies almost always want to make top executives responsible for every aspect of a company's operations. Do they really believe this will make the organizations behave more ethically? I do not believe there is credible evidence that this is true. What I do know is that it will drain the joy from those deep in the organization who have the satisfaction each day of knowing that they have responsibility for making their part of the business more productive and successful—and more ethical.

Service suppliers: For years it seemed as if every banker, insurance company representative, coal supplier, and anyone else who wanted to sell AES services of some kind called my office for an appointment. They hoped to persuade me or the CFO or some other central officer that they should get a large chunk of AES's business. This seemingly benign process can easily result in central purchasing of services for plants all over the world.

Over time, I realized that I needed to get out of the middle of these supplier relationships. The people at our various business units and on business-development teams knew far better than I what they needed and who could best supply it. I restricted my involvement to telling suppliers that we would love to pursue the possibility of using their services and products—and then directing them to the appropriate AES people.

The acquisition of knowledge and expertise: One important goal at AES was acquiring knowledge that could be applied to our business. If not approached carefully, this, too, is a process that can be a force for centralization. When people at AES learned things important to the company's success, we had a tendency to put them in charge of the area or department where this knowledge would be most essential. Our logic was simple: People usually feel comfortable making decisions about subject matter that's familiar to them. They also enjoy having people turn to them for their newly acquired expertise. The downside is that their colleagues have a tendency to stop learning and instead become dependent on them, often deferring to them for decisions. This creates its own kind of centralization, not at company headquarters but at the plants themselves, which have the ultimate responsibility for making work fun.

> *Ordinary workers need independence and a feeling of control if they are going to show initiative and risk failure.*

Tom Tribone told me of an analysis of several years of operating data at an ARCO chemical plant where he had worked as a young engineer. Operating performance was significantly better on weekends, when supervisors and other leaders and engineers were not in the plant. His conclusion was that staff technicians were more engaged and reacted more quickly to problems without bosses looking over their shoulders. When supervisors were in the plant, the technicians tended to wait for them to manage the situation.

Another illustration of this point came from the people who were building a new porch on our home. When I asked them for a progress report, they replied, "Depends on how much time the boss spends here. We get the job done faster when he is away. No one waits around for him to tell us what's next. We don't wait for him to solve the problems. We don't expect him to anticipate when we are going to need more supplies."

People become passive under the control of bosses. Ordinary workers need independence and a feeling of control if they are going to take on responsibility, show initiative, and be willing to risk failure. Putting one's talents on the line is essential to creating a healthy and fun workplace.

Boards of directors: I tread lightly in this arena for fear of being misinterpreted. My board was responsible by law for what happened inside the company just as I and other officers were. It was not particularly difficult for AES officers to rely on plant technicians or business development people to make decisions regarding environmental compliance, capital investments, or the plant reserve fund. We knew these people, worked with them every day, and trusted their judgment.

It is much more difficult for part-time board members to defer to employees. Chances are that the board members have not even met them, let alone know them well enough to have confidence in their decisions. The natural tendency is for board members to want a senior officer or plant manager to make important decisions. They argue that society and shareholders hold them responsible for the performance of the company.

It is a good argument, but only up to a point. Senior leaders and board members *are* responsible, but they cannot possibly approve— or even keep track of—every decision the company makes. If the board insists that top management make 200 decisions it ordinarily wouldn't make, that still means tens of thousands of decisions are made elsewhere in the organization. We bear the same responsibility for these decisions as we would for the 200 we made. If we delegated these 200 decisions to people deeper in the organization, who are probably better equipped to make them anyway, it wouldn't reduce our liability or our chances of being sued. It would, however, make a huge difference to the people away from headquarters who experience the joy of playing an important role and knowing that the company trusts their judgment.

Paternalism: On my first visit to Uganda in 1999, my host took me to the source of the Nile and then to the site on the river where we were planning a new hydro facility. Our third stop was a huge sugar cane plantation owned and operated by my host's family. We drove around the expansive fields where hundreds of people were working. When we passed an area of small, dilapidated housing units, he told me that these were provided free to the workers. He was particularly enthusiastic when we visited a building that served both as school and medical facility. "We provide free schooling and medical care. We have whole families who have been with us for years." "How much do you pay the workers?" I asked. "Enough," was the reply. "They don't really need much. They are well taken care of on the plantation." My host was very proud of what his family, one of the most respected in Uganda, had accomplished. "What do you think?" he asked, eager to get my reaction. "This is one of the most depressing places I have ever been," I said with only a little hyperbole. "By Ugandan standards, you are taking great care of these people, but they are not allowed to grow up and become independent adults."

This experience reminded me of the Tennessee Ernie Ford lyric: "You load 16 tons, what do you get? Another day older and deeper in debt. St. Peter, don't you call me 'cause I can't go, I owe my soul to the company store." Paternalism, whether practiced on a Ugandan sugar cane plantation, in Appalachian coal mines, or in a modern American corporation, is far from dead. Managers around the world still feel the need to take care of workers. On a superficial level, it is an admirable response. But paternalism takes on a different cast when examined more closely. It leaves people in a state of childlike dependence. It prevents workers from taking control of their work and lives. They are never in a position to take risks or make decisions, and so never develop to their full potential. In the end, paternalism kills any chance of joy at work.

When AES purchased a hydro plant in Hunan province, China, we were disturbed by the plight of the workers. Health care and education were substandard. I was pulled in the direction of doing something to help these people. Most of us have a compassionate impulse that prompts us to say: "We need to intervene." Sometimes we respond to the needs of employees by providing health care or by promising job security, higher pay, training programs, or child care. These are all "nice" things to do.

While we need to respond to the problems of our employees, we shouldn't do so for the sake of being "nice" or "good." Don't be afraid to try new approaches that give them control over how they want to live their lives. Instead of providing houses and schooling, pay them enough so they make choices about what's important to them and their families. Resist the temptation to guarantee jobs for life. Treating employees like children is not in their best interest, nor does it serve the goals of an organization.

> *The lack of freedom may be the single most debilitating and demoralizing factor in the workplace today.*

In earlier days, total concentration on production in factories and on farms was the primary reason that people hated their work. Today, the emphasis on earnings and share price has crowded out the important human qualities needed to run a healthy business— character, values, and concern for colleagues and the integrity of the larger enterprise. From individuals who judge their status in life by the size of their bank accounts to corporations that manipulate their financial results to make their stock price go as high as possible, the desire for wealth often creates systems and practices that are centralized and mechanistic—dictating everything from salary levels to cost controls—and that take the joy out of work.

Despite cosmetic improvements, the workplace has not become a more fulfilling place over the past 50 years. Economic efficiency remains the primary measure of success. Relatively few people are treated as full-fledged adults capable of making sound decisions. Workers are often treated like machines or beasts of burden, almost as if the company wanted to get the most out of its "assets" before it got rid of them. They rarely get the chance to make decisions or act on them. This lack of freedom may be the single most debilitating and demoralizing factor in the workplace today.

Inside typical modern companies, however, you get a very different view than I have suggested above. Workers, especially those at lower levels, don't seem overly concerned with job satisfaction—at least at first blush. "I like very much what you are talking about, Dennis, but what I really want is security. I don't want to risk losing my job." Then I would ask, "What is the most secure place you could be?" After a few rounds of guessing and suggestions, we usually ended up with "prisons" as the places that offered the most security, with bed and board to boot. When confronted with the logical extension of their desire for security, most people saw the fallacy of the goal. Children require security, but when they become adults, the desire for security inhibits their uniquely human abilities to make decisions, take risks, learn new things, fail, grow, make progress, experience loss, and then make progress again. We need to design organizations that encourage people to look beyond job security and seek the psychic rewards that come with a creative, enterprising approach to work. Many of the world's large organizations are filled with people trapped in the dead-end goal of seeking security. It is the enemy of joy at work.

In my experience, most people don't believe that fun and work can coexist. In large organizations, so few executives have experienced a joyful workplace that they have no idea how to create one. The result: Most employees grasp for high pay and benefits, fewer hours on the job, the mindless comfort of routine, less responsibility, early retirement, and job security. All are hollow substitutes for a rewarding, stimulating workplace.

If you're lucky, the workplace created by the Industrial Revolution may put food on the table, pay for your kids' schooling, and even provide for a comfortable retirement. But "where's the love, man?" as the old Bud Light commercial asked. Where is the love for work and accomplishment? Where are the other unique traits and gifts and frailties that make us human? Where is the passion to serve? Maybe these were left on Collin Doherty's farm, or maybe they were lost in the race for productivity and profits. I believe, however, that nothing so fundamental to human nature can be lost forever. If that is true, it will transcend even a movement as powerful as industrialization. It remains alive in many of our homes. It is preached in our churches, synagogues, and mosques. It exists in our memories of teamwork and competition in gyms and on playing fields. I am confident that it cannot be long absent from the place where we spend most of our waking hours—at work.

We are uniquely created with the ability to reason,
make decisions, and be held accountable for our actions.
When all of these factors come into play at the same time,
we feel something approaching pure joy.

CHAPTER 3

From Misery to Joy

"THERE IS NO FUN LIKE WORK." That was the motto of Dr. Charles Mayo, founder of the famous medical clinic. The key to joy at work is the personal freedom to take actions and make decisions using individual skills and talents. This is a simple concept but almost impossible to carry out because of the roadblocks thrown up by large organizations—as AES discovered with one of our early power plants.

I had just returned to my hotel room after a long day of trying to convince high-level Florida state government officials that our plant under construction in Jacksonville was following all the permit requirements (and then some). When the phone rang at 10:30 p.m., I was stunned by what I heard from Bill Arnold, the manager of the AES plant in Shady Point, Oklahoma, our newest, largest, and most profitable power-generating facility. The news he related to me would set in motion the most intense six months of learning in my professional career. It would also eventually drain the spirit of this gifted plant leader.

One of Bill's assistants had discovered that nine technicians had conspired to falsify the results of water testing in the plant. They had sent inaccurate water-quality data to regulators at the Environmental Protection Agency. While the falsification did not result in any harm to the river into which the water was discharged, it was a major breach of our shared commitment to integrity and social responsibility. A week or so later, Roger Sant and I wrote a very strong and candid letter to our employees and shareholders. Because it captures the spirit, values, and operating ethos of AES, I think the letter is worth quoting. We were still in the process of refining our values, and, as you can see, we had yet to come down hard on training programs. The job security mentioned in the letter was needed to get to the bottom of a troubling situation, and in that sense it was an exception to my larger opposition to guaranteeing indefinite employment. Here are excerpts from our letter:

Dear Shareholders and People of AES:

Some disappointing news has just come to our attention which, consistent with our values, we felt we should share with you at the earliest opportunity. On Thursday, June 18, we notified the Environmental Protection Administration (EPA) and the State of Oklahoma that we had discovered in an internal review that some water discharge reports have been falsified at the AES Shady Point Plant in Oklahoma.

It appears that no one in the management structure outside of the water treatment area was aware of these violations. The people involved say that they falsified the samples because they feared for their jobs if they reported a violation. Yet no one at AES has ever lost his or her job for telling the truth, nor will they ever, as long as we have anything to say about it.

This answer is hard to understand because these were the sort of minor excursions to be expected during the first year of operation of a new plant. Since discovering violations, we have adjusted operating procedures and are adding new equipment so that it should be highly unlikely for such exceedences to occur in the future.

What disappoints us most is that no one mentions these violations in either of the two confidential and anonymous values surveys that were conducted at Shady Point during the time this was going on.

This action raises serious questions in our minds about our performance relative to our values. One of the founding tenets of this Company is the shared values. We thought we had explained our values enough to everyone in AES that this sort of thing could never happen here. We are trying to treat people like adults, trusting in their honesty, judgment, maturity, and professionalism—rather than relying on detailed procedures, manuals, and minute supervisory oversight. We cannot comprehend why anyone would trade our integrity to make our environmental performance look better. We hope that the steps we have taken today address the problem, but are embarrassed and disappointed and angry that this could have happened in AES.

The letter was leaked to the press, and we quickly learned how candor can be misconstrued by the investing public. We were a young publicly traded company at the time, and many investors assumed that the misconduct at Shady Point was an economic disaster. In fact, it would bring nothing more than a small EPA fine because no damage had been done to the environment. Nonetheless, our stock price dropped 40 percent the day the letter was leaked. The precipitous fall was on top of the previous month's 20 percent decline from problems we were having in Florida, where a neighborhood group was mounting an effective challenge to our building permits, even though we had already begun construction on a new plant.

Before the stock plummeted, key board members and senior officers were seriously but constructively concerned about the incident. We started to investigate what happened and how. Roger and I circulated our letter. Beyond thinking about discipline and rehabilitation for those directly involved, we began asking what we could do better in hiring, leadership, and education to minimize the chances of something like this happening again.

After the stock price dropped, the nature of our response changed dramatically. We became panicky, and our emphasis shifted from disclosure to damage control. Much of our attention turned to reassuring our shareholders. A host of lawyers descended on the plant "to protect the assets."

It seemed to me that most of our leaders, especially board members, were more concerned about the drop in stock price than the breach in our values. One of the lawyers' first suggestions was to fire all nine of the people involved. When I asked why, he responded, "They will go easier on you at the Environmental Protection Agency." From my perspective, that was an unacceptable reason for dismissing an employee. Rightly or wrongly, I decided that no one would be fired if he admitted wrongdoing, accepted his punishment, and pledged to adhere to AES values in the future. Under these conditions, seven of nine offending employees left the company one way or another within one year.

Several of our most senior people and board members raised the possibility that our approach to operations was a major part of the problem. It was as if the entire company were on the verge of ruin. They jumped to the conclusion that our radical decentralization, lack of organizational layers, and unorthodox operating style had caused "economic" collapse. There was, of course, no *real* economic collapse. Only the stock price had declined. In addition, one of our senior vice presidents did a presentation for the board suggesting that "Protect Our Assets" rather than "Serving Electrical Needs" should be the top goal of the company. What he meant was that we should follow a defensive strategy, led by a phalanx of lawyers, in order to avoid legal, environmental, and regulatory wrangles. There was also discussion of adding a new layer of operating vice presidents between me and the five plant managers we had at the time. A meeting of the company's 13 top managers was convened when I was out of town. At the meeting, a senior officer of the company suggested that our outside counsel should be made vice chairman of the company, with authority over me when "compliance" issues were involved. The officers group took a straw vote that showed 11 in favor of the new organizational ideas and only two against.

Bill Arnold phoned me again about a month after all this trouble began. He asked me not to visit the Oklahoma plant anymore. Under pressure from lawyers and because of an understandable loss of confidence, the plant had decided to return to a "proven" approach to running industrial facilities. Back came shift supervisors, an assistant plant manager, and a new environmental staff department reporting to the plant manager (to make sure water treatment employees did the right thing). These steps increased our staffing level at the plant by more than 30 percent. Bill told me I would not be happy with the changes. He added that employees at Shady Point would feel "uncomfortable" if I were to visit as I had in the past. If I had not been preoccupied with the larger issues of maintaining our corporate values, I might have rejected Bill's request. I felt hurt and humiliated, but at the time I had bigger problems. I was fighting with the board to preserve our values—and to keep my job. Instead, I told people in AES I had been "fired" from the plant. I did not meet with the Shady Point managers for over six months, and even then we conferred "off campus." When I finally visited the plant a month after that, I was greeted by cheers. It was one of the sweetest moments of my career.

In the six months following the stock price decline, there was considerable pressure from some board members and officers to "tone down the rhetoric" about values. Several of them thought it arrogant of us to talk about values in public when we didn't always practice them. "Investors would not treat us so harshly if we didn't put the values out front so much and then fail to live them," said one board member. Besides, profits—not values—were what investors cared about, so "let's not talk about values outside the company," another board member said. The issue of why we put so much emphasis on values was raised again. "They didn't work, Dennis. We need to adjust," is the way one of my associates put it. We engaged in lengthy discussions about whether we should change the way the company described the relationship between values and profits in our public-offering documents. During this time I felt under-appreciated and uncertain about how much support I had among board members, who seemed to like our values only because they generated good press and were popular among employees. I felt I was alone in fighting for our values because they were intrinsically right.

All of this put an enormous strain on the relationship between Roger and me. We spent most of a day at his home discussing what to do. The board had lost confidence in me and my leadership approach. (I believe Roger had, too.) Should we split the company? Should one of us quit? He wasn't having fun and neither was I. I told him I wanted to stay and make the company work. We decided that I would visit all the board members who had been with the company since the beginning. I would apologize for what had happened and ask them to give me another chance to show that I could lead the company in a way that would make them proud.

One of the things I learned from this experience was that I had done a terrible job teaching people our values and principles. As a company, we did not understand in a practical way how those values shaped the way we organized our work and life together. Our values, perhaps most notably "fun," had become mere public-relations words. Their connection to the day-to-day operations of the company was superficial at best. Other than a couple of senior staff members and three or four of the plant managers, few people felt strongly enough about the values to adhere to the path we had started down a few years before. This was especially true whenever the share price declined or other economic problems arose. It did not seem to matter to the skeptics that there was almost no evidence that the approach we had adopted in operating our plants had anything to do with the water-treatment fiasco. If anything, most of the serious trouble—the lying and the coverup—occurred because nine AES people at Shady Point had not adhered to our values.

The breach by our Oklahoma group was minor relative to similar missteps by dozens of large, conventionally managed organizations. There was nothing to suggest that operating the company in a more conventional manner would have protected AES from such mistakes. Most important, I was convinced that weakening our covenant of values and principles would take most of the joy out of working for AES.

All this questioning forced me to examine every aspect of my business philosophy. I crammed into a few months a lifetime of learning about people and organizations. I left for vacation that summer realizing that I had nearly lost my job. I knew that if I was to continue pursuing my radical approach to the workplace, especially the highly unorthodox goal of having fun, I would run the risk of being ousted at any time. I had learned that most of the board members did not agree with my philosophy. They weren't particularly supportive of my leadership approach nor were they the least bit loyal to me. I did not forget this during the next 10 years, even when our stock price was rising rapidly and many board members sang my praises and appeared enthusiastic about my management approach. I kept saying that our values were not responsible for the run-up in our share price and should not be blamed for any downturns in the future.

On my vacation, I focused on two options for using what I had learned. I could back off, softening my emphasis on values and taking a more conventional line in my actions and communications, especially outside the company. Or I could, as one of the senior vice presidents so aptly put it a few months later, "raise the values banner high and march full speed ahead." I came back from the vacation determined to march smartly.

I committed myself to teach our values every day in word and deed. I planned regular and frequent travel everywhere in the company to do so. All outside communications would include a brief discussion of our purpose and principles and how they fit with the overall scheme of the business. I decided to return to fundamentals, especially as they related to our goal of making AES a fun place to work. A few years earlier, we had defined the assumptions about people that we believed had guided the workplaces of the Industrial Revolution. I took the next logical step and defined a new set of assumptions about people in the workplace that reflected our thinking at AES. Then I challenged myself and all other company leaders to evaluate every aspect of our existing organizational design and every system either in place or proposed. Was it more consistent with our basic assumptions, or was it less? I suggested we always choose the alternative that was more consistent with our values and in that way increase the chances of creating a rewarding, exciting, vibrant, successful, and fun workplace.

The assumptions about people in the workplace that follow were first put on paper in the summer of 1992, in the aftermath of Shady Point. I added the point about our fallibility a year or so later, but the others remained fundamentally unchanged over time. Note the striking difference between these assumptions and the ones that grew out of the Industrial Revolution.

AES people, I wrote:

- Are creative, thoughtful, trustworthy adults, capable of making important decisions;
- Are accountable and responsible for their decisions and actions;
- Are fallible. We make mistakes, sometimes on purpose;
- Are unique;
- Want to use our talents and skills to make a positive contribution to the organization and the world.

My hypothesis was that a fun workplace is one that allows people to work in an environment that is most consistent with human nature. While each person is different, some characteristics are common to all of us. The assumptions I made about AES people are intended to capture the most important of these characteristics.

Do not minimize the difficulty of matching assumptions about people with specific organizational structures and systems. It is almost impossible to do consistently. Economic realities, for example, always increase the difficulty of creating a workplace that takes into account human traits and frailties. Designing a great workplace would be difficult even if all people were the same. Because each of us is unique, it is a very tall order to create a working community that is fun and meets our individual needs—and that is also economically successful.

Compounding the problem of creating a fun workplace is the prevailing view among most people that work is, at best, a necessary evil. In my discussions about the workplace, I often ask people to play a word association game. I say "work" and ask what comes to mind. Invariably, they respond with words like "hard," "drudgery," "something I have to do," "boring," and "difficult." I have noticed that words and phrases like these are used frequently by people who have been working for 20 years or more. That is understandable given the length of time they have spent in working environments where they were rarely challenged or called on to make an important decision. What's surprising is that these same words are used nearly as often by people who are still in school and may not have had anything but part-time or summer jobs. Their parents and friends have crushed their expectations even before they reach working age.

For Christians, Jews, and Muslims, the story of Adam and Eve and the Fall often is cited as the reason that work is difficult. A few years ago, I was asked to give the commencement address at Eastern University, a Christian school in Pennsylvania. My topic was "Fun in the Workplace." In preparation, I reread the Genesis account of the Creation and realized that many of us have misinterpreted the story.

God created Adam and Eve and placed them in the Garden of Eden. In the Garden, they named and cared for the animals. They tilled the ground and harvested the fruit and vegetables. In other words, they seemed to spend much of their time "working." Their work was not hard, difficult, or the least bit boring. It was paradise.

The whole experience was sublime. Of course, they sinned and were ousted from the garden, and life became more difficult. It is this last part of the story that appears to mark our attitude and expectations about work.

Another way to view the story, however, is that God intended that the workplace be beautiful, exciting, and satisfying. Work was to be filled with joy. Work was a major reason for our creation. It was intended to be an important act of worship. It was one of the most significant ways in which we could honor our Creator. From this perspective it is our responsibility to do whatever we can to make the modern workplace the way it was intended to be. While I realize the world is not the Garden of Eden, I do believe it is incumbent on those of us in leadership roles to do whatever we can to make the workplace as fun and successful as we can.

One Latin word for work is *labor*. It is similar in meaning to the word "labor" in English. It does not reflect any of the joy of work that we see in Genesis. *Opus* is another Latin word for work, and it comes closer to the concept of work that I am championing. *Opus* connotes a voluntary act, an act imbued with creativity and meaning. The development of a fun workplace is based on the *opus* concept of work.

In many of my interactions with people in the workplace, I ask the question, "What is the most important factor that makes a work-place rewarding, satisfying, exciting—fun? The typical answers I get will not surprise you:

- "Good friends"
- "Good environment"
- "It's challenging"
- "I get to do what I'm good at"
- "Fair play"
- "I learn a lot"
- "Doing something worthwhile"
- "I'm needed"

- "I'm thought of as a person"
- "Winning"
- "Part of a team"
- "Significant responsibility"

The first thing that is obvious from these responses is that a fun workplace has a number of characteristics that help make it that way. My study and experience, however, lead me to believe that one factor is far more important than any other. First, let's review some of the important factors that don't make it to the top of the list.

Good relationships with colleagues and supervisors are almost always given as one of the answers to my question. However, when I ask people if they have ever worked in a place where they had good friends but no fun, almost everyone emphatically says yes. Although good relationships and camaraderie may be important to a good workplace, they are not the most important factor.

High pay and good benefits almost never are given as a serious answer to my question. I mention this because so many leaders spend enormous amounts of time on compensation questions. In my experience, unfair compensation can make a workplace less attractive, but fair or generous pay will have almost no effect on the quality of the work experience. People make pay an overly important factor when they choose a job, in my opinion. Most find out later that their happiness in the workplace has very little to do with the level of financial compensation they receive.

A special workplace has many ingredients. The feeling that you are part of a team, a sense of community, the knowledge that what you do has real purpose—all these things help make work fun. But by far the most important factor is whether people are able to use their individual talents and skills to do something useful, significant, and worthwhile. When bosses make all the decisions, we are apt to feel frustrated and powerless, like overgrown children being told what to do by our parents.

The difference can best be understood by considering the nature of sports. Why do people consider sports fun and exciting but view work as boring and burdensome? My longtime love of sports prompted me to look more closely at what made me enjoy playing them so much. Maybe I could gain an insight or two that could help turn work into a much more positive experience. Take basketball, for example. When I ask people what the most fun thing to do is in basketball, a few say "passing the ball." Most say "shooting the ball."

"When is it most fun to shoot the ball?" I ask.

"In a game," is the response.

"When during the game?"

"When there are two seconds left and my team is 1 or 2 points behind or the score is tied."

"What kind of basketball game?"

"In the championship game, in the NBA finals."

Most people experience game settings as "fun," "exciting," and "rewarding" when they are playing for something important and have a key role in deciding the outcome of the contest. Similarly, while young children enjoy card and board games that rely on chance, adults prefer games that require skill, strategy, or memory. In other words, the more challenging the better. While such analogies are not perfect, sports and games can help us understand what brings joy to the workplace.

In the Virginia Independent School Championship football game, my son, Dennis Jr., was the quarterback for one of the teams. His team was a touchdown behind with six minutes remaining in the game. They had the ball on their own 20-yard line. It was third down and 10 yards to go for a first down. The team needed to advance 80 yards to tie the game. I was a nervous wreck. I was pacing on the top level of the bleachers, almost afraid to watch. From a distance, however, Dennis seemed cool and confident. He calmly broke the huddle and began calling signals. He dropped back to pass and threw a perfect spiral to a streaking wide receiver for an 80-yard touchdown.

Why was I nervous and my son calm? That's simple: He was

in control and I was not. He had the ball. The outcome of the play turned on his skills, his actions, and his decisions. My experiences as a manager, coach, parent, and player are similar in this respect. The person in control of the moment has more fun than people who are less likely to affect the outcome.

Related to this point is the complaint I often hear from people dissatisfied with their work because "it is so stressful." I don't believe that stress determines whether a workplace is fun. Was Dennis's championship game stressful? Sure. Did it lessen the joy of playing? No, quite the contrary. As in most cases in which the outcome is on the line, stress enhances the experience, as long as a person has a certain amount of control

> *Stress enhances the experience, as long as a person has a certain amount of control over what happens. Debilitating stress stems from lack of control.*

over what happens. Debilitating stress stems from lack of control. The people who are probably most affected by this type of stress are middle managers caught between top executives, who won't give them the power to make decisions, and subordinates, who are constantly pressing them for answers and direction.

Similarly, I hear people complain about their work because "it is so hard" and "takes so much time." I doubt that hard work is the root of dissatisfaction. Again, I return to Dennis's athletic experience for some insight. For eight weeks in the summer before his senior year in high school, he spent three to four hours a day at school running, throwing, lifting weights, and studying film. He worked extremely hard. He was not paid a cent for this work. He wasn't even doing it to earn a scholarship to college; he had already concluded he had little chance of playing major college football. Why, then, would he work so hard? I believe it was for the opportunity that might come his way to run for a first down when it mattered or to throw a winning touchdown pass.

In basketball, football, and other games, another factor plays an important role: the scoreboard. Keeping score is a central part of the competitive experience, and it plays a crucial role in making games enjoyable. It doesn't seem to matter if the game is Hopscotch, Four Square, Horseshoes, Hearts, Boggle, or the World Cup, we keep score and care about the results. We may lose as often as we win, but at least we can measure our performance.

"How am I doing?" former New York Mayor Ed Koch used to ask his constituents. In his flamboyant way, Koch was articulating a need that all of us feel. Feedback is essential to a joyful work experience.

Failure ... teaches us humility. Failure is nearly as important as success in creating a great workplace.

Success obviously adds to our enjoyment of games and work. However, contrary to the rhetoric of coaches and inspirational leaders, this does not mean that we have to "win" all the time. A few years ago, there was an advertisement on television featuring basketball player Michael Jordan. In the ad, Jordan explained that from elementary school through his career in the NBA, he had played in 4,900 games. Thirty-nine times he had been in a position to win the game with the last shot—and *missed*. Was basketball fun for him even though he missed those shots and his team lost those games? I have no doubt that it is more fun to win the game than to lose. However, I believe the biggest source of joy to Jordan and other athletes—as well as to people in the workplace—is the opportunity to use their abilities when it really counts. From the perspective of the individual working person, the key to a great workplace is feeling wanted and important.

Failure and mistakes are also part of what makes games and work fun. In *My Losing Season*, an account of his high school and college basketball career, Pat Conroy says that failure is inevitable. It is also an essential element of learning and eventual success. Failure, in turn, teaches us humility, and because the experience is often painful, we learn indelible lessons. Indeed, failure is nearly as important as success in creating a great workplace.

Why is it fun and rewarding to play in a game or work in an organization in which you are given a measure of control and responsibility? The answer lies in the nature of human beings. We are uniquely created with the ability to reason and to develop talents and skills; we are able to apply these gifts when making decisions; and we feel it is natural and appropriate to be held accountable for the actions we take. When all of these factors come into play at the same time, we feel something approaching pure joy.

Can workplaces be structured in such a way that the maximum number of individuals have an opportunity to experience this kind of joy? Can we significantly increase the percentage of individuals who make important decisions and take key actions? Can we make work fun for people other than those at the top of the corporate ladder? Academic experts have suggested pathways toward this goal, and some business leaders have made determined efforts to reach it.

Here are some of the practices we followed at AES in an effort to make it a more fun place to work:

My administrative assistant decides what computer and software to purchase for herself *and* for me. She makes all travel plans, including airline, hotel, and car rental reservations. She decides her hours of work and schedule of activities. She decides whether she participates in or leads preparations for the next quarterly business review. She does not need my approval before making decisions. I am just one adviser among many she may consult about decisions. On purchases of furniture or machines, she routinely checks with the office accountant to see how her decisions would affect the budget, but no higher approval is necessary. When buying office equipment, she simply checks with colleagues to make sure it is compatible with the office system. She decides with whom I meet and to whom I talk on the phone. While the trend among executives is to delegate more decisions to their assistants, it is worth noting that she was not authorized to make any of these decisions in her previous job as assistant to the senior managing partner of a law firm.

A team of corporate administrative-assistant volunteers, including mine, was responsible for planning and executing the company's orientation weekends twice a year. The event usually drew 200 to 300 AES people from over 20 nations. Individuals on the team would choose the location; plan the program; arrange food, hotels, and transportation; recruit speakers; and even decide who would attend when the event was oversubscribed. The team had full and final responsibility for the entire weekend. Almost all home-office functions were managed in this way. When we held business reviews in Pakistan or South America, people in these locations took responsibility for all decisions related to the conferences.

At a plant, a technician who discovered that the heat exchanger needed repairs was authorized to schedule an outage and order the necessary replacement parts. He would routinely consult colleagues, his team leader, and the plant manager if time permitted and the amount of money involved was significant, but the final decision was his.

Recruiting and hiring were usually handled by teams, either under the direction of their regular leader or by a designated member—and always after a significant amount of consultation with representatives of other teams and possibly the plant manager.

In Oklahoma, a driver on the fuel-handling team noticed that a machine used to manage the coal pile was nearly at the end of its useful life and in any event was an obsolete model. He volunteered to lead an effort to select the best replacement machine, negotiate the purchase, and finance the $350,000 cost through a local bank. All this was done in consultation with colleagues and leaders at the plant and several financial people in the home office, but it did not require their approval.

At budget time, each team in a business unit calculated its needs. Then the teams met to hash out the plant's budget, which could run as high as $300 million. When the teams were satisfied that the budget passed muster, they sent it to the home office, which put the proposals together and sent them to all other units in the company. Several hundred individuals from local business units and the home office met together once a year to review the proposed budgets and suggest possible changes and improvements. The advice given to each business unit concerning its budget was just that—advice. The local business representatives took the advice back to their colleagues for consideration. It was up to them to make the final decisions on their budgets. Sometimes they took the advice, and sometimes they didn't. Capital and operating budgets were handled at the same time and in the same manner.

In too many organizations, charitable giving is handled by senior executives, board members, or a corporate foundation composed of current and former company executives and civic leaders. Their decisions on charity often reflect corporate goals or the special interests of the individuals involved, rather than the real needs of the community. I believe that a better approach is for the company to match the charitable contributions of its employees, whether they give to schools, traditional charities, or faith-based groups and churches. In this way, charitable-giving decisions are placed in the hands of every member of the company.

This approach both encourages the organization's people to give more and funnels money to causes that employees, in their collective wisdom, have decided are truly worthy. At AES, individual gifts were leveraged because the AES match doubled the amount given to each organization (in some poorer countries, the AES gift was triple the employee's contribution) or because employees bundled their contributions to major charities such as Habitat for Humanity or the United Way and the company matched the total.

Business development and financing decisions were almost always handled at the local level. The development of the Lal Pir generating facility in Pakistan provides a good illustration of how these decisions were made under our system.

Shahzad Qasim, who became one of the most successful developers of electric power facilities in the world, came to us as a financial analyst from a consulting firm. He was born in Pakistan and educated in the United States. A few months after joining AES, he returned to Pakistan to visit his family. While there, he noticed considerable interest in adding new electricity-generating capacity. "I was wondering if I could leave what I have been working on to make a more extensive investigation regarding the Pakistan opportunity," he asked his supervisor. "That is your decision, not mine," his supervisor told him. "Why don't you run it by your colleagues and a couple of other vice presidents. See what Dennis thinks, also." I told him I was skeptical. Several years earlier, Agency for International Development (AID) representatives from the U.S. Department of State had encouraged us to expand into Pakistan. We had told them that we hardly knew what we were doing in the United States, let alone a place like Pakistan. Besides, it ranked as one of the most corrupt countries in the world for doing business. The ethical standards at AES probably ensured that we would never get any business there.

The decision on whether to proceed was left to Shahzad. Six months later, he asked me to visit Pakistan with him to meet the prime minister and help push along the project that Shahzad and his team were planning. At each major step in the 2 ½-year development process, Shahzad asked for advice, then made the key decisions himself. Before securing the $700 million financing (including several hundred million dollars of AES equity), Shahzad consulted with the

AES board. The board reacted favorably, but the project decisions remained with Shahzad or a member of his expanding team. By this time, many of the final decisions on the development had been delegated by Shahzad to members of his team. The final decision on the construction contract and builder was not his. Neither were the final financing arrangements, including the $200 million of equity put up by AES. They all were made by people with less seniority and rank than Shahzad. As soon as the financing was complete, new construction and operating teams made all the important decisions on their respective parts of the development.

Joy at work starts with individual initiative and individual control.

Neither the idea to investigate the possibilities in Pakistan nor any important decision that followed was made by senior executives or central planners, or by the finance department or even a central business-development unit at AES. Joy at work starts with individual initiative and individual control. Individuals, not a bureaucracy, make the decisions and hold themselves accountable. The process is bottom up, but it is not a loosey-goosey, anything-goes affair. It involves creativity, careful analysis, meticulous planning, and disciplined execution. Most of those activities are done far from the home office—and with nothing more than advice from staff groups and senior leaders at AES headquarters.

The employee decisions I have described differ widely in their complexity and consequences. The goal, however, is the same: to design a workplace where the maximum number of individuals have an opportunity to make important decisions, undertake actions of importance to the success of the organization, and assume responsibility for the results.

The advice process is my answer to the age-old organizational dilemma of how to embrace the rights and needs of the individual, while simultaneously ensuring the successful functioning of the team, community, or company.

CHAPTER 4

"Honeycomb": Dynamics of a Joyous Workplace

THE KIND OF WORKPLACE we created at AES was not unstructured, much less "out of control," as some newspaper and magazine articles suggested. It was not a hands-off, undisciplined, and uncoordinated approach. It *was*, however, radically different. Information flowed in all directions within the company. More people were engaged in every aspect of the business than in other large organizations. It was transparent from top to bottom. At the same time, it was self-regulating: People given the responsibility for decisions did not want to fail. The number of mistakes we made compared favorably with that of companies that traveled a more conventional path.

Representatives from each department at AES's power plant in Houston were meeting to discuss elements of the plant's new employee handbook. It was 1986. I was at the plant as part of my "Work Week"* and had been asked to observe the discussion. The specific issue on the table was the wording of the section on "leave policy" when the parent of an employee dies. The group had already concluded that three days of leave was the appropriate amount and was in the process of drafting the exact language. Someone raised a

---

* *The idea of "Work Weeks" was inspired by the United Parcel Service, which required senior executives to spend time doing "real work" at one of the company's facilities.*

question. "What if I was raised by my grandparents or my uncle and aunt? Would that count?" Most agreed that it should. A paragraph was added for that contingency. "What if my parents live far away from Texas, maybe even in Europe? Three days isn't really enough time." After some additional discussion, more days were added to deal with this contingency. The handbook had grown by several pages in less than an hour.

While the idea of discussing the common needs of people working at the company seemed worthwhile, detailed written rules like the ones being developed that afternoon increasingly seemed out of place in a fun workplace. Where was the trust? Why couldn't reasonable people deal with each situation as it arose? What were our assumptions about people behind all the rules that we developed?

Even before the session in Houston, I was becoming skeptical about handbooks and most of the other programs administered by human resources departments. Roger Sant had set the skepticism in motion when he railed against sick-leave rules in our home office. "When you are sick, stay home. You don't need a handbook to tell you when or how long you can be sick or what you should do about it."

That evening, after all the managers had left the plant, I wandered about the facility and visited with the night crew. The meeting that afternoon was still on my mind, and I began asking questions about the handbook. What if we eliminated it altogether? What if we did away with procedure manuals? They are always out of date, and no one follows them anyway. What if we did away with detailed job descriptions? What if we didn't have an organization chart with boxes representing people and their jobs? What if we didn't have any shift supervisors? What if there were no written limits on what individuals could authorize the company to spend? What if all the specialist titles given to employees were eliminated? What if we created teams of people around areas of the plant to operate and maintain the facility, instead of letting bosses assign tasks and run the plant? What if each group could set its own hours of work? What if team members hired and fired their own colleagues? What if you could make important decisions rather than leave them to your supervisor or the plant manager? I gave no answers, just asked questions. Shortly after 1 a.m., I left the plant to return to my hotel.

When I arrived at the administration building the next morning, I noticed five or six plant leaders and supervisors hovering outside the plant manager's office. His door opened as soon as he noticed I was there. With some urgency he escorted me into his office. "What have you done to my plant?" an agitated Bill Arnold* asked. "Nothing much," I said. "All I did was ask a few hypothetical questions." "All my supervisors are ready to quit," he said. I told him I was sorry for upsetting everyone, but I was not sorry about wanting to talk about changing the way we ran plants to better fit our values and our assumptions about people.

Bill Arnold asked me to meet with his senior team to try to calm them down. In the meeting, I outlined some of the ideas about structuring AES workplaces. I called the set of ideas "Honeycomb."

This was inspired by what my Uncle Aadne told me about the bees he kept on the farm. "Denny, each of these bees can fly individually up to several miles from the hive to the fireweed on that recently logged mountain. They independently collect nectar and make the trek back home. They return to the hive with nectar, which others in the hive use to produce this wonderful honey we use on our toast." The basic thrust of my idea was to try to create an environment based on the same principles of trust, freedom, and individuals acting for the good of the larger group. These principles had guided our headquarters in Arlington, Virginia, since the company's earliest days. In Houston, the supervisors didn't begin to relax until I suggested it could take as long as two years for the plant to design and implement something in response to my questions. It marked the start of an amazingly creative and revolutionary overhaul of their industrial workplace.

---

* Bill Arnold was plant manager at Deepwater in Houston, Texas, before taking the same role at Shady Point, Oklahoma, several years later.

Within two months I was invited back to Houston to see the radical redesign of the plant. Using the Honeycomb theme, they had divided themselves into working groups with names of different types of bees (e.g., mud daubers, hornets, wasps, and yellow jackets). They had eliminated two layers of supervision (the operations superintendent and shift supervisors). Except for the maintenance department (which would break up later), the seven new teams (or families, as they called themselves) were organized around specific functions. There was a Boiler family, an Environmental Cleanup family, a Turbine Facility family, and several others. Each team leader reported to the plant manager. The teams were to be, for the most part, self-governing. They would be responsible for budgets, workload, safety, schedules, maintenance, compensation, capital expenditures, purchasing, quality control, hiring, and most other aspects of their work life. "Every person, a business person," was the way I came to describe the goal in later years.

> *Every business person needs to ask for as much advice as possible before making a decision.*

In 1997, I tried to define for the company what it meant to be an AES "business person." A business person, I wrote, must "steward resources (money, equipment, fuels)... to meet a need in society," while balancing the contributions and needs of all the stakeholder groups. This means providing a profit to shareholders, a fun workplace and fair compensation to employees, taxes and a clean environment to governments, and reliable electricity at reasonable prices to customers. "A person may very well be an engineer, or a heavy equipment operator or a financial wizard or an instrument technician, but a business person performs those functions in the context of balancing the interests of all stakeholders." In other words, a business person recognizes that every action taken by the company affects the interests of every stakeholder. "That's why I believe every business person needs to ask for as much advice as possible before making a decision to ensure the best balance of interests possible among all the affected groups, without compromising the ultimate purpose of the company to meet a need in society." Honeycomb was not the beginning, nor was it the end, of our efforts to build an organization consistent with AES values, but it was a major step forward.

Very few of the concepts underlying the AES ethos were new. Many start-up companies and other small organizations operate on similar principles. Modern high-tech organizations use some of these approaches as well. However, many of them treat administrative personnel and associates in the same way that bosses treated workers in the early days of the Industrial Revolution. Most nonprofit organizations, educational institutions, and churches seem to fall into the same traps. Nor are law firms exempt from the sweatshop, production-line mentality. A recent Rhodes Scholar, now a junior partner in a prestigious London law firm, was venting about how little control he had over his work, even as he sat in his large, wood-paneled office. "I feel like a hen producing eggs for the firm with little say over how they are used." The clever response of his superior—"I'll be here to collect the eggs"—did little to endear his workplace to the young man.

My purpose in writing this book is not to tick off a bunch of ideas for the hypothetical workplace. That's just skywriting. Corporate executives and business school professors have good ideas all the time but rarely do anything about them. What made AES unique was that we acted on our ideas. The results weren't always what we hoped, and sometimes we scrapped ideas after one try, but on the whole I think we managed to create a workplace that was fair, efficient, and—yes, I'll say it again—fulfilling and fun.

We organized ourselves around multiskilled, self-managed teams. This has been the operating style of some businesses for decades, and its popularity has grown markedly in the past 15 years. For millennia, human beings have lived and worked within communities of other people, so it's only natural that they should do so in a business setting.

What we tried to create at AES was a collection of small, interacting groups that would operate various sections of the business. Individuals on a team were responsible for everything about the "area" in which they worked. Their responsibilities might include day-to-day operations, investments, maintenance, scheduling, long-term strategy, hours of work, hiring and firing, education, safety, environmental management, risk management, budgeting and economic performance, quality control, charitable giving, or community relations. In many organizations, most of these tasks are performed by specialists. Our team system showed that complex tasks could be learned and understood by the average technicians within the operating units. At times, situations arose that exceeded their level of expertise. When that happened, team members could get help and advice from experts either inside or outside the company.

Giving teams primary responsibility for functions normally left to specialists was an approach radically different from that of most large organizations. Employees are usually grouped according to their expertise: finance and budgeting, long-term planning, safety issues, human resources, and the like. These groups of specialists often don't understand or appreciate the operating groups and their problems. Similarly, traditional operating groups have little understanding of financial and strategic planning. Typically, operations people are in awe of the specialists' skills and jealous of their salaries and status in the company.

Dividing a business into specialists (staff groups) and operating departments, as most large organizations do, blurs responsibility and decision making in ways that make work far less satisfying. The traditional structure also can make it more difficult to sustain economic success over a long period. Stories of waste caused by central purchasing or "sourcing" departments are at least as numerous as stories of cost savings.

Bobby Haft, a consummate entrepreneur, started a very successful chain of bookstores in the Washington, D.C., area in the 1980s.
After the first store took off, the company opened a second store in
another neighborhood. To stock the store with books, Haft's central
purchaser simply doubled the order of the first store. Very soon,
Bobby realized the books were not selling well in the second store.
People in that community had very different interests than those
living around the first store. He decided to scrap the idea of central
purchasing and required each store to order its own books—and be
responsible for keeping book returns to a minimum. The second
store and the ones that followed were as financially successful as the
first. Even more importantly, employees loved a working environment that put them in charge of all the important elements of the
business. Turnover was extremely low, especially compared with
that of other bookstores.

Haft recognized that a business is more responsive when workers are freed of the arbitrary limits placed on their authority. I was
told of a similar situation shortly before AES purchased its plants in
Northern Ireland. A turbine at one of the facilities vibrated above
the levels considered normal. An operator on the shift noticed the
problem. Instead of shutting down the machine immediately, he
began searching for his supervisor. Only the supervisor had the authority to decide whether to shut it down or not. Before the supervisor could be found, a catastrophic failure took place and several
hundred thousand dollars of damage occurred. Fortunately, no one
was hurt. The operator, who was in the best position to have made
the shut-down decision, could have averted the failure and saved the
plant both money and inconvenience.

I have heard dozens of similar stories. The person recounting
the incident always stresses the negative financial consequences.
Sometimes, the safety or environmental damage that could have
been prevented is included to illustrate the problem with such
"rules." Unfortunately, most of these stories are told and retold
without mentioning the negative effects on a working person's job

satisfaction, personal growth, and sense of self-worth. Rigid job definitions are not compatible with joy at work.

I have seen no credible evidence that limits on authority produce better decisions in large businesses. Yet, such limits remain standard operating procedure in most modern organizations. It is a carryover from the patriarchal system of the early Industrial Revolution. Before AES implemented Honeycomb, every individual and working unit had strict limits on spending authority. For example, the plant manager could authorize expenditures of up to $100,000, the operations superintendent $50,000, the financial manager $25,000, unit leaders $10,000, and others $1,000. In Europe, the limits were much lower for the "lower" employees. We eliminated all of these limits. Instead, staffers simply had to get the advice and perspective of colleagues and more senior people before making decisions on planned expenditures.

Along with the creation of multidisciplinary teams with broader responsibilities, we changed the way each "employee" was to be identified. We had already followed the lead of Wal-Mart and others and replaced the words "employee" and "manager," which we felt had become somewhat demeaning over time. (Let me say again that I will occasionally use these terms in this book because they are so widely applied outside of AES.) We decided we would identify every person who worked at the company as an "AES person" or "AES people." It seemed silly that we would feel compelled to identify people as "people." But it was more than a matter of nomenclature. Throughout history, especially from the onset of the Industrial Revolution, working people were often treated as less than human. At most AES plants, most of our people decided that everyone who was not a leader in the plant should have equivalent titles: "AES technician," "AES plant engineer," or something similar that would indicate general responsibility for a significant area of the plant. Most of the traditional industrial designations, such as welder or pipe fitter, were jettisoned.

In the early days of Honeycomb, we asked ourselves how many

people could work together on an ideal team. Some research indicated that 10 to 15 people was about the right number for one leader. My experience suggested that teams could have up to 40 members and still be effective, even with only one official leader. The larger the number of people on a team reporting to one supervisor, the fewer levels of hierarchy are required in the entire organization.

I was very concerned about having too many organizational layers. I set a goal of having only two layers of supervision between me and an entry-level person anywhere in the company. While that number increased to three layers and in a few cases four as the company grew to more than 30,000 people, keeping the number of layers to a minimum is important to make work fun. Each layer tends to block communication and other interaction in organizations. It also separates people at one level from those at another, sometimes physically and almost always in status. Each layer requires another leader, and each additional leader increases the chances that people will feel squelched by a boss.

Keeping the number of layers to a minimum is important to make work fun.

On the other hand, if the team is too large, it reduces the amount of individual attention and coaching a leader can give to each team member. It can also reduce the opportunity for cooperation and friendship. The "right" number is probably different in every situation. My personal preference is to err on the side of larger teams. This reduces the chance that a leader will interfere in all the decisions. It leads to a much flatter organizational structure and a lot more fun.

A question related to the size of the individual team is the number of teams that can operate smoothly in one physical location. I have found little persuasive research on this subject. My hunch is that bad things begin to happen when an organization has more than 300 to 600 people in one location. This suggests that an effective organization should have no more than 15 to 20 teams with 15 to 20 people on each team. Most of us have difficulty maintaining strong relationships with more than 20 people. Few of us can work alongside 1,000 people and manage to put names and faces together and engage in casual conversation with all of our colleagues. The CEO of Dana Corporation once told me that his company tried to limit the size of any one facility to 400 people. Above that number, people seemed to have difficulty identifying with the company.

Recent studies of mega-sized high schools show organizational patterns similar to those in business. Larger schools force young people to specialize in academic disciplines and extracurricular activities to a much larger degree than small schools, in which each individual is "needed" and encouraged to participate in several sports and numerous other school activities. In large schools, many students simply blend into the crowd, which means fewer of them are encouraged to become engaged in the life of the school beyond the classroom.

Fortunately, the huge workforces that produced economies of scale in early steel and auto plants have been replaced by automated facilities requiring fewer people. When we purchased the Ekibastuz power plant in Kazakhstan, more than 5,000 people worked at the plant. Today, fewer than 500 people produce double the amount of electricity. Teams work together more effectively, and the plant has a human scale.

Groups that perform a variety of functions are an essential part of a successful and fun workplace. This means taking these functions away from specialist staff groups. When teams handle a variety of tasks, individuals are able to make full use of their skills, and work becomes more challenging and enjoyable.

The kind of teams I am suggesting are more like banana splits than milkshakes. Milkshakes blend the various flavors of ice cream, toppings, milk, and other ingredients into one undifferentiated dessert. In banana splits, each scoop of vanilla, chocolate, and strawberry ice cream, along with the bananas and toppings, remain separate until eaten. In a banana-split team, individuals play special roles and maintain their identities. The sum of the parts is greater than the whole.

Building good teams depends on hiring the right kind of people. Dave McMillen, one of our most accomplished managers, designed a rigorous vetting process for identifying people who were most likely to succeed in the Honeycomb structure. He began with a series of questions that would both teach prospects about expectations for young people at the company and determine whether the individual would be a good fit. Skills and talent were important, but they took a back seat to the way a person reacted to the company's values, including our particular definition of fun.

> *The primary factor in determining whether people experience joy or drudgery in the workplace is the degree to which they control their work.*

The questions focused on finding self-starters who would take responsibility for their own actions. Did they understand that fairness did not mean the same treatment for everyone? Did they have the courage to make decisions? Did they understand what it meant to serve their colleagues, other stakeholders, and the company as a whole? A potential new hire might be interviewed by six to 10 people in a plant (none of them official "human resources" staffers) before being offered a position. We made some mistakes, of course, but the approach was quite effective in finding people to build and operate our special company.

The primary factor in determining whether people experience joy or drudgery in the workplace is the degree to which they control their work. By "control," I mean making decisions and taking responsibility for them. It is difficult to design a structure that allows individuals to work to their highest potential. Even more difficult is creating a community of such people who work in concert and produce something useful for society in a way that makes economic sense.

Even before we introduced the team concept into AES life, we used a "participatory" style of management. That is, the leader would seek out advice from knowledgeable colleagues before making decisions. "Suggestions" were very much welcomed and rewarded, but the boss still made the final decision. When we first formed teams in our plants, decision making shifted from the leader to the group. The teams either voted among themselves or discussed the matter until they had a consensus.

One effect was a drop in complaints about decisions. "Democracy" felt so much better than having decisions imposed by the corporate home office, or the plant manager, or a member of the plant manager's staff, or the team leader. It was a good approach, but there was an even better alternative that would both increase the fun and the chances of success.

That alternative was giving people the opportunity from time to time to make an important decision or take an action *individually*, just as a player does in a team sport. Gradually, most important decisions in the plants and in the home office were made in this manner. "Who is the decision maker?" became a common question around the company. Besides being a way to increase joy at work, it also had the advantage of being faster if a quick decision was needed. It also made it easier to hold individuals accountable, without sacrificing group accountability. Once an individual made a decision, the group, the plant, and eventually the entire company took responsibility for it.

While this approach brought extra fun to people in the organization, it posed three thorny questions.

First, it required leaders to give up their traditional right to make important decisions. Some people think decentralization can occur in an organization even while top executives make most of the decisions and sign off on others. But there are only so many decisions made by an organization, and the power to decide must be given to as many people as possible if their individual talents are to be fully utilized. This prompted an understandable question from experienced leaders: "Isn't this what we're paid to do?"

Second, this was a company, not a bunch of independent individuals. A company cannot afford lone rangers who operate apart from their leaders and colleagues. Why should one individual make an important decision for the whole company?

Third, how could a person on a team in a plant know enough to make a decision that could materially affect the entire company?

To deal with these questions, I introduced the "advice process." It is a very simple, al-

Before any decision can be made on any company matter, the decision maker must seek advice.

though often controversial, concept. It takes the "suggestion box" management approach of the 1970s and '80s and turns it upside down. Instead of the boss getting advice and suggestions from people below, the decision maker—who is almost always not an official leader—seeks advice from leaders and from peers.

Usually, the decision maker is the person whose area is most affected, or the one who initiated an idea, discovered a problem, or saw an opportunity. If it is unclear who the decision maker should be, the leader selects an individual to gather advice and make the final decision. Before any decision can be made on any company matter, the decision maker *must* seek advice. The bigger the issue or problem, the wider the net that is thrown to gather pertinent information from people inside and outside the company. In my opinion, all issues of importance need advice from the decision maker's own team. However, members of other teams in the plant or offices should also be consulted. Some decisions are so important that advice is gathered from other plants, divisions, and offices, including the home office. The board of directors should be consulted on the most important issues.

At AES, we did not always do a good job of carrying out the advice process, especially the requirement to reach beyond the team or business unit where the decision maker worked. Sometimes, the information and analysis provided to the potential adviser was sloppy and incomplete. Even with these weaknesses, the quality of the decisions using this approach was at least as good as those decisions made under more conventional management systems. Probably more important, it made work more interesting and fun for thousands of AES people.

The advice process is my answer to the age-old organizational dilemma of how to embrace the rights and needs of the individual, while simultaneously ensuring the successful functioning of the team, community, or company. I observed that Japanese companies tended to emphasize the group and consensus, while American culture pushed rugged individualism. I believe the advice process strikes a better balance. It leaves the final decisions to individuals, but it forces them to weigh the needs and wishes of the community. Parenthetically, the Internet was made to order for our advice process. The kind of wide consultations that I advocate would not be possible in large, dispersed organizations were it not for e-mail.

Five important things happen when the advice process is used by an individual before making a decision or taking action:

First, it draws the people whose advice is sought into the question at hand. They learn about the issues and become knowledgeable critics or cheerleaders. The sharing of information reinforces the feeling of community. Each person whose advice is sought feels honored and needed.

Second, asking for advice is an act of humility, which is one of the most important characteristics of a fun workplace. The act alone says, "I need you." The decision maker and the adviser are pushed into a closer relationship. In my experience, this makes it nearly impossible for the decision maker to simply ignore advice.

Third, making decisions is on-the-job education. Advice comes from people who have an understanding of the situation and care about the outcome. No other form of education or training can match this real-time experience.

Fourth, chances of reaching the best decision are greater than under conventional top-down approaches. The decision maker has the advantage of being closer to the issue and will probably be more conversant with the pros and cons than people in more senior positions. What's more, the decision maker usually has to live with consequences of the decision. Even if the decision maker comes to an issue without fully understanding its implications for the organization, that weakness can be overcome by obtaining advice from senior people. As Samuel Taylor Coleridge wrote: "Advice is like snow; the softer it falls, the longer it dwells upon, and the deeper it sinks into the mind."

The process (of making decisions) is just plain fun for the decision maker. It mirrors the joy found in playing team sports.

Fifth, the process is just plain fun for the decision maker because it mirrors the joy found in playing team sports. The amount of fun in an organization is largely a function of the number of individuals allowed to make decisions. The advice process stimulates initiative and creativity, which are enhanced by wisdom from knowledgeable people elsewhere in the organization.

Most modern organizations place extraordinary emphasis on training. While the motives might be laudable, the methods are not. Adults need education that engages their attention in an interactive way. Dr. William Glasser is a psychiatrist and psychologist who specializes in education, counseling, and business. His research on learning reinforced what I learned in the early days of Honeycomb. Glasser found our retention rates vary widely according to the ways information is transmitted. By his estimates, we remember:

10% of what we **read**
20% of what we **hear**

30% of what we **see**
50% of what we **see and hear**
70% of what we **discuss** with others
80% of what we **experience** personally
95% of what we **teach** to someone else

Education is a matter of performing tasks in an environment that encourages feedback and constructive criticism. In other words, we learn best when we discuss our work with others, make decisions that matter, and find out from others whether what we did was right or wrong. As Glasser's research shows, the people consulted along the way are apt to learn even more.

The implications seem obvious. Working and taking responsibility for a turbine is the best way to learn about the turbine; maintaining water-treating equipment is the best way to learn about maintaining the equipment; and being a supervisor or a plant manager is the best way to learn how to be an effective leader. Group projects and performance reviews are also important learning settings for everyone—certainly more important than classroom lectures or formal training programs. All these learning experiences are made more valuable when leaders act as mentors and advisers.

While some important information can be transferred using training methods, real education requires a very different approach. I was in Argentina with some of our AES people a few years ago. I asked them, "How and when did you learn to become a parent? Was it the talks you had on the subject with your mother? Was it the books you read on parenting?" "¡No, no, cuando llegó el bebé!" ("No, no, when the baby came!") they exclaimed, rocking an imaginary baby in their arms. Similarly, my wife's experience suggests that one semester of teaching is the equivalent of several years of teacher training in college.

The education tool made famous by the Harvard Business School is the "case method." The uniqueness of this teaching style is that the student is put in the position of the decision maker. Something magic happens to our learning experience when we are put in the role of seeking information because we need it to make a decision. Abstract concepts suddenly become germane and real—and a lot easier to understand.

As effective as it is, the case-study method can't match making decisions that have real consequences. It is the difference between firing blanks and firing live ammunition. When making consequential decisions, our rate of learning steps to a whole new level. This explains why apprenticeship programs have been so effective over the ages. The design of the AES workplace

People inside an organization must share all information.

somewhat accidentally created one of the finest educational institutions around. The opportunity to make important decisions after participating in an intensive advice process helped people learn in an accelerated way.

To get the most out of the advice process, people inside an organization must share *all* information. To explain this "no secrets" approach, I said that any piece of information available to me as CEO was available to every person in the company. That was probably more an aspiration than a reality, but the concept is very important. As John Case pointed out in *Open Book Management*, the decision process is rendered impotent if all information is not made available to people at all levels of the organizations.

When AES told the Securities and Exchange Commission that we intended to make available to our employees all corporate financial data, including quarterly earnings reports before they were released to the public, the SEC imposed a novel requirement. If everyone had access to financial data of the company, then every AES employee, even those working in faraway plants, would be classified as "insiders." Instead of five to 10 "insiders" at a typical company, AES had thousands. All were subject to "blackout periods" in which they could not trade the company securities. Fairly soon after AES stock began trading publicly, we asked our people if they would like to limit their access to information so that they would not be considered insiders and would be free to trade AES stock at any time. By an overwhelming margin, they chose to have full access to financial information and to remain insiders. Part of having joy at work is being "important" enough to have the same knowledge as leaders.

When the World Bank made a case study of AES as part of an internal review, I was asked to meet with a large group of the bank's employees to discuss many of the topics covered in this chapter. "How many people do you think should be employed by the bank, especially here in Washington, D.C.?"

> *Part of having joy at work is being "important" enough to have the same knowledge as leaders.*

asked one intrepid employee. "I certainly do not know the answer to that question," I responded. "But let me share our experience at AES and compare it to yours," I added. "The World Bank has about 10,000 employees. Our experience is that the typical restructured organization can accomplish twice as much with half the number of people than currently work there. If that rule held, the bank would need no more than 5,000 people. At AES we have about 40,000 people worldwide. Only about 100 work in the Arlington, Virginia, headquarters. At the bank, 8,000 of your 10,000 employees work in the Washington office. For a worldwide enterprise whose services are delivered to dozens of countries, that ratio seems upside down."

To make a large organization exciting, successful, and fun, it is crucial to limit the number of people in the home office, central staff, and senior executive offices. Most senior executives seem to believe that God or the board created them to make all the important decisions. But every decision made at headquarters takes away responsibility from people elsewhere in the organization and reduces the number of people who feel they are making an effective contribution to the organization. Remember, joy comes from freedom. When central staffs assume the lion's share of power and control, the people who are operating units don't get as much excitement and fulfillment from their work.

As CEO, I tried to limit myself to one significant decision a year (it usually involved restructuring the organization's regions and selecting new leaders for various senior positions). I wasn't always successful, but the discipline of trying made a deep impression throughout the organization. Other leaders tried to follow my example. Thousands of decisions that would have been made by leaders were spread among thousands of other AES employees. For the first time, many AES people felt needed, important, and trusted. In effect, they had become full participants in their workplace.

An analogy offered by Attila Szokol, an AES technician in Hungary, explains how they felt. Even this wooden translation of his letter cannot conceal the strong emotional reaction of a man raised under communism: "What is important is trust. When a child will jump into a parent's arms because of absolute trust that he has in the parent to catch him. Likewise, this approach requires leaders to trust those responsible to them as if the leader were jumping into the arms of the subordinate, because it is the subordinate's actions and decisions that decide the fate and success of the leader."

While having too many general managers at the center of the organization is a significant problem, the proliferation of staff offices, composed of specialists carrying out narrow functions, is an even bigger enemy of fun in the workplace. In my experience, it doesn't matter whether it is human resources, legal, public relations, engineering, treasury, or any of 15 or 20 other similar departments that pop up in most large organizations. While they are billed as "service" offices, they usually make life in the operating parts of the enterprise more difficult. Most of what they do could be better accomplished if the specialists were working as part of an integrated team of people trying to accomplish a broader mission. They can be more effective as part of a banana-split team. Central staff offices remind me of the derogatory phrase often used to describe people in the federal government who show up to audit or inspect an enterprise: "We are from the federal government, and we are here to help."

Human resources is one of my least favorite. AES did away with its HR department six months after we started staffing our first plant. All but a few of the administrative functions were turned over to the existing teams within AES's operating facilities. Recruiting, education, reviews, compensation, hiring, discipline, firing, and benefits were handled by the people who had direct responsibility for the quality of their work. Professor Jeff Pfeffer celebrated this radical decentralization in a Stanford Business School case on AES titled, "Human Resources: The Case of the Missing Department."

I sometimes explain one of the problems with central staff groups by saying, "The stronger and more competent the central staff person, the worse it is likely to be for the rest of the organization." If the central staff is believed to be very competent, operating leaders and their subordinates have a tendency to become passive, to stop learning about important aspects of the business, and to stop linking the success of the company with the success of their teams.

In one of my annual State of the Company presentations, I used a marionette as a metaphor for what happens to employees who feel controlled by staff experts at the top of large organizations. The image of being jerked around at the end of a string captured the helplessness and frustration of people in frontline units when they see dozens of specialists deal with process while they attend to business. Believe me, I experienced this in a very real way in the federal government.

There is no question in my mind that large organizations would be better places to work if they eliminated most groups organized around special functions and integrated those functions into operating groups. Not so clear is whether ridding the enterprise of all such units gives the organization a better chance to succeed. Expertise in purchasing, financial matters, auditing, engineering, strategic planning, investor relations, purchasing, and a host of other disciplines is important. The organization needs people who have expertise in these areas, if only to spread their knowledge.

How then can we best make work fun and at the same time ensure that the company has sufficient expertise to deal with any contingency? There are several approaches I recommend:

(1) As noted above, experts can sometimes be integrated into the all-purpose teams. When this happens, they quickly learn what the "real world" is like and become much more effective in teaching and applying their specialties. At various times, our top expert in fluidized bed boilers worked as a plant manager in England, our leading specialist in U.S. environmental permitting was assigned to business development in Europe, and our best gas turbine person worked in our plant in Pakistan.

People should spend 80% of their time on their primary roles and devote the other 20% to participating on task forces, giving advice, learning new skills, and working on special projects.

(2) Organization-wide task forces can handle many of the jobs usually assigned to central staff groups. Bob Waterman introduced me to the potential of task forces, but it was Dave McMillen, to whom this book is dedicated, who honed them to near perfection. He was a strong advocate of my so-called 80-20 rule. I thought that AES people should spend 80 percent of their time on their primary roles and devote the other 20 percent to participating on task forces, giving advice, learning new skills, and working on special projects not necessarily related to their primary responsibility.

My wife, Eileen, and I attended a Christmas party held in Mystic, Connecticut, near a plant managed by Dave. During the evening, Dave had members of the active task forces stand for recognition. There were task forces for Christmas party planning, annual budgeting, bonus compensation, community service, environmental work, corporate values, and others. A man at our table, whose wife had earlier commented on how much he loved his job, stood when the budgeting task force was recognized. Later, Eileen asked him where in the plant he worked. "I'm a security guard," he replied. There is no way to overestimate how much people learn by working on task forces—and how their participation makes them feel appreciated.

Task forces help people see work as a voluntary act, something they choose to do rather than something they have to do. My goal was to have everyone in the company feel like a volunteer. Volunteers are typically enthusiastic, energetic, and effective.

I have always favored using semi-permanent task forces even in crucial roles like safety, environment, and especially financial auditing. The major benefit of these audits goes to the auditors, not the audited. All of the task force members go back to their permanent roles in the organization with a wider appreciation for the work of others in the company. Needless to say, the task force leaders must have enough expertise to educate the generalists on their teams, or they must know where to find that special knowledge outside the company. Most of our important company-wide task forces were chaired by experts from inside the company, often with the assistance of outside consultants.

(3) If a permanent central staff group is deemed absolutely essential, make it small, staff it with people who have servants' hearts, and keep to a minimum the number of important corporate decisions it makes. Even central financial groups should follow this approach.

A person with a servant's heart is dedicated to serving others and bringing out the best in them. I was privileged to work with several people who were truly remarkable in this regard. Roger Naill, who was in charge of values, financial modeling, and strategic planning, led a group of about five people. He carried out his roles primarily by teaching, leading task forces, and participating in the advice process. He could have led an annual process to create a five-year strategy for the company, but such planning, in my opinion, is a waste of time because conditions change so rapidly. Instead, Roger oversaw a process that was dynamic and flexible. We tried a whole bunch of things. We collected data and analyzed the results. A few of the things worked. We wrote those down and called the result our strategic plan. Instead of looking at expected costs and returns, we focused on our mission and our values, especially our goal of bringing fun to the workplace.

We felt convinced that this approach made AES a better place. Strict financial planning often serves to centralize control of the company among a few leaders at the top of the organization.

Barry Sharp, our chief financial officer, was a servant among servants. He was also the most competent financial accounting person I have ever known. Next to the CEO, the CFO has the greatest influence on the quality of the workplace. Barry's willingness to act as an adviser, teacher, and exemplar made him the most admired person in the company. Those who worked with him were expected to act with the same selflessness. Numerous times he resisted efforts by board members to make him and others in his department act like controllers. (Controllers are not only joy-killers, but they also inhibit a company's creativity and, in the process, dampen its long-term chances for success.) His humility and service ethic, along with his willingness to delegate decisions to people in the operating businesses, helped make AES a great place to work.

Unfortunately, people like Roger Naill and Barry Sharp, who have servants' hearts along with brilliant business skills, are in short supply. Even if we intend to let others in the organization make important decisions, we often succumb to the temptation to make these decisions ourselves because we lack confidence in our subordinates. Two points are worth making. First, employees in operating units are usually wiser than executives think, and their batting average compares favorably with that of the typical central staff office. Second, even if they make the wrong decision, they derive enormous satisfaction and grow tremendously from the very act of making it.

The kind of workplace I describe in this chapter has one significant drawback. It does not easily accommodate people who cannot operate as creative, responsible colleagues because of mental, physical, or emotional limitations. The assumptions underlying the AES ethos do not require a Harvard education or extraordinary physical or mental capacities. But an AES-style workplace requires people who can reason, make decisions, and take responsibility for their actions. Some people have trouble functioning this way. It does not mean that they are not good human beings; indeed, many have other virtues that may be more important in the larger scheme of life. But it does mean that they will have trouble fitting into the Honeycomb system.

Most vibrant organizations following the philosophy I am advocating have a small number of people who do not meet the standards of the company. To varying degrees, they tend to be a drag on the organization and its teams. Leaders should try to steer them to other workplaces that are more in line with their talents and temperaments. In the end, both the organization and the individual are better off after an amicable parting of the ways.

*Keeping score is important
to the success and enjoyment of games.
The same is true in workplaces.*

CHAPTER 5

Scorekeeping, Accountability, and Rewards

MY VIEW ON ACCOUNTABILITY may be the least understood part of
my vision of a better workplace. Freedom is the key to joy at work,
but getting feedback on performance and taking responsibility for
results are also crucial. Scorekeeping is tracking what happens
as a result of decisions and actions. Accountability means taking
responsibility for outcomes. I have noted that keeping score is
important to the success and enjoyment of games. The same is true
in workplaces.

During my only face-to-face meeting with Peter Block, who influenced me greatly with his writing on stewardship, accountability,
and empowerment, we got into a discussion of how best to judge
the performance of subordinates. He told me he had once been an
advocate of "annual reviews" in which the boss would meet with a
subordinate and go over the previous year. One day, in a moment of
reflection, Block imagined calling his wife into his office at home.
"Sit down, honey. It's time for your annual review." The absurdity of
this imaginary session prompted him to change his mind about reviews. He realized that the relationship between supervisor and subordinate should be closer to a partnership of equals. He suggested a
process within organizations that starts with the subordinate doing
an extensive self-review. The leader's role in this approach is much

diminished from that of the typical supervisor-led review. The boss becomes primarily a commentator, questioner, encourager, and, to a lesser extent, an evaluator.

I decided to try a variation of this approach with my senior team. Fourteen of us gathered at the home of one of the team members. One by one, each of us reviewed our own performance during the previous year. Most people outlined their successes, failures, and problems, as well as their goals for the year ahead. In nearly every case, four or five would offer a comment or question something the person had said. Sometimes they reinforced the person's self-assessment; other times they suggested a problem or an accomplishment that had not been mentioned.

We held this type of session annually until I left the company. It became one of my favorite evenings with the senior team. There was not, of course, perfect honesty. Light did not shine on every issue. It was much too general for those who preferred specific quantifiable goals, but it was enormously valuable in other ways. It honored each individual as an important member of the team, regardless of title or status or compensation. It allowed us to show our respect for one another. It brought us closer together as a group. At the same time, I got a good sense of how people thought they had performed—and whether their self-assessments squared with the views of their colleagues.

I was a full participant in these discussions. I reviewed my own performance and chipped in comments about my colleagues. I took notes and afterward wrote a report summarizing the reviews. That report was submitted to the board of directors and to the compensation committee, which found it helpful when evaluating organizational changes and setting compensation. Doing annual reviews in a team setting was far more revealing and effective than having bosses do individual assessments of their subordinates. As Rob Lebow and Randy Spitzer wrote in *Accountability: Freedom and Responsibility Without Control,* "Too often, appraisal destroys human spirit and, in the span of a 30-minute meeting, can transform a vibrant, highly committed employee into a demoralized, indifferent wallflower who reads the want ads on the weekend. . . . They don't work because most performance appraisal systems are a form of judgment and control."

This approach did not always translate well in other countries. Paul Hanrahan, the humble, courageous, and gifted leader who became CEO of AES when I left, was leading our China business when I started this approach to annual reviews. He mentioned to some of his Chinese colleagues that he was heading back to the home office for a self-review of the year. Did they have any suggestions? They were horrified.

"Self-criticism is very dangerous," they said, remembering the experience of their parents not many years before under communism. "Don't brag about your great successes. They will not believe you, and your credibility will be destroyed. Don't talk about our problems or take responsibility for mistakes because they will blame you and you will get fired." "What do you suggest?" asked Paul. "Try using lots of statistics. Statistics are good," was their sincere and very concerned reply. If you have ever listened to a Chinese leader's speech, you will realize how widespread this simple advice must be.

After *In Search of Excellence* was published, many organizations, including AES, asked themselves some tough questions. What are we trying to achieve? Where do we want to be in five years? What kind of place do we want to become? What is the bottom line? The search for answers revitalized countless large organizations—companies, nonprofits, and governments—and helped them achieve higher levels of performance.

At AES, the primary reason we existed was to help the world meet its electricity needs. To track our progress, we started calculating the number of people who were served by our facilities. By the year 2000, AES served the electricity needs of more than 100 million people—not bad for a company that had only been in existence for two decades.

But offering an important service or serving large numbers of customers does not mean that a company will be deemed a success. Increasingly, success is defined by purely economic measures, especially shareholder "value"—as if a company's highest purpose were pumping up its stock price.

What about stock price as a measure of performance? Few non-investors believe it says much about actual performance, especially in the short term. It's worth remembering, too, that it's a yardstick that can be applied only to publicly traded corporations. This is a small minority of the universe of organizations that need a way to judge their performance. But despite its shortcomings, stock price is not only used as a measure of success but often the primary one. Even Jim Collins uses stock-price gains to separate the "good" companies from the "great" ones in his book *Good to Great*.

I do not recommend using stock-price changes, either up or down, as a significant measure of performance, even economic performance. Stock price puts far too much emphasis on one stakeholder—the shareholder—and is driven by external factors that have little to do with internal economic performance. Its use leads to poor decisions by people who work in the organization, and, as I will argue later, it distorts the real purpose of a company and discourages a more balanced approach to measuring success. Cash flow, income, and balance sheets are more reliable economic measures, but even these can be presented in a way that blurs the overall performance of a company.

The scoreboard for tracking success at AES was designed to buck this trend. Roger Sant first suggested that compensation for senior leaders be based half on whether an executive advanced the organization's values and principles and half on technical performance, which included protecting the environment, meeting safety standards, developing new business, and hitting ambitious targets for earnings and growth. I suggested that this "50/50" design be adopted by all leaders and teams throughout the organization. A good way to see what an organization really stands for is to examine the criteria used to determine executive compensation. You quickly find out whether companies put their money where their values are.

We evaluated performance on "technical factors" in a straight-forward way. We kept track of emission rates of pollutants at every plant. We compared these emission rates with the limits specified in our permits. We also compared them with the emissions of similar plants operated by U.S. companies, even if the plant was in South America or Asia. We established a process of regular internal audits by task forces. Similarly, we tracked all safety incidents and accidents. Results were compared with those of U.S. companies in our industry. A rigorous internal audit process was also in place to review our safety record.

Financial performance was tracked using Securities and Exchange Commission standards and generally accepted accounting principles. Even before going public in 1991, the company adopted accounting and financial reporting standards that conformed to those used by publicly traded companies. In addition to independent audits by a major public accounting firm, AES organized task forces to do internal audits.

We had the hardest time measuring success in business development. While we certainly celebrated "wins" and mourned "losses" in creating business opportunities, it was difficult to assess in a timely fashion the long-term value of new undertakings. For example, it sometimes took four or five years to determine whether a new project was an economic success. Timely evaluations of noneconomic aspects of new businesses were troublesome as well.

Judging performance on our values and principles was more subjective and required greater creativity. In the first place, we had a difficult time finding a basis of comparison. No other organization put as much weight on these factors as we did. Among the companies that did stress values, few had methods for determining whether individual employees were practicing them. Because our values were so central to the way we did business, we had to come up with a tool for evaluating our employees.

We finally settled on a company-wide annual values survey. The questions changed somewhat over the years, but the thrust remained the same. For instance, we asked employees what we meant by fun and social responsibility. They also rated themselves and their supervisors on how well they were living our shared values. (See Appendix A for sample questions from various surveys.) In the early years, we devoted a lot of attention to quantifying the responses. But we gradually learned that most important information was contained in individual comments. When we began doing the surveys in the mid-1980s, I blithely promised to read the comments of all of our employees. That took me less than an hour the first year. By 1993, it took me a plane trip to Europe and back to get through them. Five years later, it took several months to review the tens of thousands of comments that poured into our central office.

After we read and summarized the results, we required each business unit to review and discuss them as well. This process was essential to achieving joy at work. Here are some facts and observations about the surveys:

The corporate survey was designed by a couple of people from the central office with advice from all around the company. Many of the business units added a local survey, designed by employees without HR experience.

Most surveys were completed anonymously, although people had the option of signing their names. This was probably out of fear that their comments could get them in trouble or even result in the loss of their jobs. Unfortunately, even after AES assiduously followed a "hold harmless" policy for years, most employees continued to withhold their names.

The fact that I read the comments on every survey reminded people that they were important members of the AES community.

While the survey was designed to encourage accountability, it was equally effective as an educational tool. Each survey reminded people what our shared values were, how they were defined, and why they were important to our life together.

The surveys helped identify problems, omissions, and misunderstandings in our values. They sometimes identified leaders who were acting in a manner inconsistent with our values and principles. Similarly, comments often revealed major misconceptions about how the values should be practiced.

Over the years, the survey results were overwhelmingly positive and the interpretation of values was very consistent with my own understanding of them. However, the responses from almost every business unit pointed out problems and significant issues that needed attention. We could never come close to perfection. "Negative" comments were much more prevalent from people or units that had been part of the company fewer than three years. Some examples: "Some leaders are too hands off in enforcing our values." "AES belongs to someone else; not me. It operates independent of me and my actions." "Bakke doesn't care about vacation and hourly employees." "It is amazing how many people push these principles yet it's the same people who choose not to follow them." "I don't agree with the fun philosophy. Why do people have to take on other challenges in order to have fun?"

The survey results and comments were comparable regardless of nationality, religious affiliation, political system, wealth, or education level. This was an important finding because by the mid-1990s only 8 percent of the company's employees spoke English as their first language. "These are Islamic values." "This is consistent with my Christian faith." "These are human values." Among business units that had been actively part of AES for three years or more, the comments generally were outstanding. AES employees on every continent had nearly identical attitudes about our shared values and about what makes work fun. "Cultural diversity," it would seem, tends to melt away when it comes to basic human traits.

The surveys reminded us that AES was very unusual, if not unique, among companies. "You have to be blind not to realize what the corporation has done to change the way people view their workplace," said one of our U.S. employees. " I am very happy because today I'm practicing values that were hidden before," said a Brazilian. "My plant is by far the best ever plant in Pakistan and my job is of course the best I have ever had," said another respondent. "The AES values at work are basic human values and are similar to what we tell our families at home," said a Pakistani. "This is the most amazing corporate doctrine I have ever seen," said an American about leaders who willingly give up authority. "AES is a great place to work after coming from a place with a class system. AES has taught me a whole new way to look at life and work as a whole," said another American.

The values and principles survey was the most important score-keeping mechanism we had in the company, even though it was not basically quantitative in nature.

Finally, the surveys convinced me that we were well on our way to becoming the most exciting and fun large workplace ever devised. "AES is still the best job I've had and barring any disasters I hope I will be able to work with AES for the rest of my life. Why do I like it? The freedom, the challenge, the opportunities, the values, the goals, EVERYTHING!" "The hardest job I ever loved." "I'm free to develop myself, I feel I can reach the moon." I was most moved by this one: "If making decisions and taking responsibility are major contributors to fun, [the plant] must be the most fun place in AES!" "The working environment is so excellent that I really look forward to coming to work in the morning." "Great learning, great responsibility, great fun." "The common principles of integrity, fairness, fun represent AES culture."

The values and principles survey was the most important score-keeping mechanism we had in the company, even though it was not basically quantitative in nature. It confirmed what I observed on hundreds of visits to the company's business units. I estimate that over 90 percent of the survey comments from people who had been with AES for three years or more were positive.

One of the most important side benefits of the survey was the discussions it prompted in all our business units around the world. These sessions celebrated the year's progress on shared values and addressed problems described in the comments. This process was as crucial to AES as our budget deliberations and our compensation reviews.

No matter how it's delivered, though, feedback on performance is always a touchy matter. Once, on a visit to our Thames plant in Connecticut, I asked how people felt about our shared values and principles. One of our people complained about "Monday morning quarterbacking." "I thought it was against the rules to throw this thing back in my face after the fact." "No, it is not," I said. "After getting the appropriate amount of advice from colleagues, you always have the unquestioned right to take actions. However, once the action is taken or decision is made, we all look at the results. We use that information to hold you and ourselves responsible for those results." Of course, the whole team, even the entire organization, should join in taking responsibility for what happens, but the individual who made the final decision bears a disproportionate share of that responsibility. That is what made AES so rewarding and worthwhile. It was the work equivalent of keeping score in basketball or in a card game.

I have noticed that the people who say that others in the organization are not being held accountable for their actions are usually referring to people who are not being held responsible for poor outcomes. Sometimes I wish they were as concerned about celebrating good decisions and good results. Both are equally important in the accountability equation. We tend to spend less time talking about the positive side and instead simply give tangible rewards: promotions, raises, and bonuses. And if we forget to reward good performance, people usually find a way to remind us of our oversight.

We are much less comfortable, even in games, holding people responsible for negative results. When is it appropriate to fire or demote people, eliminate their bonuses, or cut their pay? I do not have a simple answer except to say that each course is appropriate under certain circumstances.

At AES, leaders had another way to deal with individuals who didn't perform up to our standards. We simply didn't assign decisions to them as often as we would have under normal circumstances. If abused, this is a form of control that can make work as demeaning as it was during the Industrial Revolution. But used judiciously, this approach can send an effective message to the underperformer while keeping work fun for the other members of the team.

I believe the best and most appropriate response to most mistakes in life and within an organization is to admit the error, ask forgiveness, and promise to try not to make the same mistake again. Most of the time, this is sufficient "punishment." Parents who try this approach with their children know how hard it is to pull off. It is no less difficult in work settings. It requires that people in the organization understand what it means to forgive. And after granting forgiveness, they should then act as if the problem or action never took place.

Many times I have been asked, "When should someone be fired?" I am quite sure some people posed that question thinking that I didn't believe firing is ever warranted. My answer has been consistent. Firing is appropriate when people do not accept responsibility for transgressions and refuse to ask forgiveness. This is especially true if the problem is a major breach of an important principle or value. Losing a million dollars or causing an injury to another person are terrible mistakes, but they would not necessarily result in dismissal unless the person refused to admit his error and ask forgiveness.

As every organization leader knows, mistakes often are not clear cut, and it can be difficult to assign blame. For example, it can take six to eight years between deciding to build a new power plant and getting sufficient operating data to learn whether the decision was a good one. Business-development efforts on AES's first plant started in 1981, but it was not until 1986 that we realized the business would lose $20 million a year. If we had fired the rascals who dreamed up that business, AES would have lost its top four officers, including me.

Holding people accountable requires enormous humility. There are more questions than answers, and many gray areas require Solomon-like wisdom to navigate. For too long, organizations have confused accountability with controls. As Lebow and Spitzer point out, "The more you try to control people, the less responsible and accountable they become." My experience is that no one wants to be controlled but that most people want to know how well they performed. Working people are much more willing to be held accountable than most leaders and board members assume. Keeping score, reviewing performance, assigning responsibility, and distributing rewards and penalties are crucial to creating a great workplace. But it takes preternatural discipline by an organization to make these processes work in a fair and consistent manner.

Pay classification systems used by governments and often advocated by unions are inherently arbitrary and unfair. They benefit underperformers and insufficiently reward star performers.

Rewards can take many forms. Honors, promotions, and the esteem of colleagues count for a lot. However, compensation is the most important reward in every organization except voluntary associations. As I have already pointed out, compensation usually does not have a major effect on increasing joy at work. It is a reward for work accomplished, not a predictor of future happiness. You should not expect to enjoy work more because you are given a significant pay raise. If the workplace is miserable, the people who work there are likely to push for extra pay to compensate for the drudgery they have to endure. I am convinced, for example, that assembly-line jobs command much higher pay than warranted by the skills of the employees because the work is boring and even demeaning.

Above all, compensation is an individual matter. It takes into account a person's contribution to an organization and the success of the organization. It usually involves some rough comparisons with how much people are paid in similar jobs in similar companies. But no two people are the same, and it is up to company leaders to make sure employees are paid according to their skills, accomplishments, and ability to work with other people. The pay-classification systems used by governments and often advocated by unions (and sometime management) are inherently arbitrary and unfair. They benefit underperformers and insufficiently reward star performers. Worst of all, these systems are a form of group control—"corporate communism," in the words of an executive I know—in which everyone is dragged down to the lowest common denominator.

In keeping with my desire to make the workplace fun, the compensation issue that caught my attention most was the practice of paying salaries to executives and other "important" people, while everyone else in the organization was paid an hourly wage. In 1993, as I was first reading Peter Block's *Stewardship,* I found myself in a self-congratulatory mood. "I could have written this," I thought. "This is consistent with everything we are trying." Then I came to his chapter on compensation. Block suggested that a class system existed in most organizations. Managers got paid salaries and were eligible for bonuses and some form of ownership participation. Everyone else was paid for the number of hours spent at the workplace, including overtime if they couldn't finish their work within the "normal" time allotment.

The system was so ingrained that I had never considered its implications. I was perpetuating a pay system based on assumptions about people that were totally inconsistent with the ethos of our company. Even though we had long ago rid ourselves of time clocks and similar vestiges of the class system, a main dividing line remained in the pay system.

This was a throwback to the Industrial Revolution that separated the workforce into two arbitrary groups—labor and management.

The structure had been codified in "labor laws" early in the 20th century. The gulf between the two groups often is aggravated by the elitism of management and the militancy of unions. Today, federal and state wage-and-hour laws are one of the major hindrances to creating a fun and fulfilling workplace. For many workers, physical labor and time spent on the job are put ahead of innovation, output, and achievement.

As a young man I lived near an Indian reservation and went to school in a building originally on the property of a Native American tribe, a group of people subjected to considerable discrimination. In my late teens and early 20s I watched the civil rights movement make great breakthroughs for African-Americans. I am convinced that the next form of discrimination that needs to be overturned is the second-class treatment accorded to working men and women. The division between elites and workers was evident everywhere we did business, from former European colonies in India to South America to Communist countries such as China and Kazakhstan. Western democracies were no better than former Communist states or nations with emerging economies. This class system can be found, in some form or another, in every industrialized country in the world.

It took me nearly three years to persuade our plant leaders to experiment with an "all salary" approach to reduce and possibly eliminate this discriminatory behavior. The biggest obstacle was that it had never really been attempted in a significant industrial setting. It was also difficult to structure a program that fit with the existing labor laws in the United States. For example, by U.S. law if I carry a wrench for 20 percent of my work time, I am not "exempt" from the hourly limits and overtime requirements, no matter how much I am paid or what my title is.

Because of these antiquated laws, we couldn't simply junk the hourly wage systems. Instead, we created a voluntary program in which people who chose to take salary and no overtime could opt back into the traditional system of hourly pay and overtime at any time, no questions asked. Even the voluntary approach was seen by some experts as running counter to labor laws. These laws were designed to protect people working in sweatshops, but they were being applied to AES technicians, fuel handlers, and engineers who often earned between $40,000 and $60,000 annually (in 1990 dollars).

I wrote to then Secretary of Labor Robert Reich asking permission for AES to experiment in this area. I received a letter from him, probably written by an underling, saying that while it was an interesting subject, he couldn't do anything because management couldn't be trusted to treat these people fairly. President and Mrs. Clinton were gracious enough to listen to my plea, but they also found the issue too difficult politically to advocate a change in the laws. Sen. Don Nickles of Oklahoma was very knowledgeable about and sympathetic to the problem from his experience in his family business, but he couldn't get Congress to support the idea. Despite encouraging words from many politicians, no movement toward change occurred in the eight years I pushed the issue.

> *Everyone should be made eligible for bonuses and stock options, just like bosses.*

Finally, our smallest plant in California, with only 26 people, made the switch to all salary. Every person decided to make the change, although one decided a year or so later to return to hourly wages and overtime. The original salaries were equal to each person's hourly pay plus the amount of overtime worked by the average plant employee during the previous year. Everyone was made eligible for bonuses and stock options, just like bosses. Their pay packages included the same contingencies that all company leaders, including me, already had in ours. Bonuses and options were not guaranteed. They were based on individual, plant, and corporate performance.

In an attempt to stay within the spirit and letter of the applicable laws, the plant kept a record of hours worked, just in case the government complained that people were being exploited. About six months later, one of the control room operators called me to let me know how well the new pay approach was going. "We love it," he said. "One surprise was that we now have a higher base salary. This has helped a couple of us get better home loans than we could have before. Most of us are spending less time in the plant than we did before as well. That's more time to be with our kids. By the way, we also quit keeping time records." "What about the government?" I asked. "We've gone to reading Martin Luther King on civil disobedience," he responded.

A more dramatic conversion of "workers" to "business people" occurred at our Tisza II plant in Hungary. For three months the AES people there debated whether to convert from hourly wages to a salary system that would also make them eligible for bonuses and stock options. On one of my visits to the plant, Attila Legoza, a plant technician, tentatively approached me. Through an interpreter he asked if I would sign his contract converting to "all salary." Within minutes, dozens of others had run to their lockers and returned with contracts for signature. It felt as if the Berlin Wall of labor-management relations were crumbling before my eyes. The impromptu ceremony ended in enthusiastic applause.

When we started this change in AES compensation policy, only 10 percent of our people worldwide were paid a salary. The other 90 percent received hourly wages and overtime. By the time I left in 2002, over 90 percent of 40,000 people in 31 countries were paid a salary, just like the company's leaders. It was a giant step in breaking down barriers between management and labor and in bringing us together as AES business people. On average, people were paid about the same amount of money as before but spent less time at their plants and offices. There was no reason to take four hours on a Saturday morning to make a repair instead of staying an extra hour on Friday evening to get it done. In most cases employees took more responsibility, initiative, and pride in their work. The most important result was the self-respect that it engendered among AES people.

It was a revolution in our workplace—and one of my proudest accomplishments.

In strictly economic terms, it probably does not make much difference who in the organization determines an individual's compensation. Some organizations use computerized formulas to determine pay. The president of the United States sets a percentage salary increase for every worker in the federal government. In some organizations, the human resources department sets pay for employees. Many organizations still use union and management bargaining teams to determine a person's compensation. The most common decision maker on compensation matters has traditionally been the individual's supervisor.

At AES, supervisors were generally given responsibility for making pay decisions for everyone who reported to them. I was convinced that compensation decisions could be made in a more satisfying way. The first big question was whether individual compensation information should be kept confidential. Roger Sant and I both advocated transparency on compensation matters, something that we felt was consistent with our idea that all important financial information should be shared among AES employees. We also believed it was a myth that people didn't already know what the next person was paid. Many leaders did not like having to explain why one person was paid more than another. I responded that responsible leaders should be able to give a legitimate reason for all decisions they make, including those involving compensation. Unfortunately, few business units within AES decided to provide salary information to all team members.

AES had several interesting experiments allowing people to set their own compensation. The first one took place in a small business-development group and lasted only a year. The supervisor asked people in his group to set their own salaries. He judged the exercise a failure. The best people paid themselves too little, and the poorer performers paid themselves too much.

In the early days, bonuses for people in the plants were set by "objective" criteria using formulas. The formulas gave way over time to a more subjective approach, which included an employee's adherence to our values and principles. Bonuses were often calculated through a consensus process involving all team members. I heard few complaints about this approach.

One of AES's most innovative leaders, Paul Stinson, rejuvenated the experiment to let people set their own compensation levels. He too limited the experiment to business-development specialists and other executives who reported to him. After several interactions, the process that seemed to work best required each person to propose a compensation level and then send it to others in the group for comment before making a final decision.

The most radical and possibly the most important AES compensation experiment was led by Pete Norgeot, a veteran plant manager and a protégé of Dave McMillen. First, the members of a group put together a plant budget that was consistent with their business plan. The budget had a line item for the total compensation expense for the entire staff. They decided that the total compensation paid to everyone in the plant could not exceed the budgeted number. A task force from the plant had already researched comparable pay levels in the area where the plant was located. That information was shared with everyone in the plant.

Each individual was asked to propose his or her own salary for the year ahead and then to send the proposal to every other person in the plant for comment. After a weeklong comment period, each person made a decision on his or her own compensation. When the amounts were tallied, the sum exceeded the budget, but not by much. As it turned out, only one person had settled on a pay level substantially higher than others of comparable responsibility, skill level, and experience had. He was also one of the few who had not followed the advice of colleagues to adjust his pay. After he was given this information, he agreed to reduce his proposed salary, and the revised compensation total allowed the plant to meet its original budget.

The individuals who participated in this approach were changed by the process. They had a much better understanding of how compensation affected the overall economics of the organization. They learned the value of seeking advice when they had to balance competing interests. They put the interests of other stakeholders on a par with or even ahead of their own. The process pulled team members together and helped some make the transition from workers to business people. It made them "owners" of their business. For the first time, they understood what it meant to be stewards. This method of setting compensation was stressful, successful, and fun.

While I was writing this chapter, a national magazine published its annual review of the best places to work in America. AES never made many of these lists, mainly because the evaluators were more interested in glitzy extras than in the crucial intangibles that make work fulfilling and fun. This particular *Fortune* article, titled "What Makes It So Great?" was typical. It touted one company that offered $500, a limo, and an extra week of vacation to employees who get married. Several highly rated companies pledged not to lay off any employees—a promise that reeks of paternalism and that is impossible to keep because of constantly changing economic conditions. Another company got high marks because it had a piano in the company lunchroom. Free Thanksgiving turkeys helped another company secure a high ranking.

I described my visit to the sugar-cane plantation in Uganda where the owners practiced the ultimate in benefit compensation by paying people almost nothing in cash, but giving them "free" schooling, "free" housing, and "free" medical care. Many companies in this country took similar approaches in an earlier era. Textile mills had company towns, and many factories had company stores. Ostensibly they were to benefit workers. In reality, they often indentured them by offering easy credit.

We have a similar approach to "helping" the poor in this country. A small percentage of the money designated for the poor and disadvantaged reaches the targeted people in the form of cash that they can decide how to spend. Everything else is spent on government workers administering programs for the poor, on social workers, and on services such as health care, education, child care, and food. Poor people have little or no choice or decision-making role regarding the use of these "benefits." If growth, responsibility, adulthood, and fun come from making decisions and being held accountable for the results, then we have done a great disservice to the poor. We have treated them like children who are unable to think for themselves. In the process we have made them dependent on us and turned them into the wards of society.

The benefits systems used by most companies are similarly paternalistic. Postwar inflation prompted the federal government to impose wage controls. Because this prevented companies from raising the amount of pay to individuals they wished to hire in a tight labor market, clever organizations started offering "benefits" that were exempt from wage controls.

The wage controls ended, but benefits remained. In most cases, benefit decisions are controlled by the company. But employees are loath to complain because government taxes cash wages but generally not benefits, since they are not classified as compensation. This is another law that hurts working people by giving them less control over how they can spend their money.

I think companies and the people who work in them should look for ways to be paid in cash or cash equivalents so employees can decide for themselves how much they want to spend on vacations, health care, child care, weddings, and a host of other gimmicky extras offered by many companies.

Almost no employee I've talked to seems to understand that the amount of money available to spend on staff is basically fixed by the economic realities of the organization. That fixed amount is made up of cash wages and salaries plus the cost of benefits. If the benefits increase, the cash wages must decrease. They would increase and decrease in equal measure were it not for the favorable treatment given to benefits by the tax code. Even so, it is important to remember that benefits are not free. I hope that someday the tax laws will be changed so that companies no longer have an incentive to provide "extras" and instead will replace them with direct compensation that can be spent any way an employee sees fit. For example, wouldn't it be better to receive cash to pay a relative to care for your children than to use the company's child-care center?

Organizational discipline is the glue of a successful workplace. By discipline I mean self-discipline. I am not referring to punishment or holding someone accountable. Discipline means making important decisions and carrying out everyday responsibilities in good weather and bad, whether you're sick or well, and even when you've been asked to simultaneously perform other duties.

My high school basketball coach had a rule that no member of the team could snow ski during the basketball season. The rule existed because he feared injuries to team members. The school was small and had only a limited number of competent players. There was an excellent ski resort less than 20 miles away. During my junior year, one of our better players broke the rule almost every weekend. The coach knew what was happening and did nothing about it. The results were insidious. Our practices were sloppier. I lost some of my respect for the coach and responded less enthusiastically to some of his instructions and suggestions. We seemed to play our games more as individuals than as a team. We lost more games than we should have based on our basketball talent. It doesn't take much to ruin organizational discipline.

Discipline is checking the pressure gauge on the boiler every hour, even though you have never found it out of its normal range in the three years you have been responsible for the boiler area. Discipline is going to a plant to celebrate its remarkable values survey results, even when the poor financial performance by another business unit makes it unlikely that the company will reach its financial targets for the quarter. Discipline is refusing to take a bonus for your latest business accomplishment because you received a bonus for a previous project that did not live up to performance projections.

Discipline is staying humble when everyone around you is singing your praises because the stock price is rising. Discipline is sticking to the organization's shared values even when the company's economic performance has been less than stellar. Discipline is putting the interests of invisible shareholders and faraway customers on a par with your own. Discipline is having the courage to say you don't know the answer and to seek advice from your colleagues—or to seek advice even when you're sure of the answer. Discipline is taking pure joy from the assist, not the basket. Discipline is always remembering you're part of a team.

*The most important character traits of a leader
are humility; the willingness to give up power;
courage; integrity; and love and passion for the people,
values, and mission of the organization.*

CHAPTER 6

Leading to Workplace Joy

IF THE KEY to joy at work is the freedom to make decisions that matter to the organization, then the key to good organizational leadership is restraint in making decisions of importance. This is easier in theory than in practice. From my early childhood I was encouraged to be decisive. My mother helped me start little businesses that honed my decision-making ability. When I was a quarterback in high school, my coach allowed me to call all my own plays. I held numerous leadership roles during my school years. Then I attended Harvard Business School, where the case method teaches students about decision making. I was good at making decisions, and this ability was affirmed many times at school and at work. I enjoyed taking responsibility and living with the consequences.

Then came AES and the realization that this enjoyment should be spread around. I came to understand that as co-founder and later as CEO, I had to adopt a leadership style that left most of the important decisions to others. I tried to make my attitude reflect Max De Pree's admonition that leaders should introduce employees as the "people I serve." I had to find a way to remind myself daily that giving up many of my executive powers was essential to the goal of creating a fun workplace. I often fell short of the standards I set for myself.

When I left business school, I thought I was an expert on leadership. I seem to have gotten less smart on the subject ever since.

My objective is not to explain what it takes to lead people in a positive direction. Scores of books explain it better than I can. My focus is to show how a leader can make principles and values, especially fun or joy, a significant part of an organization's definition of success. My views may not get high marks from many top executives. Few embrace the central organizational principles I advocate in this book, especially giving up power.

Leaders serve an organization rather than control it.

My notion of leadership does not require a John Wayne or a General Patton or a Jack Welch to swagger on to the scene and save the day. In fact, the superhero style of leadership is not conducive to creating a joyful workplace or to putting the same emphasis on values as on the bottom line. The systems guru Edward Deming once said that a leader's job is to drive fear out of the organization so that employees will feel comfortable making decisions on their own. Most leaders of large companies do not make driving out fear a high priority.

Today, there is almost too much focus on leadership, mainly because it is widely thought to be the key to economic success. In fact, the degree to which a leader can actually affect technical performance has been substantially overstated. I subscribe to Warren Buffett's theory that when good management meets a bad business, it is the business that maintains its reputation.

On the other hand, the importance and impact of moral leadership on the life and success of an organization have been greatly underappreciated. Moral leaders serve an organization rather than control it. Their goal is to create a community that encourages individuals to take the initiative, practice self-discipline, make decisions, and assume responsibility for their actions.

This form of servant leadership is often misunderstood as

being hands off, even passive. It is just the opposite. In the company's annual budget "advice" meetings, I sat in the front row of several hundred AES people. I frequently asked tough questions of the presenter in an effort to find weaknesses in analysis and assumptions. I was not at all shy about giving my views on our budget performance during the past year or our spending plans for the year ahead. Other AES leaders did the same. Good servant leaders are engaged in every aspect of an organization's life, from suggesting radical new ideas and strategies to teaching the organization's principles and values. The kind of leader I have in mind makes few, if any, final decisions on business matters but is never passive or far from the center of the organization's important plans, processes, or actions.

> *One of the most difficult lessons I have had to learn is that leadership is not about managing people.*

One of the most difficult lessons I have had to learn is that leadership is not about managing people. People are not resources or assets to be managed. Nor is leadership about analyzing issues and making big decisions. As I'll discuss later, these are not the qualities that produce a joyful workplace or give an organization its best opportunity to succeed. It is a shame that most leaders give little thought to how their decisions affect the working environment for their employees.

A leader's character is far more important than his or her skills. Jerry Leachman, a former linebacker for Bear Bryant at Alabama and leader of my men's Bible study group, says, "Good leadership starts with a person's character." I am not sure whether character necessarily boosts profits and share price, but I am convinced that it is essential to creating a fun place to work. The most important character traits of a leader who embraces the principles and values championed in this book are humility; the willingness to give up power; courage; integrity; and love and passion for the people, values, and mission of the organization. It is not essential to be a great visionary. A leader must communicate a vision, but that vision can come from a colleague or someone outside the organization. Nor does a leader have to be an accomplished strategist or analyst. Again, strategy and analysis can be undertaken by others inside or outside the organization. A leader doesn't even have to be an effective communicator.

Aristotle said, "We are what we repeatedly do. Excellence, therefore, is not an act, but a habit." I believe these words describe the essence of how we learn and transmit the values that guide an organization. This is the way I put it in a message to AES employees: "Character and virtues do not come to us primarily through exploring our own and others' feelings, nor are they best learned through impersonal analysis of ethical choices or even intensive classroom training on right or wrong. For the most part we 'catch' character and virtue and values by practicing 'right' behaviors and actions so that they first become habits and then part of our character. We catch these behaviors and actions from leaders, parents, mentors, teachers, and friends, and by repeatedly acting in ways consistent with the espoused principles in all aspects of our lives."

A person's character speaks far louder and with more lasting effect than any speech or letter to employees. Elliot Richardson refused to carry out President Nixon's order to fire Archibald Cox during the Watergate scandal. He showed courage and integrity that marked him for the rest of his life. This simple act will be remembered far longer than the book he wrote or the five cabinet posts he held during his years of public service.

"Beware of bosses who treat subordinates differently than superiors" was the advice given me by Jonathan Moore, my mentor and boss, early in my working years in the secretary's office of the Department of Health, Education, and Welfare in the U.S. government. "It reveals a major leadership character flaw."

Our character is transparent to those around us. Leaders must realize this. The people who work for us absorb our character in both positive and negative ways. They are not fooled even if we try to cover up our flaws. We are an open book.

Finally, a leader doesn't even have to be inspirational. I have had people graciously describe me or my talks as inspiring. Sometimes I have been credited with motivating and influencing people. While it is flattering to receive these compliments, it is arrogant to think that executives can control people in this way. There are historical anomalies—demagogues who somehow move people by force of their personalities—but people usually possess the motivation, discipline, and inner strength to act in a way that is true to themselves. The role of leaders is to create an environment that allows these qualities to flourish.

Humility is at the core of a leader's heart. Humility is understanding who you really are, regardless of your title or education, your wealth or status. Humility underlies the impulse to make others do better. Being a leader is like being a good point guard in basketball. In Pat Conroy's book *My Losing Season,* he describes the joyful role of a playmaker who makes everyone else on the team perform better than even the team members thought was possible. "I wanted to luxuriate in the waters of pure and free-floating human joy," he wrote. Conroy was not the best shooter or the best defender or the best rebounder. He did not make decisions for his teammates. But he was their leader. He served his teammates and made them better.

The most important aspect of this leadership style is letting others make important decisions. When that happens, leaders dignify and honor their subordinates. At the moment power is shared, everyone is in a position of equality. People feel needed and valued because they *are* needed and valued.

Max De Pree writes, "Not having the chance to make decisions within the organization in which one works is a great tragedy, leading to hopelessness and despair." This is a sober warning. When a leader acts in a manner that assumes he is the best decision maker— in other words, the most knowledgeable and responsible member of a group—everyone else feels extraneous. The intoxicating effect of exercising power can pervert even the most selfless executives. The more decisions they make, the more comfortable they feel making them. They begin to lose touch with the people below, who end up feeling like pawns being moved around a corporate chessboard.

In a discussion with AES people in Bahía Blanca, Argentina, I asked, "What happens to you and how do you feel when your boss makes a decision on an issue in your area of work?" "*No tengo traba-jo*" ("I don't have a job") was the poignant and illuminating response. In *Good to Great,* Jim Collins writes that companies that seemed to do better in the long run were run by understated leaders. "Self-ef-facing, quiet, reserved, even shy—these leaders are a paradoxical blend of personal humility and professional will. They are more like Lincoln and Socrates than Patton or Caesar." At AES, John Rug-girello had these characteristics. He was the most natural leader in the company. He had a quiet contentment; nothing seemed to rattle him. And when a wrong needed to be undone, John had the courage and skill to say and do what was truthful and right.

I have a friend, George Long, who epitomizes this kind of leader. He was the force behind the creation of an adult softball team in our community. The team encourages the participation of young men who have had difficult teenage years. If he had wanted, George could have assumed the role of manager and made all the decisions regarding the team. Instead, he did whatever others couldn't do or didn't want to do. He raised money, played when needed, and provided transportation—and he did it without asking anything in return.

I noticed the same characteristics in George when we shared little-league football coaching duties for a half-dozen seasons. He would spend hours each week giving the kids rides to practice after encouraging them to do their homework first. As a coach, he always deferred to others even though he clearly had every right to call the plays and make the important decisions. You can imagine how much everyone loved being part of his teams and how successful those teams were by almost every measuring stick. It is possible to have financially and technically successful organizations with self-aggrandizing or even arrogant leaders, but it is highly unlikely that these workplaces will be filled with joy for everyone involved.

Let me give you an example of a leader acting without humility. When I was president of AES and testifying at a public hearing in Florida on a proposed power plant, I made this grand pronouncement: "Our plant is so environmentally clean that you could stick your head down the stack and no harm would come to you." This is a classic example of a senior leader speaking on an issue when the assessment should have been left to a lower-level employee with firsthand knowledge. Not only is it more fun for people from various units to speak for the company on important matters and to lead important initiatives, but it also gives the organization a better chance to achieve business goals and financial success.

The idea that top executives or financial experts should make key decisions is so ingrained in our corporate cultures that it is nearly impossible for leaders to delegate important roles and decisions. Indeed, governments often require that senior people take responsibility for these decisions, as Dave McMillen found out. Dave had given the ultimate responsibility for the plant's environmental compliance to our best technicians in each of the relevant areas of the plant. Unfortunately, federal and state governments require that an officer of the company sign the compliance documentation regarding these matters that we send to the government every month. Obviously, none of the responsible technicians were corporate officers. Dave felt it was vital for the technicians to take responsibility and be accountable for AES's environmental performance by signing the monthly compliance documents. After all, they understood the rules better, knew of the company's commitments and values regarding the environment, and had the best information regarding our performance. Our solution was simple but unorthodox. The technicians were made officers of the company so that they could legally sign the documents. One of the satisfactions of this style of leadership is that we share, for better or worse, the consequences of the decisions made by subordinates.

Courage would probably not be among the four character traits highlighted in this chapter, except for the radical nature of my prescription for a fun workplace. Not only are these proposals new to most executives; the idea of carrying them out can be downright scary. So, it takes no small amount of courage for an organizational leader to embrace them intellectually and then put them into practice.

Courage is also required when senior executives are asked to surrender a large portion of their authority to others. The exercise of power validates big titles and high salaries. When executives give power away, they often feel insecure, as if they are not doing their jobs. In fact, they are meeting the highest requirements of their jobs when they delegate decisions to subordinates. Not only are decisions being made by the people who are most familiar with the facts, but the act of making them gives more people a real stake in the organization's performance.

At one of my lectures at the World Bank discussing the AES approach to work, I met Isabel Guerrero, a delightful and skilled manager who was in charge of the bank's Bolivian operations. She asked me a question often raised by mid-level managers of large organizations. It is a question for which I do not have a very satisfactory answer. Roughly, it goes like this: "What you have said about organizing the workplace and making decisions makes sense to me. However, I am several layers from the president and other senior leaders of the bank, let alone the directors and all those specialists in legal, planning, financial control, human resources, the environmental department, women's affairs, etc., that now have the right to veto what I do. What do you recommend I do in this situation?"

I gave her a few rather weak suggestions about trying to delegate responsibility to subordinates while simultaneously trying to sell her bosses on the idea of spreading the authority to make decisions. Then I told her the same thing I tell everyone in a similar position:

"Be prepared to lose your job, because this is radical stuff." The color drained from Isabel's face, and she visibly slumped as she walked away. Later I learned that she was the sole breadwinner for her household. I did not expect to hear from her again. About two weeks later, my assistant buzzed me to say that Isabel was on the phone. She was her bubbly, enthusiastic self. "I decided to go for it, Dennis. I know it's risky, but it is a change that needs to be made. I am going to move to Bolivia and try to operate according to the organizational principles you suggest."

What courage she seemed to have. I discovered something else that day: No person is freer and stronger than one who has faced the worst possible consequences—in this case, the chance of getting fired—and decided, "I am going to do it anyway." I don't know if Isabel really tried the radical approach I suggested, but at least at that moment she had thrown off the shackles that make corporate hierarchies so stifling. In her mind at least, no one could stop her from doing what she believed was right.

"Love" is not a word used much in the rough-and-tumble corporate world, perhaps because it sounds soft and sentimental. But as Max De Pree says in *Leading Without Power*, "We are working primarily for love." Love prompts us to visit our employees around the world. Love makes us want to work extra time. Love pushes us to do whatever it takes to help others succeed. Love forgives mistakes and binds up the hurt and frustrated.

Some of us love winning. Some love competition. Some love analysis and strategy development. Some love to make machines do more than anyone else thought possible. Some love the exercise of power over others. Some love to design and implement intricate systems. Some love money, the more the better.

Leaders who create dynamic, rewarding, enjoyable workplaces love *people*. Love is an act of humility that says, "I need you." Love affirms that the other person is worthy and important. Most of us know what love demands. I will not dwell long on this leadership characteristic. As a young person, I learned that one way to spell love is T-I-M-E. If I love the people who work in my organization, I will allocate time to be with them. In some organizations there are sanctions against "fraternizing with subordinates." I believe refraining from forming friendships or taking time to know and love people does immense damage to the spirit of everyone in the workplace. Setting executives apart from everyone else certainly does not make work more enjoyable.

Leaders can't serve the people under them without spending time with them. They need to visit them often.

Leaders need to spend time with the people for whom they are responsible—in effect, the employees they serve. Needless to say, this task becomes more difficult as you move to higher positions in an organization, for the simple reason that each promotion makes you responsible for more people. But leaders can't serve the people under them without spending time with them. They need to visit them often, preferably in their place of work. I could fill this book with the expressions of gratitude I received for regularly visiting our plants around the world. I estimate that over 80 percent of the people who came to AES from other large organizations had never met and talked with their previous CEO.

Early in AES's history, we brought AES people and their spouses from our business units around the world, without regard to rank or time of service, to the company's home office in the United States. Our intent was that every person would have at least one chance to connect with the people in the home office, as well as with colleagues in other locations. Another purpose was to talk to them about the history and shared values of the company. Roger Sant and I took turns hosting receptions in our homes during this twice-yearly orientation. Every time I visited a facility, AES people who had visited my home and had been part of an orientation weekend in Washington, D.C., would tell me it was one of the most significant events of their lives.

I also used the orientations and the visits around the world to update AES people about what had been happening in the company and to celebrate their work. Above all, these interactions gave me a chance to express how much I respected and cared for all the people who had committed themselves to AES.

The professionalization of management has sometimes led to improvements in the leadership of large organizations, but in many cases it has squeezed out the passion that leaders need to make their companies great places to work. Mark Fitzpatrick, a senior VP at AES and one of our most accomplished power-plant engineering experts, had a knack for finding new business opportunities. He also was a great developer of leaders within the company. One of the reasons was his passion for people. He cared deeply for each one. I had the privilege of attending several ceremonies during which he celebrated the successes of his people. He was not afraid to show emotion. Often tears would flow as he championed someone's character and accomplishments.

Bill Marriott, CEO of Marriott International, Inc., is famous for his habit of going to dozens of hotel properties in a short period of time. He visits with staff members, checks the kitchen, tests the food, and looks under beds. His passion for the important details of Marriott's business is well known. Being passionate about your people and what they do is a key characteristic of a leader who can make work a joyful experience. Showing passion communicates to others in the organization that they are important and that their work is vital to the success of the enterprise. It is crucial for people to know that they really matter to those in leadership positions.

Earlier in this book, I gave my definition of integrity. Integrity implies a reasonable consistency between beliefs and actions. I once worked with a board member who was very bright, experienced, and dedicated. But he was often dismissed by colleagues because he continually changed his position on important issues for no logically articulated reason. For example, he would make a statement to one person and say something totally different to someone else. Leaders who act in this manner are not trusted. They might be tolerated because of their position, but subordinates will most likely follow out of necessity, not out of respect. It is not a fun way to work.

CEOs frequently send one message to employees, another to Wall Street, and still another to customers. For example, on Monday morning a CEO might visit a business unit to tell employees that they are the company's best asset and that their welfare is his top priority. On Wednesday he goes to Wall Street and lists everything the company is doing to increase value for shareholders, saying, "That is our major purpose. It's all about you." On Sunday his company runs a TV advertisement claiming that customer-service quality is its highest concern. Other leaders communicate different messages to colleagues than they do to subordinates. Some of this is accidental, and some of it comes from following the advice of public-relations experts who push a philosophy of "tell the audience what they want to hear." This sort of pandering undercuts an executive's credibility and his ability to lead.

Dave McMillen sometimes introduced me to his people by saying, "You can be sure of how Dennis will come out on an issue because his beliefs, actions, and words both here and at home are nearly always in sync." One of my irreverent colleagues suggested that what he meant was that I was a hardheaded, inflexible Norwegian.

At AES, we chose "integrity" as one of the company's shared values, but not because it would get us ahead of the competition or improve our image. We chose it simply because it has a moral consistency that carries over to the way we treat our people and operate our businesses. The traits of good leaders—humility, courage, love, passion, and integrity—are essential to the roles they play in the workplace. I believe that leaders have three main roles. They are responsible for interpreting the organization's shared values and principles. They are senior advisers to everyone in the organization. And they are the collective conscience, pushing the organization to reach its goals and live up to its ideals.

After everything I've said about good organizational leaders having to give up power and delegate decisions, it may seem inconsistent that one of the roles I assign to leaders is to make decisions regarding shared values and principles. Let me explain.

Waterman and Peters posited "tight" and "loose" leadership in *In Search of Excellence*. They suggested that "tight" matters should be decided by the most senior people and that others should be delegated. In general, I subscribe to their thesis.

However, I suggest that leaders exercise tight control only on issues that affect the shared values of an organization. These shared beliefs are the bedrock of an organization's sense of community. They are the glue that holds everything together. All other decisions, including those with major financial implications, should be delegated to the team members who are closest to the matter under consideration.

Shared values are not necessarily the same as the values held by individuals within the organization. This potential discrepancy means two things. First, an organization's values must be clearly and thoroughly defined. Second, when a conflict arises between the values of an individual and those of an organization, the shared values of the larger group must prevail.

It is important for leaders to distinguish an organization's unchanging principles from its constantly changing strategy. The former is a function of moral precepts that have been tested and proved over the millennia. The latter is tied to market conditions and the strengths and skills of an organization.

The following comments about leaders from an AES shared values and principles survey show how seriously they were taken by our employees—and how difficult they are to live up to:

- "About half the superintendents and the plant manager should have the words 'Give up control' played on a tape as they sleep, because they keep forgetting. It is not fun when all of the decisions are made for you."

- "One of the values we aspire to is integrity. ... I think the commitment from our leaders ... needs to be raised in this regard. Long-term AES people need to understand the impact of the example that they project."

- "In general, I think we have grown so fast that we are having difficulty implementing the principles and culture. Several of the existing group managers are not well equipped or inclined to work hard on principles and culture. Their performance is based more on how fast they grow the company."

- "I have serious concerns about maintaining our values. With speedy growth, senior leaders are not maintaining importance of values. They are spending more time on business development and less on values."

Board members should practice the same values as everyone else in the company. Because they are among the most senior leaders of the organization, they can have an enormous impact on fun in the workplace by the way they approach decisions. I suggested that AES board members, including me, become active advisers on every important issue facing the organization but not make decisions except when required by law to do so. Persuading board members to exercise restraint is no small feat. Most are accomplished decision makers in other organizations. They will not easily give up decision making when they join a board. Ironically, because the AES board was so involved in giving advice on every important decision facing the company, I believe the directors were far more influential, committed, and engaged than those of more conventional companies of similar size who perfunctorily and automatically vote yes on every proposal put to them by managers and corporate lawyers.

To minimize the number of times they must intervene in decisions about values, leaders must devote a lot of time and energy to instilling them throughout the organization. To some people, AES's

e Bakke family moved to this farm in Saxon,
ashington, after their first home was destroyed.
nnis owned 29 cows, including these, during
s high school years.

*ES and every other energy company were hit by a
ies of events that were as powerful–and as
avoidable–as the flood that swallowed my
yhood home."*

Cousin Gordon Bakke, Dennis, and
brother Ray Bakke playing in the
Nooksack River

arilyn, Dennis, and Ray Bakke

Ray, Marilyn, Ruth (mom),
Dennis, and Lowell Bakke

Dennis Bakke, 1964

Ruth and Tollef Bakke at Dennis's Mount
Baker High School graduation in 1964

Dennis Bakke in 1964 as quarterback at the University of Puget Sound before deciding to go to the Harvard Business School

"I don't recommend you do it, Denny. It's very far away, and I have never heard of it. It can't be a very good school."

Tollef Bakke

"My dad was a lifetime union member, a source of great pride to him."

Ruth Bakke celebrates her 80th birthday at a Safeway in Puyallup, Washington, where she enjoyed working into her 80s.

"She gave us enormous freedom to work and make decisions. Somehow she made work so attractive..."

Dennis, Eileen, and Dennis Bakke Jr. several weeks before the Virginia independent schools championship game in 2000

"I was a nervous wreck, [but] Dennis Jr. seemed cool and confident. Why was I nervous and my son calm? That's simple: He was in control and I was not."

Helen and Brantley Harvey (Dennis's in-laws) on the porch of Marshlands, their home in Beaufort, South Carolina

Football coaches George Long (left) and Dennis Bakke. Dennis Jr. is No. 6.

"As a coach, George always deferred to others even though he clearly had every right to call the plays and make the important decisions. You can imagine how much everyone enjoyed being part of his teams..."

Dennis Bakke's Saturday morning basketball group

"Being a leader is like being a good point guard in basketball."

Bakke and John Sawhill during a press conference at the Federal Energy Administration during the 1974 energy crisis

"It was during those years that I learned that having a purpose made work meaningful. I also came to understand the destructive tyranny of most central staff operations."

President Bill Clinton and Dennis Bakke enjoy a round of golf.

"One of the most difficult lessons that I have had to learn is that leadership is not about managing peopl..."

Bakke visits the White House and makes the case against wage-and-hour laws.

"President and Mrs. Clinton were gracious enough to listen to my plea, but they also found the issue too difficult politically to advocate a change in the laws."

Dennis Bakke with AES
co-founder Roger Sant
"Because we hold very differ-
ent worldviews, the kind of
bond we have forged is some-
thing of a miracle."

nt and Bakke play trombone at the AES
ristmas party in 1986.
Vhen Roger Sant first used the word 'fun' to
pture the kind of working environment we
inted to create, neither of us could have
essed at its layers of meaning."

Shahzad Qasim with Eileen and Dennis Bakke at
the dedication of a school that AES founded near
its plant in Pakistan
"In making 'social responsibility' one of our core
values, we recognized that every corporation is given
certain rights and privileges by the state."

Shahzad Qasim and
Dennis Bakke sign
a contract to build
a power plant
in Pakistan.
"A joy-filled organization
starts with individual
initiative and
individual control."

Dennis Bakke and Leith Mann (with back to the camera) with Pakistani President Pervez Musharraf at a state dinner he gave in honor of AES

"The AES values at work are basic human values and are similar to what we tell our families at home," said a Pakistani on the AES annual values survey.

AES Chief Financial Officer Barry Sharp

"Barry was a servant among servants. His willingness to act as an adviser, teacher, and exemplar made him the most admired person in the company."

Benazir Bhutto, then prime minister of Pakistan, with Bakke at her home in Islamabad

"AES employees on every continent had nearly identical attitudes about our shared values and about what makes work fun."

Dennis Bakke discusses AES at the Bahía Blanca plant in Argentina in 1998.

"One of my most important tasks at AES was to teach people inside the company about our shared values.

Dennis Bakke meets with then President Eduard Shevardnadze of the Republic of Georgia, who thanked AES for keeping electricity running in the middle of the winter.

"The company's ability to operate in Georgia was in jeopardy because we were not yet close to breaking even financially, never mind making a fair return for our investors. The goals of service and economic health are each essential parts of a company's purpose."

andan Ambassador Edith Ssempala, Dennis Bakke, John Ruggirello, Ugandan esident Museveni, Peter Woicke of the World Bank, Eileen Bakke, and AES's ristian Wright, who worked diligently to bring the company to Uganda

the Uganda power plant is eventually built, this profit-making venture will very ely do more good for the people of Uganda, especially the poor, than all the aid the ernment has received over the past 25 years..."

AES's Christian Wright at Bujagali Falls in Uganda

"He and his colleagues at AES and in the Ugandan government were doing God's work."

The Bakke family with spouses and grandchildren at a family gathering in Hawaii, 2001

Members of Dennis and Eileen's church covenant group tour the AES Thames facility.

Ray Bakke, Lowell Bakke, Marilyn Bakke Pearson, and Dennis Bakke are developing Bakke Graduate University (www.bakke university.edu), which plans to offer both a doctorate in ministry degree and a master's in business administration.

"Most of the heroes of the Bible are people called to secular vocations."

Dennis and Eileen Bakke, co-founders of Imagine Schools

"When Eileen, a lifelong educator (she started her first school when she was 12 years old), agreed to join me in the venture, Imagine Schools was born."

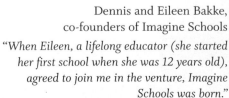

shared values were natural and easy to understand. But interpretations of the values varied widely among other employees. Most of the differences were resolved through teaching and discussion. As a result, people either adopted the common interpretation of the values or accepted the company's right to apply them in the workplace.

One of my most important tasks at AES was to teach people inside the company about our shared values. I advised other senior leaders to do the same. Of course, the most important way to teach the values was to live them personally, both inside and outside the organization. Thus, I ended every Leaders Conference with a paraphrase of St. Francis of Assisi: "Go and teach the values every day and, if necessary, use words."

The role of adviser is a natural one for leaders in a big organization. After all, they often are chosen because of their experience with the issues that the organization is likely to face. Their expertise is integral to making an organization successful. Asking leaders for their input on pending decisions and actions should be made mandatory. At AES we did so through our advice process.

Being a senior adviser also restores a little of the fun that usually comes with being a boss. Not having control and not making the key decisions detract from the fun that leaders experience in the workplace. But as we know from the research that led to participative management, people like to be asked for their opinions and suggestions, and leaders, including senior ones, are no exception. I believe that leaders, as well as board members, should be consulted on all important matters.

Being an accountability officer is like a kid keeping score. When we were children, my younger brother, Lowell, and I built a lighted, dirt basketball court near our rural home. We played over a hundred one-on-one basketball games each year, and I had great fun outscoring him in most of the games— until he grew bigger and became an all-state player. I decided not to play him anymore or keep score.

In organizations, scorekeeping is difficult, but not nearly as hard as holding ourselves and our colleagues accountable for the results. Unlike in my basketball games with Lowell, we can't just quit when the scoring goes in a negative direction. In the early days of Honeycomb at AES, I assumed that individuals and teams would hold themselves accountable for the scores they got on their performance. It was not always a good assumption, especially when the results, either on values and principles or on technical and financial matters, were poor. I came to realize that leaders have to step forward and put a high priority on encouraging accountability among all employees. When a member of my team fails to hold himself responsible for poor results, I believe I have failed as a leader.

Although it isn't always easy to take responsibility for our actions, we need to do so if we are to experience the feelings of joy and accomplishment that the workplace offers. If individuals are to become the best they can be, leaders must hold them to account when they fail and express gratitude when they succeed.

This is part of what Max De Pree refers to when he suggests that leaders need to "define reality." Where do we stand relative to our goals? How are we doing relative to our competitors? Who is most responsible for our success—or our failure? What are the consequences of our performance? It would be wonderful if each of us routinely answered these questions and adjusted our work habits accordingly. In a perfect world, that might happen, but my experience is that it doesn't occur automatically. Leaders must find ways to stimulate self-discipline, self-assessment, and individual and team accountability.

A crucial part of this process is leading by example. When our people in Oklahoma lied to the EPA in 1992, I took a 30 percent reduction in my own pay that year as the most senior person responsible for adherence to our values. Other corporate officers and leaders in the plant also took reductions ranging from 10 to 20 percent. Taking responsibility for a "bad score" is a leader's role, even if he had no direct responsibility for what happened.

Turning traditional corporate executives into servant leaders can be a wrenching process. After the radical leadership approach at AES was described in dozens of magazine and newspaper articles, numerous executives decided to "benchmark" the AES approach. They were impressed by the vibrancy, creativity, loyalty, and joy that were evident in the company. But when they realized the key to creating this kind of workplace was limiting *their* power and decision making, most reverted to business as usual. Their reaction was similar to that of the rich young ruler when Jesus told him to sell all he had and give it to the poor; he was unwilling to give up what he had to gain something much better.

Most organizational leaders experience great satisfaction in their roles and are reluctant to give up their perquisites. Many executives think the excitement and thrill of being a leader is centered on the wins they chalk up for the organization. The opposite is also true. When things aren't going well, especially financially, you will hear leaders say, "It isn't fun anymore." While winning and losing do influence how we feel about work, they are not the key to fun, which I illustrated with the story of Michael Jordan's last-second shots that win or lose games.

The primary reason leaders experience joy at work is not prestige or status or even financial success. It is the control they have, the decision-making authority that gives them a chance to make organizations succeed. Why do you think it is so difficult for many senior executives to retire, even though they have more than sufficient financial resources? The reason is that in retirement they don't feel useful or able to use their unique skills and creativity. I wonder how many of these leaders ever stop to realize that 90 percent of the people in their organizations never got a chance to exercise their natural gifts and fulfill *their* potential. Many retire without ever experiencing the joy that meaningful work can bring.

One of the jobs of a great organizational leader is to make everyone on the team better. This is especially true in an organization that puts a premium on a fun workplace. At AES, I noticed that former schoolteachers seemed to adapt to our concept of leadership more quickly than people from other backgrounds. The reason, I believe, is because the best teachers are rewarded by the performance of their students and the success of former students. Leaders who want to increase joy and success in the workplace must learn to take most of their personal satisfaction from the achievements of the people they lead, not from the power they exercise. The prayer of St. Francis of Assisi captures the intrinsic joy of being a servant leader:

> *Lord, make me an instrument of your peace;*
> *where there is hatred, let me sow love;*
> *where there is injury, pardon;*
> *where there is discord, harmony;*
> *where there is doubt, faith;*
> *where there is despair, hope;*
> *where there is darkness, light;*
> *and where there is sadness, joy;*
>
> *O Divine Master, grant that I may not so much seek*
> *to be consoled as to console;*
> *to be understood as to understand;*
> *to be loved as to love;*
> *for it is in giving that we receive,*
> *it is in pardoning that we are pardoned,*
> *and it is in dying that we are born to eternal life.*

*People want to be part of something greater
than themselves. They want to do something
that makes a positive difference in the world.*

CHAPTER 7

Purpose Matters

THE HISTORIC Chesapeake & Ohio Canal towpath runs along the
Potomac River for 184 miles from Washington, D.C., to Cumberland, Maryland. In Washington's Georgetown neighborhood, a com-
memorative plaque gives credit to George Washington for having
inspired the canal. Long before he became our first president, he
came up with the idea of building a series of locks around the falls
just north of Washington that were blocking commercial navigation. He formed the Patowmack Co., a profit-making corporation
with investors, to carry out his scheme.

What was Washington's primary motivation for starting the
company? To make money for himself? To make money for investors? To make a name for himself? To test his engineering skills?
To open the river to navigation for the betterment of Maryland and
Virginia and their citizens? From what I have read of Washington,
I suspect his purpose was primarily to improve navigation and only
secondarily to make profits.

I have learned that one measure of a good society is that it makes
doing good deeds easy and makes bad behavior difficult. Shouldn't a
company be the same way?

During the past several centuries, large organizations could
choose from a wide variety of missions, goals, and purposes. This

excerpt from John Steinbeck's *The Grapes of Wrath* sums up his belief that companies ought to exist for the sake of workers:

> "Sure," cried the tenant men, "but it's our land. We measured it and broke it up. We were born on it, and we got killed on it. Even if it's no good, it's still ours. That's what makes it ours—being born on it, working it, dying on it. That makes ownership, not a paper with numbers on it."
>
> "We're sorry. It's not us. It's the monster. The bank isn't like a man."
>
> "Yes, but the bank is only made of men."
>
> "No, you're wrong there—quite wrong there. The bank is something else than men. It happens that every man in a bank hates what the bank does, and yet the bank does it. The bank is something more than men, I tell you. It's the monster. Men made it, but they can't control it."

On the other hand, capitalists tend to assume that the primary purpose of a company is making profits for shareholders. This mission is besmirched by some executives who use their enterprises to make themselves rich, powerful, and profligate, or all three. In the old Soviet Union, most large organizations had yet a different mission. They were primarily a means of carrying out state policy. In the United States, the rhetoric and behavior of some government leaders suggest they believe the primary purpose of profit-making companies is to generate tax revenues to fund government programs. Other government officials believe businesses exist to create jobs. Finally, some not-for-profit organizations write lofty mission statements about helping society, without any reference to their own economic activities.

People tend to act in ways that are consistent with their personal goals. Similarly, a company's primary purpose—the real one, which isn't necessarily the one written in official documents or etched on wall plaques—guides its actions and decisions.

If board members and senior executives react with enthusiasm when the stock price goes up and turn grim when it drops, the organization's uppermost priority quickly becomes clear to its top executives. Did the goal of maintaining a high stock price or increasing profits lead some Enron officials to bend or break the rules? I can't say for certain, but I do know that goals and missions tend to shape the behavior of organizations and the people in them.

Nineteenth-century philosopher and economist John Stuart Mill said, "Those only are happy who have their minds trained on some object other than their own happiness—on the happiness of others ... on the importance of mankind, even on some act or pursuit followed not as a means for profits, but as in itself an ideal."

> *Selecting a mission is crucial because it becomes an organization's definition of success.*

Selecting a mission is crucial because it becomes an organization's definition of success. If a company chooses as its primary goal "adding value for shareholders," then success is typically defined by stock price. If a publicly traded company chooses the goal of creating long-term value for shareholders, success would probably be measured by stock price plus cash dividends paid. Jim Collins, for example, used stock price appreciation over 15 years to separate the "good" companies from "great" companies in his book *Good to Great*. Unfortunately, stock price appreciation is, at best, an incomplete definition of greatness. At worst, it is misleading or even dangerous because it encourages executives to make decisions that are not in the overall interests of the company or society.

If a company states that its main goal is providing good jobs and employee satisfaction, growth of the workforce will probably define success. If a firm's goal is providing a certain vaccine to children, it will most likely measure itself by how many children it inoculates. If an organization decides that its primary goals are to act with integrity and create a great working environment, it will grade itself according to how well it achieves those intangibles.

Every organization has a unique mission. Still, every modern, progressive, and socially responsible organization should strive to achieve three goals:

- To serve society with specified services or products;
- To operate in an economically sustainable manner;
- To achieve these results while rigorously adhering to a defined set of ethical principles and shared values.

The goal of meeting a need in society should be central to every organization incorporated by the state. Most firms and the people who work in them acknowledge that their organization exists to do something useful for society. Unfortunately, the current fad of putting shareholder value at the forefront of mission statements has made serving society a secondary goal, at least for many publicly traded corporations. Many executives forget that "value" doesn't necessarily have a dollar sign in front of it.

Some companies seem to exist only for profits. Selling a product becomes the means to that end. In my opinion, a much better case can be made for reversing the means and ends. The end should be selling a product, and the means to keep doing so should be making a profit.

Both investor-owned and nonprofit organizations have been given special status by the state, with associated rights and responsibilities. Both types of organizations exist to manage resources in such a way that a useful product or service will result. Serving society is an organization's main reason for existing. This is why I prefer the words "serving" and "stewardship" to "selling" and "management." The distinction in language makes clear that employees are guardians of resources, not owners. In the workplace, I make no distinction between "managers" or "management" and other employees. All employees are managers; all managers are employees. All are stewards. This is the ethos I tried to instill at AES, as articulated in our goal of making "every person a business person."

The manager/employee is a caretaker. "This is not mine, but I will steward it as if it were" is the proper perspective of every person who works in a moneymaking operation. "Serving" conveys an element of humility that is absent from "selling." A manager's work should be of service to someone else. Service not only helps an enterprise succeed; it also satisfies the altruistic impulse that is in all of us.

When a company gives a high priority to serving society, its employees are energized.

The concept of service is crucial to the creation of a joyful workplace. As I've already mentioned, people want to be part of something greater than themselves. They want to do something that makes a positive difference in the world. Most employees do not consider making a profit for shareholders, or even making money for themselves, sufficient to satisfy this goal. My hope was that the people at AES would be motivated primarily by the satisfaction of meeting the electricity needs of others, not by a desire to make profits or to fulfill the requirements of their jobs. One AES person described this as "love in work clothes."

When a company gives a high priority to serving society, its employees are energized. At AES, our people took satisfaction from being stewards, and many became passionate about their work. They incorporated as their own the organization's goal to serve society. Most did whatever it took to ensure that the company accomplished this goal.

There is another argument for making serving society the cornerstone purpose of every business. It is nothing less than the survival of private enterprise. I fear that free capitalist societies will one day reject their own systems if economic gain is the only goal of business. Sooner or later, societies will demand an end to the selfishness that in recent years has motivated so many companies, shareholders, and senior executives. Corporations exist at the sufferance of society and consequently must have a broader and more meaningful purpose than simply making money.

The importance of the role AES played in society was indelibly etched in my mind when Roger Sant and I met with then President Eduard Shevardnadze of the Republic of Georgia. Shevardnadze began the meeting with a gracious thank you: "Delivering electricity to the people of Tbilisi [the capital of Georgia] in the middle of winter kept people from rioting, and it also saved my job. It is the first year in many that we had light and heat for a significant part of the winter season."

AES's mission in Georgia was the same as it was everywhere else—to serve society's need for electricity in a way that allowed us to make enough money to sustain our company. We told Shevardnadze that we were pleased to assist the people of Tbilisi but that the company's ability to operate in Georgia was in jeopardy because we were not yet close to breaking even financially, never mind making a fair return for our investors. The goals of service and economic health are each essential parts of a company's purpose.

My experience in corporate boardrooms is that the noneconomic goals are often considered "soft." Noneconomic factors carry far less weight than stock price or profits. "Remember, Dennis, this is a business" was a refrain I heard often at AES during the past 20 years. I agree. Every business should seek to make a fair return as part of its goal to achieve economic sustainability. Profits reward shareholders for the equity capital they provide. Profits also provide an objective measurement of a company's ability to steward its resources, particularly equity capital, in a successful manner.

A healthy profit is an integral part of any successful business, but it should not be the sole or even the primary reason the business exists. I like Max De Pree's analogy: "Profits are like breathing. Breathing is not the goal of life, but it is pretty good evidence of whether or not you are alive."

I began to understand the difference between maximizing shareholder value and seeking economic sustainability during negotiations on our second plant, AES Beaver Valley, in 1994. Roger Sant and I had approached Allegheny Power (a utility we hoped would buy the power from our plant) one last time to negotiate the price for power from Beaver Valley that we believed was due us under the federal energy laws.

Our counterpart at Allegheny, Stan Garnett, a gentleman and astute businessman, was not interested in paying the government number. He told us to name a number, and he would give us a yes or no answer. Roger and I deliberated about 10 minutes and came back with a figure. Stan said, "No." Roger and I got up to leave but, just before we walked out the door, I asked, "What range are you thinking about?" Stan named one substantially lower than the figure we had suggested.

On the way to the airport, Roger and I quickly did another set of projections for Beaver Valley using Stan's number. It reduced the value of the project by $100 million, but the economics for AES still worked.

Our decision was easy. The goal wasn't to make the maximum amount of money. All we needed was enough to finance the deal, pay projected operating expenses, and get enough profit to offset the investment and risks involved. The lower price was certainly better for the customer as well.

Stan had left immediately after the meeting to go fishing. I located him by phone in a lodge in northern Pennsylvania and told him AES would accept his price. Within two weeks, AES and Allegheny signed a letter of intent—the first of its type in Pennsylvania. No arbitration. No tedious round of appeals. Allegheny was impressed. Our lawyers were aghast at what we had done. From their perspective, AES had just "thrown away" $100 million.

Profits should have the same priority as paying interest to financial institutions, salaries to employees, taxes to governments, and discounts to customers. Why should enriching shareholders be more important than producing quality products and selling them to customers at fair prices? What logic says that a company should put creating value for shareholders ahead of the economic well-being of its employees? The legendary lawyer Clarence Darrow reinforced this view when he said, "The employer puts his money into ... business and the workman his life. The one has as much right as the other to regulate the business." Employees should share in the value they create.

As "individual citizens" of the state, corporations are given certain rights and responsibilities in order to serve society. Most modern corporations rely on various groups and institutions to help them meet this goal.

The diagram below identifies the stakeholders that help the company achieve its goals. These stakeholders are not necessarily "owners" in a legal sense, but each possesses legitimate interests and many ownership characteristics.

Stakeholders

Classical economics suggests that all "residuals" (profits) should go to shareholders or owners. Some students of the modern corporation have used this economic theory as the basis for suggesting that making money for shareholders is the primary goal of investor-owned corporations. Some legal scholars also support this theory, although the courts have not consistently held that the "shareholder is king."

Margaret M. Blair, the Sloan visiting professor at the Georgetown University Law Center and a nonresident senior fellow at the Brookings Institution, analyzes the legal, economic, historical, and practical issues in *Ownership and Control: Rethinking Corporate Governance for the Twenty-First Century*. Her book supports the idea that shareholders are only one of many important stakeholders in corporations. "What troubles me most about the shareholder primacy argument is the glibness of it all," she wrote in *The Financial Times* in 2002. "Anyone who runs a business on the basis of fundamentals knows that they have to pay attention to human capital, their suppliers, franchise operators, all the different parties involved." During the past two decades, several states, including Illinois, Massachusetts, New Jersey, New York, and Pennsylvania, have added language to their laws of incorporation that give expanded rights and other considerations to these stakeholders. The shift was evident even in the conservative *Board Alert* newsletter, which in February 2003 published an article titled "Board Focus Shifts From Shareholders to Stakeholders: Employees, Customers, Communities Become More Important to Directors." The article stated: "Corporate boards are rethinking whom they represent as they draft governance principles required by new regulations."

Regardless of the economic and legal issues, however, most CEOs of large organizations know that the classical economic view and a strict legal interpretation of corporate ownership have little relevance to how the modern organization does and should work in reality. Each stakeholder is crucial to a company's success. Obviously, the company depends on investor capital, but it also needs lenders, customers, productive employees, rights and protections provided by government, and products and services from suppliers. The value created is the sum of the contributions of all these stakeholders. In return, each stakeholder deserves a portion of the value created.

In reality, "residuals" are seldom given only to the shareholders. When value is created above some theoretical minimum level, the premium is often reflected in dividends and higher stock prices. Employees get raises and bonuses and sometimes ownership shares. Financial institutions benefit because the company represents a lower risk. Governments and communities receive higher taxes and larger charitable gifts both from employees and the corporation.

Shareholders don't even choose the board members of the corporations in which they hold a interest. They vote on or ratify a slate of board members recruited by the existing board. No candidate for the board is ever put forward unless the CEO approves. As a result, not only are boards self-perpetuating, but they are ultimately controlled by the people who work full time in the organization. This is the only pragmatic way for the modern corporation to be managed. It is a myth that shareholders control companies through the board of directors.

Corporate-governance experts often discuss shareholder rights as if modern corporations were still "owned" or "controlled" by a few large shareholders. Not many years ago, most of these controlling shareholders were also senior executives in the firm. Today, shareholders are seldom a cohesive group with the same goals, objectives, and values. Even after our stock price dropped in 2002, there was no consensus among AES shareholders on what caused the problems or what to do about them.

There is also a tendency for board members and senior leaders of a company to listen to the shareholders who agree with their point of view. They then cite shareholder opinion as the rationale for taking actions that just happen to coincide with their own views.

I was guilty of that behavior, and I believe other company insiders were as well. I spent more time with shareholders during our time of turmoil than with anyone else connected to the company.

I could see that they held widely diverse opinions regarding the cause of the stock price decline and the steps that should be taken to remedy the situation—disparities that were confirmed by a survey of shareholders at the time. For example, there was not even a consensus among shareholders that major leadership changes were needed within the company.

A few years ago, it was popular to analyze any given situation by "following the money." I decided to try the idea on my own company. Which of the stakeholders got the corporation's money? I thought this information would help me figure out which group was most important and should be given highest priority. I traced how much of the company's annual revenue went to each of our major stakeholders. The following diagram shows the results.

Where the Money Went
Percentage of Revenues

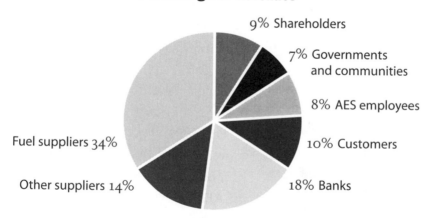

9% Shareholders

7% Governments and communities

8% AES employees

10% Customers

18% Banks

Fuel suppliers 34%

Other suppliers 14%

While every organization would allocate its revenues differently than AES did, many would show a similar result regarding profits. A fairly small percentage of revenue generated by companies is allocated to shareholders in the form of profits. Investors are important to any organization, but most of the time they get only a small piece of the corporation's revenue. This reinforces my argument that the interests of shareholders should not be paramount. Other stakeholders receive more significant economic benefits from the corporation than shareholders.

Maximizing value for just one stakeholder—i.e., shareholders—is probably easier than creating value for all stakeholders. But just because it's easier doesn't mean it's right. Justice demands that companies balance the interests of every stakeholder and allocate a fair share of the rewards to each.

Because of the importance of each stakeholder to the success of AES, I changed the salutation in my letter in the annual report from "Dear Fellow Shareholders" to "Dear Friends." For several years I included separate sections for our various stakeholders. I felt I owed each important group, not only shareholders, a report on how our business was conducted.

Creating economic value is a prerequisite to being a viable business, but the value created cannot be limited to shareholders. Shareholders do not "own" a company in the way that I own my house. They are more akin to investors in an apartment building who receive a portion of the rental income after paying for maintenance, heating, security, and other expenses. Other stakeholders in the apartment building—the renters, doormen, and superintendent, for instance—also receive benefits from the enterprise. Likewise, the stakeholders in a corporation deserve returns for the contributions they make to the company's effort to serve society. Value needs to be created for *all* major groups that assist the corporation in achieving its purposes. To sustain itself economically, a company needs to generate enough value over the long term to "pay" stakeholders an amount consistent with their contribution to the enterprise. Giving an outsized return to any single stakeholder effectively cheats the other stakeholders.

We don't need businesses that primarily "add value," which is just another way to say making money for shareholders. Simply put, we need businesses that perform well. That means that they need to serve society by providing customers with a valuable service or product and make enough money to pay employees, banks, share-holders, governments, and other stakeholders what they deserve for their assistance in making the enterprise successful.

As Harvard Business School professor Lynn Sharp Paine says, "superior performance in today's world has both a moral and a financial dimension."

We gave AES a moral dimension by making certain values and principles a central part of our purpose. It was a relatively new idea to me when we started AES, and I'm sure many people in business find it strange and inappropriate even today. Why, they ask, should a profit-making organization put such emphasis on shared values instead of letting employees follow their own values in their personal lives?

This letter, which was sent to me by an AES plant technician in Hungary, answers the question better than I ever could: "Keep living the principles and values even if no one else goes along with them or acknowledges your good work. We are trying to live this way, not because it will make us popular or successful or get others to go along with us. We are trying to live this way because it is the way we think life in our Hungarian business ought to be lived."

If serving society is given the same priority as creating value for stakeholders, it will most likely change the behavior of corporate leaders in a positive way. It might well reduce the pressure to "cook the books" or indulge in other illegal and immoral actions. The chances of such unethical behavior will be reduced even further if companies make certain values and principles their highest priority. Integrity, excellence, service, and social responsibility often are mentioned in company annual reports and other promotional materials. But nonfinancial considerations rarely come into play when a company decides to buy or sell assets, open a new plant, or eliminate a line of business. These decisions are usually made on the basis of what's good for shareholders. When I ask why there's no talk of values and principles, most board members and executives respond along these lines: "There is no need to spend time on principles.

Everyone understands that they're a given." I am quite sure that some business leaders would never even think of making decisions that are inconsistent with their company values. But when you listen to top executives talk to Wall Street analysts or you eavesdrop on a typical strategy session among board members and senior corporate executives, it's clear that financial security, profits, growth, and stock price are the only important goals of all but a handful of companies. This is especially true in times of financial stress.

Does the goal of making profit for shareholders, in the process boosting the financial rewards to executives, lead to cheating, lying, and other unethical behavior? We all have a tendency toward selfishness and greed. Most of us are tempted by power, money, and fame. Some of us will act in inappropriate ways to get these things. A clear set of corporate values helps protect us from ourselves. When our mission is to serve others, we don't think as much about ourselves. Channeling our energy toward worthy pursuits is infinitely more effective in governing behavior than draconian compliance programs.

A mission statement that challenges people to create the world's most fun place to work is essential for organizations that want their employees to have one of the most gratifying experiences in their lives. This end requires no other justification. However, for executives who can't get the dollar signs out of their eyes, it's worth noting that the link between fun and superior performance is extremely strong. Research shows that when employees feel like tightly controlled robots, with no opportunity to make decisions or take action on their own, productivity and performance decline.

Even so, at AES it required constant attention—and a lot of agitating—to keep fun and our other shared values at the top of our list of priorities. I tried to make our principles central to all of our hiring decisions, acquisition discussions, editorials in the company newsletter, annual reports, values surveys, compensation decisions, new business launches, investor meetings, and business review sessions. Listing the key principles of an organization on a wall plaque will never make them part of a company's collective thinking. If values and principles are to set the tone for organizations and guide their decisions, they must become part of every task, plan, discussion, and operation.

Most employees make corporate decisions on the basis of what they believe their leaders value. How do they determine what their leaders think is important? They pay attention to criteria used for determining compensation. They read company presentations to shareholders and banks. They consider what factors their bosses use in making decisions. They track how leaders steward corporate resources. They watch how leaders live their private lives.

If shared principles are not discussed when making important budgeting decisions—cutting costs, allocating capital, devising strategy—everyone will quickly understand that the company's real priority is not values and principles, even if they are extolled in the CEO's annual letter or on the corporate Website.

In *Accountability: Freedom and Responsibility Without Control*, Lebow and Spitzer suggest that "values statements, especially those imposed from the top, are seen by most as mere wallpaper that, at best, are ignored; at worst, create cynicism." I agree. Corporate values are worthless unless they are: (1) shared by the majority of people in the organization, (2) lived with some consistency by leaders, (3) considered at least equal to economic criteria in all major decisions of the organization, (4) taught to employees by senior leaders at every opportunity, and (5) constantly communicated to people and stakeholders *outside* the organization, including shareholders.

It takes courage to present the company's shared values and principles to financial institutions, shareholders, and even governments because these constituencies expect "serious" businesses to focus almost exclusively on the bottom line. I have already mentioned the reaction of the Securities and Exchange Commission when we said AES planned to give the highest priority to our shared values. In 1992, when our stock price dropped 65 percent primarily because of problems at our Oklahoma power plant, some investors chastised AES for not adhering to its values. As a result, several of our board members suggested that we "low key" our principles. "It is arrogant to make such a big deal about the values, especially since we have trouble living up to them. Let's just keep them to ourselves," was the way one director put it.

The same thing happened in 2002–03 when the stock price again dropped precipitously. Some investors blamed the goal of serving society, and others blamed our effort to create a fun workplace. I'm convinced that these analyses of AES's problems were far off the mark. Giving the appropriate weight and attention to all aspects of a company's mission, not just the economic measures that interest shareholders and banks, is difficult. I learned from these experiences that top leaders should always remind stakeholders that their companies are fallible and that, no matter how diligent or well-intentioned, they occasionally fall short of their values or economic goals—and sometimes both.

Three purposes or goals— service to society, economic health, and ethical values— should drive a company in equal measure.

Three purposes or goals—service to society, economic health, and ethical values—should drive a company in equal measure. Major business decisions should be evaluated both on the basis of economic and noneconomic criteria. Strategic planning should start and end with an assessment of whether a plan serves all three elements of a company's purpose. Compensation decisions should reflect "performance" in all three aspects of the company mission. Board members and other company leaders should stress the reasons that the organization has goals beyond economic success. In hiring and firing decisions, a person's performance in non-economic areas should get heavy consideration. Communications with investors, banks, communities, and other stakeholders should describe the major aims of the organization and include a note of humility concerning its ability to live up to the standards it sets for itself.

From 1981 to 1989, my wife and I had the marvelous opportunity to help start a church, a charitable foundation, the AES Corporation, a neighborhood learning center for disadvantaged children, and an independent elementary school. I have come to realize that the primary purposes of each of these organizations have much in common. Each one was created to serve a need in society in an economically sound manner, and each has a set of well-defined values that guide its operations.

Is it too much of a stretch to suggest that all organizations incorporated by the state, both profit-making and nonprofit, have similar purposes? Both should seek to steward resources entrusted to them in order to serve specified needs in society with integrity and in a way that makes economic sense. In this respect, profit-making organizations and not-for-profit organizations are quite similar. They both do good things for society, and they both must pay attention to their income statements and balance sheets. The only substantial difference is how the two obtain their capital. Both rely on customers for a portion of their capital. But companies get the balance from investors and lenders, while most not-for-profit organizations look to donors and governments.

I am a staunch advocate of free competitive markets in which customers, not governments or even corporate executives, effectively set prices by their individual decisions. It is a lot more fun to live in a market society because of the freedom it gives the individual to make the important decisions. That sounds similar to what makes a fun workplace, doesn't it?

I also believe that private, profit-making institutions rather than governments and nonprofits can supply most of the products and services needed in society. If profit-making companies make "serving society" an important corporate purpose, organizations might even do a better job of providing services to the public than governments or nonprofit organizations. Moreover, capital is more easily obtained by profit-making companies because investors and financial institutions have the incentive of making a return. Non-profits are limited to donations or government allocations, which are often more difficult to obtain. Paying returns to investors tends to make corporations disciplined and effective, so it is a mistake to assume that governments and nonprofit organizations are better at delivering social services than profit-making institutions. There is no reason profit-making organizations cannot be just as effective as their nonprofit cousins in operating schools, hospitals, welfare organizations, and other public services.

Organizations place enormous emphasis on being successful. Words like "winning," "excellence," "great" (not just "good"), "best," "first," "super," "superiority," "competitive advantage," and "premier" are used ad nauseam to describe the goals of organizations. As a young athlete, I used many of these same words to describe my own ambitions. The teams on which I played also used these words to set goals for performance.

It's perfectly appropriate for individuals, teams, and organizations to aim high. Using our God-given talents and acquired skills to accomplish significant positive results is a natural impulse. Problems sometimes arise, however, when we define success strictly in terms of achieving goals. Goals can be set in a way that virtually precludes an organization from being successful. For example, if the goal of every company were to achieve a higher return on shareholder investment than any other company in the world, then only one company would be considered a success. When goals are set in a realistic way, there can be many "winners" even if the standards are demanding. Excellence is less a competition against other organizations than an internal measure of quality.

My daughter, Margaret, ran cross-country for her high school. From her behavior at meets, I concluded that she had three primary goals. First, as a senior, she took the responsibility of being the chief cheerleader for other runners on her team, which included girls who were stronger and faster than she, as well as some who were younger and less experienced. Second, she tried to record better times each time she ran. Third, she wanted to be as high in the order of finishers as possible to help her team score well. Against those measures she had a very successful season. The three organizational goals I suggest in this chapter—serving society, achieving economic sustainability, and meeting the highest ethical standards—lead to a definition of success that has similar characteristics to Margaret's cross-country goals.

Ethics and service are often considered too squishy at a time when quantification of goals is increasingly popular. In *Corporate Governance*, shareholder advocates Nell Minow and Robert A. G. Monks advocate using profits as the primary way to measure a company's performance because they are "objective and quantifiable." Obviously, the book was written before the financial shenanigans of the recent past. Quantifying results is a good thing if the numbers promote real understanding of an important area of the organization's performance. But choosing a measurement just because it is quantifiable is like choosing a spouse because of height or SAT scores. No matter how many data points are available, you also need to consider intangible information to make a good judgment.

> *The most important questions*
> *in business are often*
> *never asked:*
> *What is our motive?*
> *What is our purpose?*
> *Are they worthwhile?*

Experts on organizational behavior usually urge simplicity in selecting purposes and goals. My goals would probably strike them as too complicated. Granted, it is more difficult to rally the employees around a mission that has multiple components. It also makes evaluating success far more challenging. But goals should not be set according to whether they're easy or hard to measure. They should be set because they're right.

The most important questions in business are often never asked: What is our motive? What is our purpose? Are they worthwhile? Motive and purpose guide behavior, color decisions, and add or subtract joy from work. Keep asking these questions, and use the answers to measure success.

Every job is or should be
in a constant state of change.

———————— ✦ ————————

CHAPTER 8

Potholes in the Road

ATTEMPTING TO DESIGN the most fun workplace ever by trial and error was difficult, to say the least. At times there seemed to be more trials and errors than success. From my reading and my studies at the Harvard Business School, I had been exposed to some of the best research and theory available on organizations, human behavior in work settings, and shaping the workplace. I was familiar with the scientific management theories of Frederick Taylor. I had studied Abraham Maslow's needs hierarchy, as well as Douglas McGregor's Theory X, Theory Y, and his ideas about the psychological manipulation of workers. Most of these theories were helpful, primarily for what they taught me about why people dread work.

Peter Drucker was the first of the great organizational scholars whose ideas fit with my view of the world. He suggested such radical ideas as having the same person be responsible for both planning and execution. He advocated self-discipline and individual responsibility. Under his approach, supervisors would be assistants to the people they supervised. None of these ideas, or others that I later picked up in books I read, gave me a complete blueprint for making AES the kind of place that would be rewarding, stimulating, productive, and successful, not only as a business but also as an environment for the people who worked there.

The key to reshaping AES was experimentation. As problems and issues arose, we would improvise, learning what worked and what didn't. We didn't create a joy-filled workplace but rather stumbled toward one. At one point, I summarized some of what we were learning in a series of articles for our internal AES periodical. I titled the series "Potholes in the Road," which I've dusted off and used as the title of this chapter. I will recount a number of the questions we faced for two reasons: first, to demonstrate how my theories were tested and refined by practice, and second, to show how much learning occurs when leaders are willing to try new approaches, evaluate them honestly, and learn from their failures as well as their successes.

————————

The man was about 6 feet, 4 inches tall and appeared to weigh close to 250 pounds. His size and strength reminded me of the 6-foot-8, 280-pound defensive end from Whitworth College who, in my first varsity start at quarterback for the University of Puget Sound, "helped" me rethink my career as a football player. The union leader standing in front of me asked the question I had dreaded for several years: "Mr. Bakke, what do you think of unions?"

I was, by nature, sympathetic to unions. My father had been a union laborer all his life and was very proud of his membership. My study of the miserable work environment that most laborers had to endure convinced me that unions were essential to ensuring justice in the workplace. I believed that unions were needed to offset the inherent power of management. I had also been schooled by my wise and experienced plant managers that "bashing" or saying anything derogatory about our unions would set back any chance we had of implementing our radical ideas about work.

"I don't think much about unions," I said. "My job is to eliminate management. If I succeed in doing that, I don't know what unions are for." The union leader sat down and before I could move to the next question, he said, "You sound like a union man." "I'm not," I said with a smile. "But thank you anyway." For the past 16 years, I have responded in the same way whenever this question arises.

AES's relationship with unions has been one of the most amazing and seldom told stories about the company and its culture. Our first union experience came at the Beaver Valley facility near Pittsburgh, Pennsylvania. We had purchased the facility and renovated it while operating parts of the plant. The operating people transferred to AES from ARCO Chemical, the previous owner. Except for the supervisors, all were members of the Oil, Chemical & Atomic Workers International Union. Most had worked at the plant and belonged to a union all of their adult lives.

From the beginning, we told the people of AES Beaver Valley that life for them would be different at AES, although at the time we did not really have a good idea what the differences would be. At first, the changes were simple. In my first visit to the plant, we invited all the employees and their spouses to dinner at a large restaurant. I was told this was the first time that union and nonunion members and spouses had ever been together at this type of social gathering. From then on, all celebrations and special events—golf, Pirates baseball games, Steelers football games, dinners, picnics, plant strategy sessions, and evaluations of our values survey—were open to managers and union members alike. All information about the plant was shared with everyone. We said we would respect the union as an entity and would try our best to treat each individual working at the plant with the same dignity and status regardless of union membership.

Later, we decided to pay year-end bonuses based partially on how well the 50-year-old plant boilers and turbines performed. Everyone in the plant, union and nonunion, would be eligible to participate. Some of the union members were skeptical. Francis was one of them. In one of my periodic nighttime visits to the plant, I found Francis in the main control room, operating the facility. He had worked at Beaver Valley for 30 years. During the course of our conversation, I mentioned that the data I had seen indicated that some of the earlier boiler problems had diminished, with the likely result being a bonus for everyone at the plant. It would be the first bonus ever for union members like Francis.

"They're going to shut it down," he grunted. "They're going to do what?" I asked incredulously. "By the way, who is 'they' anyway?" But Francis was convinced. "There is no way that they will allow us to get that bonus. The boilers will be shut down sometime before the end of November." I muttered something to the effect that it didn't make economic sense to shut the boilers down to avoid paying a bonus and then left. The bonus checks were handed out at a plant celebration a little over a month after my visit. As Francis received his check, the plant manager reminded him of his earlier conversation with me. "The boilers didn't get shut down, and you got your bonus," the plant manager said cheerily. Without any hesitation or hint of a smile, Francis said, "Yeah, but *they* took out taxes."

It took years to change the victim mentality engendered by Industrial Revolution assumptions about workers. Some people were never able to change. Early in our encounters with people who had worked in industrial settings for more than a few years, we noticed a strong tendency to blame some unnamed and invisible "they" for every decision the employees didn't understand or agree with. Eventually, that led to a company-wide "anti-they" campaign expertly designed and implemented by my colleague Bob Hemphill. Our purpose was to find the "theys" who seemed to be in charge of all injustices in our company and expose them as quickly as possible. The company's success was evident less than a year later when a reporter visited our Placerita plant in California. "Everyone talks about 'we' around here. What a difference from other businesses I visit."

During my visits to Beaver Valley I met Terry Gould. He had worked at the plant for over 20 years, mostly as a utility technician. That meant he did a little of everything, especially jobs that didn't require highly honed technical skills and that others didn't especially want to do. He was probably the best student of revolutionizing the workplace I ever had.

We became friends and ran in the Marine Corps marathon together in Washington, D.C. After AES had owned the Beaver Valley facility for several years, Terry was elected leader of the union by his colleagues at the plant. Once, when I visited the plant to participate in a celebration, he pulled me aside. "Dennis, please don't introduce me as head of the union anymore. I don't want anyone to know there is a union here." He didn't want union people to be considered different or to set themselves apart. He wanted everyone in the plant to be trusted as a business person.

A couple of years later, Terry led the effort to allow Beaver Valley union members to choose to be paid a salary without overtime pay, just like supervisors. He had a provision placed in the union contract that allowed the company to offer an "alternative pay package." Within two years, nearly 70 percent of the union members had chosen to be paid salaries. This was a major step in converting workers to business people, including members of the union.

As he was approaching retirement, Terry called me to say that before he left he wanted to give something back to the company, as if he hadn't already given enough. He wondered if someone could use him as an ambassador, teacher, and worker in some of our recently acquired facilities.

We took him up on his gracious offer and asked him to join the 1,000 people working in our deep coal mine in Hungary. For nearly a year he worked 1,500 feet below ground, teaching union members that they were valued and respected and could become business people just like him. Terry did several other successful stints in the company, working in unionized locations that had particularly troublesome histories. He then retired. Terry will always be one of my biggest heroes. I can't imagine that there's another union leader in this country who did as much to make workplaces fun for union members.

In *Stronger Than Steel: The Wayne Alderson Story*, R. C. Sproul cataloged the leadership efforts of a middle manager in a Pittsburgh steel foundry. It describes the love and respect he had for his men and the peaceful relations between management and labor that re-sulted. It is an inspiring story, but I think it misses a larger point. I believe that dividing people into management and labor is morally unsupportable. It results in an unfulfilling workplace regardless of whether the two groups get along.

Most of the businesses we acquired around the world were unionized. Our way of viewing working people was usually greeted with suspicion, but over time it was overwhelmingly and enthusias-tically accepted by everyone except some of the union leaders. When we purchased a group of hydroelectric facilities in Brazil, almost all the people working in the company were part of a union. To show our trust in our people and to signal our desire for a radical new approach to the workplace, we sent a team of union members to ne-gotiate with union leaders on the new contract. No "management" people or legal representatives were present. A confused group of union leaders and an empowered group of members quickly settled on a contract that looked more like the personal contracts manag-ers might negotiate for themselves. The amount of money paid to the employees by the company was almost identical to the amount we earmarked in the economic model developed for acquiring the business. The typical fear in situations like this is that the business economics will suffer if management does not exercise strict con-trol over all aspects of worker compensation. It is an unwarranted fear. In fact, I can think of no instance at AES when taking the steps needed to create a fun workplace had a long-term negative effect on the economics of the company.

The other benefits to the employees and to the company were also very positive. All three of the plants we bought in Southern California in the late 1990s were being operated under union agree-ments. Because another company had a contract to operate the facilities for two years, union members had an extended time to choose whether they wanted to work for AES. They could transfer to another facility operated by their incumbent employer, retire with a healthy severance package, or find a job in another company. It was the only time in my experience when a large group of union people had so many options. AES leaders were very candid about how the company planned to operate the facilities. We suggested that the employees talk with AES people at other facilities to help them understand our philosophy and its implications for them.

The report below was prepared by a team of union members from the California plant that visited AES Shady Point, a large, coal-fired facility in Oklahoma. Joe Arias, who wrote the letter, was a union member and one of the best control room operators at Redondo Beach. He was also one of the biggest skeptics about AES and its philosophy when we purchased the California plants:

If you're looking for an end-of-the-world report, you better stop here. What I found was a really good experience and we should thank God that our station was bought by AES and we have been given the opportunity to advance our careers. Everywhere we went, we were treated cordially and our accommodations and meals were first class.

The people at AES are very self-motivated and highly dedicated to the company values, which are: Integrity, Fairness, Fun, and Social Responsibility. Team work and leading by example are key traits to have. Most that have been hired by AES had to go through a very lengthy interview process. I would warn some Edison O&M employees that they shouldn't think we're going to be assimilated by AES just because we work at Redondo. If you don't have the above values, not a team player, don't know your job, or can't do your job without someone watching over you, then AES won't be needing you. Better start looking for another job now.

Speaking for myself, I'm more than ready for a change, where I could learn more about the plant and cross craft. I'm looking forward to the days when I won't have to work someone else's shift because he has a headache. Once we're working for AES, we are subject to peer reviews. So if you're a poor relief, don't make good rounds, have bad safety habits, these will be identified ... At the AES plants, they don't work anywhere near the over time we do. Vacation scheduling is not a problem. Since they have highly qualified people, they have plenty of people to pull from. They don't have people calling in sick like we do. They do have an on call system, but it's rare when they have to come into the plant.

I would like to thank AES [for] letting me go on this field trip. Without seeing this with my own eyes, I wouldn't have believed it. I feel much better about the future, and have my goals set for tomorrow.

At two of the California plants, AES was not required to negotiate a union agreement because more than half of the employees were new and not part of the previous union. The third plant retained more than 50 percent of the workforce from the original union and required a standard union contract to be in place. Nine months later, union members at the third plant voted overwhelmingly to decertify. This was enormously gratifying, both because it showed that they agreed with our view that a union wasn't necessary if we could eliminate management and because the decertification vote came without any encouragement or support from AES.

————————

One of the questions I'm frequently asked is how far down should a company go when it gives its employees the freedom to make important decisions. I'm not sure if there's a precise answer, but my experience has given me a good idea about the process a leader should use in making this judgment. My colleague Roger Naill and I often teamed together on visits to AES plants around the world, especially to meet with people at facilities recently acquired by AES.

People would listen politely to our "pitch" on the approach AES was hoping to apply to their workplace. It did not help that the business had typically been in existence for 20 or 30 years, even though it was new to AES. When it was time for questions and comments, invariably one of the first statements we heard was, "This sounds very interesting, but it won't work here because…" Most of the reasons involved the history of the facility and its location. We heard: "This is a Communist country," "This is a developing country," "We have been here too long to change," "Our leaders will never let it happen," "Our plant's too old," "This is not America," "There is a union here," "We can't afford this," "We do a pretty good job already," and "We are Dutch." Rog Naill and I would share a knowing smile from across the room when these objections to the AES approach were recited. We had learned that if we were persistent and were able to install AES-style leaders in these organizations, the objections would usually melt away within three years.

In almost every setting, we would also hear that "people here don't want what you are talking about. Most people do not want to make decisions." At first, this objection stymied me. After all, making decisions was at the center of our entire approach. I noticed, however, that most comments of this type came from supervisors.

Our experience shows that some people do resist taking responsibility for significant decisions. Sometimes this results from a lack of education or experience. However, the people who tend to be most reluctant seldom have been given real freedom to exercise their natural talents. They have not been allowed to reason, decide, and take responsibility. The result is low self-esteem and self-confidence, which inhibit them from embracing decision-making roles.

Surprisingly, I often find that these people are completely different away from work. They don't hesitate to make decisions at home or in community activities that require good reasoning skills and that entail significant consequences. They are clearly not afraid to make decisions, but the culture of the workplace has somehow discouraged them from doing so.

The most commonly proposed way to overcome an employee's distaste for making decisions is to "train" him. I have already mentioned my strong preference for education over training and for giving the employee, rather than the organization, responsibility for learning. I recommend that training be used sparingly. I also believe that learning how to make decisions is far more rapid when it takes place on the job while a person is actually doing it. When this happens, trainers become coaches, mentors, and friends. It is an education process that makes the workplace more effective and more fun. Top-down classroom training, by contrast, is just another form of control that limits freedom in the working environment.

Arbitrary prerequisites for jobs are a terrible way to decide when a person is ready to take on positions of responsibility. Organizations often have written or understood prerequisites for jobs that involve making important decisions. For example, AES's first three plant managers had college engineering degrees. They formed a "union" and decided that in the future all plant managers had to be college graduates with engineering degrees. It took me four or five years to break down this needless barrier.

Similarly, after the stock decline in 2001, one of my board members seriously suggested that we establish a rule that no one could be given responsibility to make a decision on a significant business issue—an acquisition of a power plant, for instance—unless they had been with the company for seven years. I couldn't help remembering how women, people of color, and even individuals who went to the "wrong" schools had been excluded from decision-making or leadership roles that they deserved.

While there is no doubt that certain specific skills and experiences may be very helpful in preparing a person for a particular job, we should be careful not to require these skills. We will not find the people most capable of making important decisions by instituting arbitrary or inflexible prerequisites. On the contrary, these requirements end up excluding some of the best possible people.

If prerequisites and training are not the answer, what is? As discussed above, most leaders decide ahead of time what backgrounds, education, and skills are needed for the people who will work in the organization. It is fascinating to see how many times we hire people whose backgrounds are similar to our own. If I went to the Harvard Business School, I tend to recruit at that school to fill roles that I think require skills similar to mine. If I am a man, I recruit men. If I worked at McKinsey, I recruit people from McKinsey. Part of this is based on existing relationships. Part of it is because we think that if our backgrounds were good for us, similar backgrounds will be good for everyone else.

The strategy of hiring clones is questionable to begin with, but it is especially inappropriate when we are trying to find people for jobs unlike our own. My friend Bob Giaimo founded and leads a group of quality family restaurants in the Wash-

People generally know best when they're ready to take on a particular responsibility and, in the process, contribute to the team.

ington, D.C., area. He and his leadership team have adopted many of the organizational principles outlined in this book. Many of his employees work only part time, and frequently they come from foreign countries. He asked me a series of questions. "How should my leadership team and I decide to trust people from such backgrounds with important business responsibility? How much decision making should be delegated to these folks? When do I know they are ready?"

As I pondered his questions and searched my own experience, I realized I could not answer the questions. Leaders can never know enough about the skills, motivation, ambition, and values of people to determine if they're ready for making business decisions. Knowing their backgrounds might be useful in getting a rough idea of potential, but the most important clues come from the employees themselves.

Employees should indicate their readiness by requesting to take on a role. Bob Hemphill called this the "choose me test." This characterization comes from the playground pickup games when the designated captain chooses from a group of children, some of whom are jumping up and down with their hands in the air saying, "Choose me, choose me." Effectively, they are saying, "I'm ready. I want to be on your team." This is not a foolproof test, but people generally know best when they're ready to take on a particular responsibility and, in the process, contribute to the team.

Bentley Craft and Byron List were young teachers at Rivendell School in Arlington, Virginia. When the school's headmaster of 10 years decided to leave for another position, Byron and Bentley came to the board with the unexpected request that they be made co-headmasters of the school. Neither of them had experience in leading organizations, nor were their educational backgrounds in school administration. They did possess numerous qualifications necessary to run the school, but I believe it was their unequivocal willingness to step forward, together, that swayed the board. They passed the "choose me test" with flying colors.

David Flory had just graduated from college as a liberal-arts major. His father had suggested he come visit me to see if I might have a job for him at AES. I told him I didn't do the hiring and at any rate, I doubted we had a place for someone who was fresh out of college with no experience. Besides, the only place we might need somebody was in Belfast, Northern Ireland (a war zone at the time), where we had recently bought a couple of power plants. "I'll go," he said, "and I'll work for no pay." I called one of our leaders in London and told him I had a smart kid who was willing to work for nothing in a war zone. David passed the "choose me test" and became one of AES's finest and most productive people. We paid him, too.

———

This book has focused almost exclusively on people who work in a way that is consistent with our assumptions about human nature. What about those who don't?

At AES, this was a problem, but not nearly as significant as most people imagine. When we first took over the old power station at

Monaca, Pennsylvania, I estimate that fewer than 20 percent of the people working there appeared to be operating according to AES assumptions about people. Few of them seemed to be capable or willing to think creatively and make decisions. Few thought of the job as anything but a way to make money to support their families. They concentrated their psychological energies on activities at home, at their churches, or in other community associations. Fun was primarily associated with bowling, deer hunting, and golf.

It took longer to change the culture at Beaver Valley than in other places. However, within five years, more than 80 percent of the people there were operating in a way consistent with the AES mission. At the end of 10 years, many people in the plant began to retire. Most had made a great deal of money from stock options and 401(k) investments. They no longer needed to work for money. I listened carefully to the reasons the people were retiring. I visited the plant and announced that I had failed in my plan to change people's minds about the nature and purpose of work.

At a lunch gathering, most of the plant people disagreed vehemently with my position. They didn't budge me. "I believe that between 5 percent and 15 percent of the people are leaving for the wrong reason," I said. "They are retiring primarily to get away from this place, rather than to move on to another exciting opportunity." These people were never able to see the great contribution to society they made through their work at the plant. They did not fully experience the joy of using their skills, making decisions, and taking responsibility.

This experience and dozens of similar ones in our operations around the world taught me some valuable lessons. First, most people will flourish in a liberated workplace. Age, sex, educational background, political inclination, union membership, color or ethnic background, and even IQ have little effect on whether someone will come to love and succeed in this kind of workplace.

Second, there will always be exceptions. Some people are scared of change for fear that they cannot survive or do well in such an environment. Others are beaten down by the years of being regarded as little more than a machine—a "human resource." Some never become fully adult in the sense that they shy from responsibility and accountability. A few have emotional or behavioral difficulties that prevent them from reaching their potential. Many of these people are uncomfortable in a workplace where individual achievement and fulfillment are the paramount goals. They often retire early and take a less taxing job.

Intelligence and education are not as important as an organizational culture that treats people of every background as creative, capable, responsible and trustworthy.

Third, the current emphasis on hiring "the right people" in order to be successful is oversold. Of the 40,000 people who worked at AES, fewer than 10 percent were actually hired by the company. The rest came to us through acquisitions. I learned that the performance of an individual at AES was more a function of work environment than the hiring process. McKinsey believes in hiring only "smart" or well-trained people. That's effective only up to a point, as illustrated by the example at Enron, which followed the same philosophy, even hiring dozens of McKinsey people. Intelligence and education are not as important as an organizational culture that treats people of every background as creative, capable, responsible, and trustworthy. A fun workplace trumps careful hiring when it comes to performance and personal satisfaction.

One of the fundamental questions for a business is how many people to employ. Most leaders rely on economic criteria. This means that an organization needs as many people as it takes to do a job, while operating within budget constraints. Unfortunately, this usually results in a three-way struggle among workplace leaders who believe that having more employees increases the chance of success, financial specialists who are trying to hold down costs, and people who need jobs.

I come at this problem as someone who is mainly concerned with the quality of the workplace. At AES, I found that a place with too few people is likely to be a much more fun place to work than one that has too many. This is easy to understand when you shift the paradigm from "work is hard, difficult, and something I have to do" to "work is my calling, a chance to exercise my gifts, and an opportunity to make a positive difference in the world." The latter model requires far fewer people.

After AES gave people freedom in the workplace and got rid of central staff specialists, we discovered that we could double the effectiveness of new acquisitions with half the original number of employees. As I reported earlier, when we took over Ekibastuz in Kazakhstan, the plant had 5,000 full-time employees and contractors and produced less than 500 megawatts of electricity. Within three years, the plant employed 500 people and was producing over 1,000 megawatts of electricity. In other words, with one tenth the number of employees, the plant produced twice as much electricity as it had under rigid Communist control.

Even our new coal plants in the United States had 30 to 40 percent fewer people than the industry average. To ensure that we were giving our people the best chance to maximize their enjoyment of work, I pushed every plant, even the ones we had just built, to reduce staffing levels by another 15 to 20 percent. One of the most modern coal-fired plants in the world is AES Shady Point in Oklahoma. It went from 135 employees early in its history to about 75 today. The plant has a world-class economic and environmental record.

While visiting an electric-generation business AES had recently acquired in India, the first question I got from nervous employees was, "Are we going to lose our jobs?" Not too diplomatically, I answered, "Yes, every person here will lose his job." That got their attention. My explanation—that losing their jobs meant that they would be doing something different, not that they would be out of work—calmed some of them a little, but not completely.

Job security is the chief concern at many businesses. I found that discussing the AES philosophy was enjoyable for most employees, but it was often overshadowed by the fear of losing their jobs. To them, this meant losing their ability to support their families, losing their identities, even losing their friends. They worried about failure, embarrassment, and not finding a new role in the world. This fear often causes pain, but it is a false fear.

My personal belief is that seeking job security is an illusory and empty goal.

My personal belief is that seeking job security is an illusory and empty goal. This view, no matter how elegantly presented, does little to dissuade people who cling desperately to their jobs. There is often a powerful conflict between an employee's desire for job security and my goal of maximizing joy, freedom, and success in the workplace.

It is popular in societies around the world to argue that we should go the extra mile to keep people employed. The people who hold this view believe it is kind, just, and generous. They believe it is not fair to fire people from the source of their livelihood. To their way of thinking, a company is not socially responsible if it puts people out of their jobs. I hold a contrary view, based on a half-dozen considerations:

- In the dynamic world in which we live, every job is or should be in a constant state of change. Some jobs change faster than others. Each of us has to keep adjusting our work to keep up with the changes in technology, operations, and regulation.

- Every individual changes constantly. We gain new knowledge and skills, and we develop new interests and goals. These changes make it imperative that we move to different jobs that offer challenges that fit our personal growth.

- At AES, I encouraged people to broaden their responsibilities, to educate themselves in new areas, to seek opportunities to make important decisions, to practice self-discipline and accountability, and to learn from specialists so that everyone could be part of multidisciplinary teams. Thus, even if people worked at the same organization for many years, their jobs would keep changing.

- It is counterproductive to let people stay in jobs when they're not needed. Even one extra person reduces the amount of responsibility available to others in the organization, making it difficult for co-workers to use their talents and skills to the fullest extent.

- It is not in anyone's interest to retain a supernumerary employee. In effect, it is withholding this person's talents from the rest of society. That person's creativity and energy could prove valuable in another job.

- Keeping too many people in an organization also raises operating costs above what they should be. The company increases prices to customers, pays less in taxes to governments, becomes a bigger risk to banks, reduces profits to shareholders, and lowers annual raises. These consequences are unfair to stakeholders and to society.

The right size of a workforce is equal to the number of people needed to make the workplace fun. When each person is given a measure of responsibility for the business, when "every person is a business person," the number of people needed diminishes dramatically. When the controllers, shift supervisors, and staff departments are eliminated, the remaining employees have a lot more fun—and the economics of the enterprise improve dramatically.

Having too many employees demoralizes colleagues and causes

turf battles. A very astute AES plant manager in Northern Ireland told me that arguments over turf are good indicators that the facility has too many people. No one worries about who does what when there is more than enough work to go around.

My belief that business should not carry unneeded employees does not mean that they should be given pink slips and hustled out the door. Departing employees need time to make the transition to new work. Organizations should be generous with severance arrangements. We encountered overstaffing almost every time we made an acquisition. One of the first things we did after acquiring a business was to set up a generous and voluntary severance program. Only rarely were individuals asked to leave.

In Panama, AES created a loan fund for employees who took the severance package. A year later, I traveled to a celebration lunch with former employees who had left the company. Seventy-one new businesses had been started by these former employees, most of whom tapped the AES loan fund. Even with generous, voluntary severance arrangements, the changeover from a company you know to one you don't can be traumatic. I strongly believe that these difficult transitions are a necessary evil that forces employees and organizations to adjust to a dynamic world. Part of the joy of work is learning new roles and taking on new responsibilities. Job security is attractive gift wrapping, but seldom is there anything of lasting value inside. Joy means using our work skills to meet fresh challenges.

―――――

When reporters wrote about AES, they all seemed to ask the same "last paragraph" question. One day a reporter came to interview me, and I saw at once that it was on her mind. But she began with broader questions about the "strange" philosophy of a profit-making business that gave people the opportunity to make decisions and take significant responsibility. I spent an hour or so with her and then suggested that she visit one of our facilities and find out firsthand what was happening.

A couple of weeks later, she returned a different person. She was surprised and excited about her findings at the plant. She accused me of not being forthcoming enough about the overwhelming joy, passion, and feeling of success that she observed among AES people at the plant. Then came the question: "Aren't you taking a significant risk that big mistakes will be made?"

Almost every article written on the company extolled the virtues of creating "turned-on," self-motivated people who were dedicated to service and excellence. Almost always, however, toward the end of the article the writer would make the following point: "AES is taking a big risk with its approach. Its people may make mistakes that will damage the company." Then the article would conclude with a simplified characterization of my view of this situation. "But Bakke thinks that freedom in the workplace is worth the risk of mistakes."

This simplistic assessment of the AES risk profile was neither fair nor accurate. By the time I met with this reporter, I was determined to take a tough line. "What's over there?" I asked, as I pointed across the Potomac River toward the grand buildings of Washington. "The federal government," she responded. "I used to work there," I continued. "They have more sophisticated control systems, more inspectors general, more risk-assessment people, more experts and specialists in every subject imaginable, a plethora of highly skilled and motivated leaders at the top of their organizations, and training programs ad nauseam. Do they make fewer mistakes than we do per person, per dollar of revenue, or whatever measure you want? I do not know the answer to that question, but until you do, I suggest you not write that we are taking any greater risk than anyone else is taking. Unless you can prove that others are doing better with a different approach, don't add the paragraph to the story." She left the paragraph out of her story.

I know of no credible evidence that an organization that chooses to allow important decisions—such as purchasing, planning, hiring, and budgeting—to be made "low" in the organization experiences more mistakes than those who use traditional central management and financial controls. Nor have I found any credible evidence that organizations with a control mentality perform better economically over the long term.

To the contrary, most recent research reaches just the opposite conclusion. From Drucker to Waterman to Block to Spitzer, leading business analysts suggest that a decentralized approach creates a much higher probability of economic success. More important, it also leads to a radically more rewarding and fun workplace. Yet most large organizations continue following rules of management that date to the Industrial Revolution. They are either unaware that there's a better way—or unwilling to try it. This has had a negative effect on economics worldwide, and it has been tragic for working people everywhere.

How can an organization with so many decision makers ensure that everyone is pursuing the same goal in a fair and just manner? Consistency is the key, as long as it's not imposed from above. The traditional way to achieve consistency is to have senior executives make all important decisions and set all company policies and procedures. Trouble is, this process often leads to defining fairness or justice as "sameness." It tramples on the idea that each individual who works in the organization is unique and special and deserves to be treated accordingly.

My experience indicates that we can have our cake and eat it too, as long as we share information across the company and make sure that everyone has a chance to offer advice. At AES, people who set compensation levels for others or for themselves gave evaluation data to everyone involved and asked colleagues for advice before deciding what people should be paid. Sometimes inconsistencies occurred, but they tended to be corrected rapidly. No HR person or senior executive ever had to intervene in the process.

———————

It would be easier to sell AES's approach—and this book, for that matter—if I stressed the economic effectiveness of companies in which everyone, not just senior executives, is expected to make decisions, act independently, and assume responsibility. In other words, why not write about companies that become economic winners by getting rid of top-down control?

I am reminded of a luncheon conversation many years ago with Bob Waterman. At the time, he was writing *The Renewal Factor: How the Best Get and Keep the Competitive Edge*, which argued that companies that place a priority on "high-minded" values and principles performed better than those that didn't. His list of exemplary companies included Rubbermaid, Merck, Hewlett-Packard, Levi Strauss, and AES. These companies were also very successful financially. "Bob, are there any companies that try to live these values but are not in the top 10 percent of economic performers at the current time?" I asked. "Yes," he said. "I can think of some companies that fit your description." "Why don't you write about them?" I asked. "It won't sell," he replied.

I've never been comfortable with his answer and the philosophy of life that stands behind it. Even if it is true that companies have a better chance of succeeding economically when they create a fun workplace, I have always tried to avoid the impression that we adhere to values and principles simply to make money. Again, it comes down to a question of means and ends. If our values were simply a means to an end, they would lose their meaning and importance. Our people would have every reason to be cynical about them. To me, it is like the old TV preachers who declare that a religious approach to life leads to good health and financial security. The message is not very subtle. While there may be some truth in the preacher's message, it is secondary. A man of the cloth should know better than anyone that virtue is an end in itself. So it is with companies. If they happen to make money while living their values and principles, it is a happier but incidental reward for conducting business in an upstanding and joy-filled way.

Over the years I have offered three major arguments to support this view. First, living by shared values and principles does not automatically lead to financial success or make a "great" company. Even if adherence to certain principles gives an organization a better chance to succeed financially, it is a meaningless objective because it would take so long to show up. In addition, the exceptions are numerous. The *Harvard Business Review* article titled "It Doesn't Pay to Do Good" found little correlation between "goodness" and economic performance. Lynn Paine makes a similar case, with a lot of supporting data, in *Value Shift*. Many of the companies singled out in *In Search of Excellence* have had spotty economic records since the research was completed. I have been told that a similar fate has befallen some of the "great" companies in *Good to Great*. Does this negate their greatness? Keep in mind that I believe price and other economic criteria are lousy indicators of success, excellence, or greatness.

Leo Durocher, the irascible manager of the Dodgers and later the Cubs, famously said, "Nice guys finish last." I don't think there is much credible evidence to back up his claim. But neither is there convincing reason to believe that nice companies with great values and selfless purposes finish first. Financial success is the function of many forces, including luck.

Second, linking values and principles to economic success will most likely lead to eventual rejection of these same values and principles by board members and other leaders of the organization. We all know the principle of basic logic that says: If A, then B. If not B, then not A. If A (certain principles and values), then B (financial success). If not B (financial success), then not A (it's time to junk principles and values). In other words, if a company links values to high profits and share price, it should logically reject these values when the stock price or profits fall. Because all companies experience financial fluctuations, this logic would require them to adjust their values and principles every time they experienced a downturn. That is very close to my experience at AES. In the midst of our economic difficulties in 1992 and 2002–03, voices inside and outside the company called for less idealism and more pragmatism. So if an organization champions the link between principles and economics, it will almost always have to compromise its most fundamental principles in the drive to increase value for shareholders.

Finally, linking principles and the bottom line diminishes the company in the eyes of its employees. Our effort to create the most fun workplace was built on trust and respect for every person at AES. This appreciation was based on who these people were, not on what they could do for the organization. If our senior leaders had gone to Wall Street and said that creating a fun workplace was simply an important strategy for achieving financial success, the hypocrisy of our shared values would have destroyed any chance of establishing relationships with employees based on mutual trust and respect.

This phenomenon is easier to understand in close personal relationships. Imagine that I tell my son I love him unconditionally for who he is, but in reality I feel close to him mainly because his athletic success or his outstanding academic record give me status with friends. My motivation is built on a hypocrisy that will inevitably damage our relationship.

I am afraid that many CEOs like me are guilty of this sort of hypocrisy when we push the latest "management technique" among our people. We know that jacking up our profits or stock price will not stimulate loyalty, productivity, initiative, creativity, and discipline among our employees. But Wall Street looms over us, and it can be difficult to be consistent about our goals and motives when speaking to our various constituencies.

When a company has an emergency that requires a rapid and coordinated response, it is difficult to operate under the principles that underpin a fun working environment. It may not even be appropriate. There usually is not enough time to get advice from people throughout the organization. Even participative management, in which subordinates advise bosses before decisions are made, may have to be short-circuited when time is at a premium.

When I think of emergencies, I picture an army heading into battle. Under enemy fire, soldiers can function effectively only if they follow the orders of their commanders. Employees are not cut out to blindly follow instructions from senior executives. However, in some emergencies there's no alternative. The threat to the organization is so imminent and significant that extraordinary approaches are warranted.

If the organization survives the emergency, the short-term suspension of collegial and decentralized decision making—the hallmarks of a fun workplace—need not result in permanent damage. To mitigate the potential harm done by a switch to emergency management, leaders should take two important steps.

First, they need to assure the people in the organization that the suspension is temporary and that ordinary operating procedures will resume as soon as possible.

Second, they should pick a leader for the emergency who is not currently a major line manager or even an obvious candidate to be a senior leader in the future. The skills required of a top-down emergency manager are very different than those needed to be a servant leader who brings joy to the workplace. When the AES stock price fell dramatically and capital markets were suddenly closed to the company, many coordinated actions were needed immediately. We put our brilliant, young general counsel, Bill Luraschi, in charge. Bill is a person of great integrity, courage, and decisiveness who had no senior line management experience or aspirations for a higher management position in the foreseeable future. His appointment was a signal to the people at AES that the crisis would be temporary.

Most organizations go through periods of crisis. Almost nothing about the management approach that is needed during emergencies applies to the long-term needs of a company that stresses service, decentralization, and collegiality. The fun and excitement of work might temporarily increase during a crisis. However, joy at work will dissipate if the central decision making needed in a crisis continues too long.

International students are well represented in the best American graduate business schools. This was especially noticeable to me when I visited Stanford to give lectures. I found it more than a little ironic when, on my second visit to the school, a young American woman asked, somewhat indignantly, "What right do you have to force this approach on other cultures?"

I believe this question comes out of the academic fad to hold all values equal and to evaluate a society only on the basis of its own values and beliefs. It is assumed to be morally imperialistic to claim that a particular set of values and behaviors are right or best. This attitude has changed the definition of tolerance. In the past, people could argue about the superiority of one culture or belief over another in a spirit of tolerance. But the "new tolerance" requires a person to acknowledge that the other person's perspective has as much merit as his own and that no one has the right to assert the primacy of his culture and values.

I cannot abide the new tolerance. As one of my AES colleagues put it, "the new kind of tolerance is mush." I believe that certain values, principles, and beliefs transcend time and culture. As a result, I have sometimes been labeled a cultural imperialist. I believe that basic principles—integrity, justice, and freedom in the workplace, for instance—apply to every culture and every organization. These values are not "American" or "Western." It is not sufficient to say that values guide the life of an individual or organization. I believe there is Truth with a capital "T." The choice of values is what counts.

My belief in transcendent values does not help overcome the difficulty of applying them in different situations. We need to be sensitive to differences in language, heritage, and education, and we should show humility when preaching our values both at home and abroad. Even so, I give no quarter to the Stanford student or to other relativists. Not only do we have the right to carry our basic principles across borders, but we must do so if integrity and justice are values we hold dear.

I am not talking about materialism, which is an impulse, not a value. I refer to ethical standards. In my experience, these are more often questioned by Americans and Europeans than by people in other parts of the world. "These are the values of Islam," was a familiar refrain in Pakistan about AES principles. "This is what we were taught at home," was often heard in other parts of the world. Stanford professor Jeffrey Pfeffer told me of an evening class where he taught the Stanford AES case to a group of advanced management students. The issue of cultural imperialism and the right of AES to impose its values was raised. After a spirited discussion, a black South African student ended the argument when he said, "These were our values before you came to our country."

Another threat to joy at work is "24-7" operations that necessitate shift work, a reality that many businesses deal with daily. I have already mentioned that shift workers often feel so estranged and dispirited that they start thinking about retirement in their early 20s, almost as soon as they begin working. I have never figured out how to eliminate the problems posed by shift work. Human beings were meant to work during the day and sleep at night. It isn't easy to reset your body clock for a substantial portion of your working life. The poorest results in our annual values and principles survey almost always came from shift workers. Working at night caused the most severe problems, but almost as troublesome was the cycle of working a week on daylight, then a week on the evening shift, followed by a week on "graveyard" (10 p.m. to 6 a.m.). The fact that almost all senior managers and staff people opt for regular day schedules indicates what hours people work when given a choice— and why it is difficult to make shift work fun.

Like most issues involving the workplace, the solutions depend on a company's priorities. If profits are the main goal, the problem probably will be addressed differently than if working people are the first priority. If the employees and shareholders are given equal priority, yet another approach will be used. Outlined below are several ideas we tried at AES to mitigate the problem. Most of them originated with the people working on shifts. They know best how to balance their own lives with the need to run costly equipment for the maximum number of hours.

First, most of AES's approximately 150 plants reduced the number of shifts from three to two and expanded the average time per shift from eight hours to 12. In almost every case, this decision was made by the people who worked on shifts, not by the plant leaders. Like most modern workplaces, power plants now require more mental than physical work. A 12-hour shift does not seem excessive for most people. Not only does it give people bigger blocks of time to accomplish projects at work, but it also provides longer stretches of time for family, recreation, and community activities. Moreover, communication at the plants improves when there is only one shift change instead of two each day.

Second, we minimized the number of people who had to be at the plants during the night. Modern automated facilities often can be controlled and maintained by fewer people at night than would be prudent for a full 24-hour period, 365 days of the year. Over the past 10 years at AES, we reduced the average number of people on night shifts by half. During this time, plant availability, or the average time the plant was available to produce electricity, increased appreciably. At several plants, the night shift consisted of only two people.

Third, we encouraged people to learn the gamut of skills required to keep the plant operating during the night shift. Managers, maintenance experts, and office people should all aspire to acquire these skills. When employees are versatile, a schedule can be devised that requires them to be on the night shift for only a few weeks a year.

Finally, a few people actually prefer to work at night. Allow them to take a disproportionate share of the night shifts. They might even prefer working exclusively at night. This will free up even more day work for others.

These ideas will not eliminate the negative aspects of shift work, but they can make a huge difference for a large proportion of employ-ees. We should also remember that the key to a great workplace is the freedom to make important decisions and take responsibility for the results. Other elements of the work environment contribute to the joy of work, but none, not even the absence of shift work, compares with being treated as an important and trusted decision maker.

One spring, Eileen and I were in her beautiful childhood home-town of Beaufort, South Carolina. On this particular afternoon we were visiting numerous shops to purchase household items for our beach house on nearby Fripp Island. After our third or fourth stop, Eileen had an epiphany.

"What a difference it would have made in this town if the own-ers and managers of these stores could have, over the past 50 years, adopted your philosophy of creating a fun workplace. I bet imple-mentation of the values of AES would have doubled the benefits of desegregation. It would have made these shops much more success-ful and a whole lot more enjoyable to work in." Her upbringing had given her an instinctive understanding of how the legacy of segrega-tion has affected the economic habits of Beaufort.

"What do you mean?" I asked, hoping my mind was tracking her correctly.

"That clerk at the hardware store," she said, "knew that the item we wanted had been out for several weeks, but he had done nothing about it because he wasn't responsible for ordering. The person at the paint store couldn't answer our question about the kind of sealer we should use on the deck rail, either because she didn't know or she was in a hurry to get off her shift. When I was a little girl in this town, none of the small-business owners and managers were black. That was understandable because of the official and unofficial seg-regation policies that still had a significant hold on the area. Today, those racial discrimination policies are not nearly as powerful in shaping life in Beaufort, but there are still few African-Americans who own these small businesses. I think this stems not from linger-ing racial discrimination, but from owners and managers not allow-ing employees to make decisions and take on major responsibilities within the businesses."

"Wow!" I said. I had never looked at these principles of work as they relate to retail service jobs and other small-business positions. Eileen suggested that I include a section in this book on how I would change the structure of these jobs and the effect those changes might have on people and the businesses in which they worked.

I have no experience in small business, except in agricultural jobs, and I suppose this book would be more credible if I had. That said, I think my views on the workplace apply just as much to a Beaufort hardware store as they do to an AES plant. In my experience, working people share many of the same traits, needs, and aspirations. In Beaufort, the majority of retail employees are paid low wages, have a high school education or less, often work fewer than 40 hours per week, and have few of the skills and traits that employers are taught to look for when hiring people for their organizations.

Imagine that I purchased and managed a general merchandise store. Say I had six people who worked a full schedule year-round and 10 others who worked part time. The realities of the competitive market require that the average compensation be just a little higher than minimum-wage levels. This store had been in business for 30 years and had survived despite the entrance into the market of Home Depot and Wal-Mart less than 10 miles away. The average employee had been working at the store for less than three years, although one older gentleman has been there since the store opened.

I'd spend the first few months getting to know the employees, customers, and suppliers personally. I'd ask what they knew about the business and about their hopes and fears for the business and for themselves. I'd share my own dreams and fears as well, along with my ideas about decentralized workplaces. I'd work alongside people to see how they run the cash registers, keep the books, order and receive new merchandise, pay bills, secure the facilities, pay employees, clean and maintain the building, hire and schedule employees, track inventory, and promote and advertise the business.

After four to eight weeks I would announce our first regular business review meeting. We would probably have to close the store early or open it late to make time for the meeting because some of the employees would have great difficulty changing schedules for reasons of family, school, or other commitments. There would most likely be two identical review meetings each month to accommodate people who work just on weekends. Everyone would be expected to attend one of the two meetings, each lasting an hour to an hour and a half.

Everyone should be shifted from hourly wages and overtime pay to a flat salary.

In the first few business review meetings, I would teach the principles that would serve as the foundation of our business. We would assume that each person was thoughtful, creative, trustworthy, and capable of making decisions; that each person was willing to take responsibility for his or her work and actions; that each person would make mistakes but wanted to make a positive contribution to the store and help make it successful.

Together we would also define the purpose of the company. The idea that the business existed to serve the needs of the community in an economically strong manner would be the centerpiece of the mission and the goal of the store. We would also define in terms all of us could understand the organization's shared values. Because I would again lead this discussion, these shared values would very likely include integrity, fairness, and a rewarding, stimulating, and fun working environment.

All of us would be given the chance to discuss and possibly put in writing ideas about our personal roles in achieving the purpose and goal of the company. Colleagues would be allowed to comment on these "job descriptions." In each subsequent year, employees, including me, would restate our own purpose and job description in relation to the firm's purposes and values.

Everyone would be shifted from hourly wages and overtime pay to a flat salary without overtime. This would help employees understand that their compensation was primarily for their skills and accomplishments, not for the time they put in at work.

The organization would consist of one team, with me as the only official leader. Everyone else would be a business person reporting to me. The group would work together on important issues such as setting compensation and benefits, ordering new merchandise, purchasing a new financial system, and hiring new people. We would establish a potential company bonus pool for the end of the year. The bonus pool would be shared among all employees, including me, based on an individual's annual salary. All employees would get a bonus equal to the same percentage of their salaries. Equal weight would be given to both economics and shared values.

We would adopt the 80/20 rule for work responsibilities. All employees would be expected to spend approximately 80 percent of their time carrying out their primary responsibilities. The other 20 percent would be spent working and learning the other areas of responsibility.

For example, everyone would be given the opportunity to work the cash register, stock the merchandise, oversee the storeroom, greet and assist customers, purchase and return merchandise, develop store advertising and promotion strategies, handle employee benefits and compensation, clean the store, and open and close it. This would be considered the ongoing education program for the company, although employees would be encouraged to take classes at the local community college or attend a seminar on something related to the business.

I would let everyone know that I would try to refrain from making any significant decisions related to purchasing, hiring, firing, advertising, or compensation. Every business decision would be assigned to a team member. The assigned decision maker would be required to get advice from colleagues before he or she made a decision or took action. If decision makers did not do an adequate job of getting advice, they could be fired. In the first year, all significant issues would require my advice. That rule would probably be relaxed to some degree as time passed. I would always reserve the right to overrule a decision that, in my judgment, was substantially inconsistent with our purpose or principles. I doubt that I would ever have to use that authority. (I never did at AES.)

By the second year, we would experiment with people setting their own compensation, after getting advice from all colleagues and completing a local survey of what people were paid in similar organizations. All information on salaries would be shared with all employees.

One of the business-review sessions would be used to establish the year's budget. Another meeting would be used for annual reviews. At that meeting, each person would be required to do a self-evaluation, and colleagues would then be encouraged to comment on the individual's review. Every person, including me, would be required to participate in this review process.

As soon as possible, we would begin the process of having a different employee present the financial report of the company at each business review. The person most responsible for keeping the books would teach the presenter the essence of the numbers and what they meant. This would force each of us to understand the financial implications of everything we did.

After all this, I would be surprised if we were not well on our way to creating the most fun and successful workplace in Beaufort County, South Carolina. Within 25 years, a dozen or more entrepreneurs and managers might come from the store. Some would stay and become managers and owners of my store. Some might be hired by other organizations, a few might start their own businesses, and still others would be encouraged to complete more formal schooling before moving on to other work. The community could be changed in a significant and positive manner.

———

I was often asked how my personal philosophy and the beliefs of colleagues blended with the shared principles and values of AES. Were there conflicts? How did we reconcile differences? A dialogue between Roger Sant and me on this subject was published in the AES newsletter.

Dear Dennis:

Great speech you gave at the Eastern College commencement [the school, now called Eastern University, is a Christian college in Pennsylvania], especially to that audience. However, it does raise a question regarding AES. Given that your context is Christianity, how do you reconcile that with the global nature of our business?

- 2-3% of our people are American
- a minority of folks are Christian
- ?% are Muslim
- ?% are agnostics
- ?% are other

Articles written about AES often refer to yours or my personal religious [beliefs] or other important philosophical underpinnings of our approach to life (e.g., environmentalism). It makes me nervous that some people might confuse these personal beliefs with our corporate values and principles. Do you have any words of clarification?

Roger

Dear Roger:

Thanks for your generous comments on my Eastern College speech, "It's Sunday—But Monday's Coming!" but you could have thought of easier questions for me to answer. You are correct that we live in a pluralistic world and our company reflects that world to a remarkable degree. We have great diversity of "worldviews," "belief systems," "faiths," or however one wants to title them. We have Christians of various persuasions, Hindus, Communists, Jews, Muslims, secular humanists (both selfish and generous), pantheists, atheists, Buddhists, environmentalists, capitalists, and many others.

Many of us have belief systems that encompass elements of more than one of these worldviews. I don't think the percentages are very important. All views deserve to be listened to and analyzed. It should be similar to a market for ideas. Where the various systems are in conflict, we as a company must choose. Fortunately, for our purposes, they are not often in conflict.

We have chosen not to focus primarily on the conflicts because AES's shared principles and values tend, to a great extent, to fall within the common intersection of many of the great philosophies of life. We didn't really design them that way; it just happened. That's why so many Christians, Muslims, capitalists, environmentalists, and humanists feel somewhat comfortable with the most important values that shape the company. It does not mean that we adopt all aspects of any one belief system, but it does mean that much of what we believe is not in conflict with so many of these philosophies.

We do have critics and those who will feel uncomfortable with our corporate beliefs—including some Christians, both on the left and right, some conservative capitalists, some strong environmentalists, orthodox Socialists/

Communists, elitists, self-centered humanists, and many others.

My view is that we compete to have our personal ideas become part of the shared intersection of what we call AES. It's a market. Labeling the ideas as being Christian or Buddhist, or environmentalist, or humanist, or scientific "facts" is probably not helpful or necessary. Sometimes our personal ideas are accepted into the intersection and sometimes they are not. It is a rigorous and stimulating process. Ideas should be accepted or rejected, not because they are Christian, or science-based, or environmental in their origin, but because of their merit, advancing and guiding our life together at AES.

I do not try to justify an idea I promulgate primarily because it is "Christian," or because it is consistent with my faith relationship with Christ. It is true that I am unlikely to push for values and policies that are inconsistent with my worldview and this relationship. I believe this is the essence of integrity and entirely appropriate. When asked about the basis of my beliefs, I am open and candid about them. I also let people know that they are personal, not corporate. Others who hold to these same AES shared values and principles come at them from a different set of beliefs. I often mention you in this regard, because of the major role you played in influencing the company's (and my own) interpretation of the shared values and principles.

Dennis

*At age 10, I learned
that when the river flooded at a 100-year level,
it didn't matter how well our house was constructed.*

CHAPTER 9

Another Crisis

AFTER THE DRAMATIC DROP in stock price in the summer of 1992, I began a campaign. My objective was to convince the leaders of AES, especially board members, that there was a broader and better definition of success than a Wall Street report card. I took every opportunity to make the case that stewardship, service, principles, and economic sustainability were the real underpinnings of the firm. I believed that AES's stock price was an inadequate indicator of our overall success, even of our economic performance. Almost every time I had a chance to speak inside and outside the company, I tried to explain what was required to make our company principled, fun, and successful. I used my annual report letter, investor meetings, worldwide phone calls with AES people, visits to AES businesses, and internal business review sessions to communicate the same message. In many of these settings, board members were in attendance. However, when the stock price dropped precipitously again in the fall of 2001, I quickly learned that I had failed. My efforts to change the views of my colleagues on the board had been fruitless.

In 2000, AES's share price hit its all-time high of $70, outpacing the upward movement of the stock market. Then it began a downward drift to $26 in September 2001. No one panicked because the $70 level was unrealistically high, and the decline tracked the market. But when the share price dropped to $12, the board grew alarmed. Within a few weeks, Enron and all the unregulated companies involved in the electricity business had suffered huge drops in price as well. By December, Enron had declared bankruptcy. By the end of February, the price of AES stock had fallen below $5. The market was afraid that AES and other companies in the sector would succumb to bankruptcy like the once-mighty Enron.

The reaction of the AES board was the same as it had been in 1992, though magnified several times. The most salient emotions were fear and loss of confidence. Some directors were worried about the financial consequences for them because many had much of their wealth tied up in AES stock. Some were concerned about their reputation as business leaders. Others focused on their legal liability as directors and officers. We hired scores of lawyers, consultants, and advisers to protect ourselves and to show that independent opinions validated the actions of the directors. The board called for a major reorganization of the company. Important decisions were centralized. While most leaders verbally supported the company's shared values, they proposed new definitions of our principles and new ways of implementing them. Several of my board colleagues suggested that putting so much emphasis on creating a fun workplace was a major cause of the company's problems.

It was painfully evident that some of our board members and leaders had supported our values because we had "won" in terms of growth and stock price. Then, when the stock price dropped, our values and philosophy of decentralization were blamed, and pressure mounted to change to a top-down management structure.

While many of these reactions were understandable and maybe even unavoidable, they were, in my view, directly related to my inability to persuade my closest colleagues on the board that we were on the right path. They had never fully adopted my view that business has obligations to society and to various stakeholders that go beyond the bottom line. My failure to win the hearts and minds of board members was not obvious to people outside the company.

Over the years, board members were quoted in prestigious national magazines supporting the company's approach. Nearly all board members participated in "Ask the Board" sessions at our annual investor conferences. They were articulate and passionate in support of the "upside down" decision-making structure of AES. A couple of members even took personal responsibility for the company's adoption of some of its more radical approaches. One of them told people that the company's emphasis on serving the world was the major reason he joined the board. "It is a special place" was a refrain I often heard from board members in both public and private settings.

Most board members loved the AES approach primarily because they believed it pushed the stock price up, not because it was the "right" way to operate an organization.

Nearly every board member traveled with me or with other senior leaders to company facilities around the world. They sat through meetings with a governor in Kazakhstan and then President Shevardnadze in the Republic of Georgia. (AES's struggle to live out its principles and serve the Republic of Georgia's need for electricity is documented in the award-winning film *Power Trip*, produced and directed by Paul Devlin.) They saw firsthand the despair of workers in Hungary and Argentina as we acquired facilities in these countries. They also experienced the joy that filled our workplaces only two or three years after we took over traditionally run companies. Most observers would have concluded that AES board members were both knowledgeable and supportive of the company's approach. After all, most of them appeared to be genuine ambassadors of AES's unique way of doing business.

I was not surprised, however, by the reaction of board members and a few other AES leaders to the large drop in stock price in September 2001. I had predicted to colleagues and business students that everything would change if the stock price fell sharply. I suggested that the 1992 reaction was likely to be repeated. Because of this experience, I surmised that most board members loved the AES approach primarily because they believed it pushed the stock price up, not because it was the "right" way to operate an organization. I had several clues that my campaign to win over my board colleagues had been ineffective. One senior board member told me several times in private that he did not appreciate my characterization of the "absolute" nature of the shared values. "You are too dogmatic, especially with the religious stuff. You need to be more flexible and pragmatic," he said. Even while some board members were telling shareholders that they loved "giving up power," I could see that they found it difficult to give advice rather than make decisions. In addition, board members often suggested I tone down the "rhetoric" concerning our shared values and purpose, especially when writing the company annual letter and in meetings with shareholders.

I never knew whether my failure to convince board members resulted from not being able to get them to understand my philosophy or from not being able to convince them of its merits. In the end, it didn't really matter, because the results were the same. The hard truth was that I had failed as a leader: I couldn't inspire them to follow me when things got tough.

When I started this book I had no intention of admitting that I had failed so miserably with my board members. Nor did I expect to analyze the economic woes that battered AES in 2002 and 2003. After all, this book is about fun and high purpose, not board politics or the vagaries of economic cycles. Friends wiser than I gently suggested that I couldn't advocate a radical business model without discussing what happened to AES during the dramatic economic downturn and stock market decline.

I believe we made four major mistakes that led to our economic problems during 2002–3. I will also discuss our stock price decline, although the two issues are only tangentially related. The principal causes of the underlying economic problems are very different from the reasons the stock price dropped so quickly.

We made our first big mistake in the early 1990s when we abandoned our ceiling on investments in any one market. Previously, we restricted ourselves to 10 percent of cash flow and invested capital. This limit, which originally was 5 percent, was to make sure that we would not overinvest in South America, Pakistan, or other developing areas. I even suggested that we ought to apply it to the developed world as well, even the United States. But when business opportunities began to come our way in bunches during the second half of the decade, we abandoned the limits.

Ridding ourselves of this self-imposed ceiling was not done without considerable discussion at the highest levels of the company and substantial input from large investors. I took advantage of every meeting with investors in New York and elsewhere to pose the question as to whether we should take advantage of promising new opportunities or let them pass so we could stay within our limits. Investors, board members, and senior leaders in the company were nearly unanimous in favor of taking advantage of the opportunities in Argentina, Brazil, Venezuela, California, Britain, and nearly everywhere they might occur, even if they breached our arbitrary internal limits.

In hindsight, this was an act of arrogance. Underlying the cap was the assumption that our company, no matter how diligent and prudent, was likely to make mistakes. The diversification mandated by the limits was a good way to protect ourselves against bad decisions. Limiting investments and cash flow in certain markets would have reduced our upside economic potential, but it would also have reduced dramatically the losses and asset write-offs that came later.

Our second mistake grew out of the financing philosophy that we followed for most of our existence: "Debt is cheaper than equity." I was a particularly strong proponent of the idea of maximizing debt rather than diluting the equity shares of the company by selling more to the public market. But after 1991, financial institutions would no longer allow us to "project finance" facilities with 100 percent debt. In order to finance new plants and acquisitions, the company had to invest equity. The share of investment required from the parent company in the 1990s ranged from 20 percent to as much as 100 percent in a few cases. Because we were still working on the assumption that debt was cheaper than equity, we often funded our equity commitment to these new businesses with debt that was on the books of the parent AES company. By the time the financial crisis of 2002 effectively barred non-investment-grade companies from obtaining new debt, AES had over $6 billion of debt that it had invested in businesses around the world. The parent company, not our subsidiaries, was responsible for repaying this money.

A much smarter financial strategy would have been to sell AES shares to investors more frequently and in larger amounts than we did during the '90s. We could have used those funds to fulfill our investment requirements in projects and reduce the amount of debt on the books of the parent company. Even a reduction of $2 billion from the $6 billion would have made for a much easier transition during the liquidity scare that occurred later, caused primarily by the collapse of Enron.

Our third mistake can be traced back to our humble beginnings. When AES came into existence in 1982, we had plenty of ideas but no money. "You have no balance sheet" is the way some financial analysts politely described our condition. Because we were not a publicly traded corporation, it was also difficult for us to raise equity. Before a bank would give us money to build or buy a plant, we had to have a series of contracts with established companies. For instance, one contract required a long-term agreement with a creditworthy company that pledged to buy the electricity that our plant would produce. The contract needed to be of sufficient length and price to guarantee that we could pay back the money that financial organizations loaned to the project.

Late in the 1990s, power companies in the U.S., U.K., and a few other countries began to build or purchase facilities without these long-term contracts. These so-called merchant plants planned to sell into the open market on a daily or slightly longer time frame. AES resisted this approach for several years and never did make it a major part of its strategy. The company did, however, acquire or build several dozen of these facilities, the biggest of which was the 4,000-megawatt facility in northern England called Drax.

The approach we took was flawed. We invested too much money either building or acquiring these merchant facilities given the uncertainties of price and volume of electricity that the facilities would sell over the long term. The problem was exacerbated by the excess electricity-generating capacity that developed in the United States and Britain. This excess capacity drove electricity prices down considerably.

Our last mistake was that we put too much emphasis on new business development. My passion for serving the world with clean, safe, reliable electricity prompted me to support creative, new ways to accomplish this goal. Others in the organization, as well as board members, became equally enamored of doing good things around the globe. This desire exacerbated the three mistakes discussed above and undoubtedly reduced somewhat our focus on the economic sustainability of some of the proposed new business opportunities.

We made other mistakes, of course, but none of them had a major effect on our economic performance. For example, we didn't thoroughly canvass AES for advice before making some important moves. I doubt this would have changed many of the decisions, however. The information we used could have been better and its distribution broader. Here, again, I doubt these defects had much of an effect on our decisions. Some board members and investors suggested that our financial controls were too loose. I question the validity of this assessment, but, even if true, it would not have changed important decisions. The advice given by individual board members and most other senior staff on all major decisions was nearly always unanimous.

The most frequent criticism of AES was that it was too decentralized. No credible evidence supports this judgment. Senior AES people, including me, and members of the board were primarily responsible for two of our four major mistakes. Non-officers had almost no responsibility for ignoring the market limits or using central debt instead of equity. Remember, I was a champion of making acquisitions in as many markets as possible, so our overexpansion was not something that could be blamed on business-development people traveling the globe looking for new opportunities. Finally, most of the other companies in our industry had much more conventional top-down management structures. Yet, they made at least as many mistakes as AES did, and most of them made even more. Decentralization didn't cause our mistakes.

Even from the rosy perspective of the good old days at AES, there was little evidence that the best and the brightest, to borrow David Halberstam's description of the men who led America into Vietnam, made fewer mistakes than the people who later participated in our collegial system. Our first three businesses were developed by Harvard and Yale graduates. We had the strongest banks and advisers that money could buy. Yet all three businesses were financial duds. None came even close to our expected pro forma economics. The first business lost $20 million a year. The second made less than half of what we had predicted over the first 10 years. The third ended up in the red after 10 years. Roger Sant, Bob Hemphill, and I were the key planners and decision makers. I don't suggest from this that decisions made at the highest level had a worse chance of economic success. But it is also difficult for me to stomach the argument that AES stumbled because decisions weren't all made by the three of us and other senior people in the company. Hundreds of project decisions made by people lower in the organizational hierarchy turned out to be greater financial successes than any of the early ones made by the company's founders.

Board members, including me, offered advice on every key decision and effectively signed off on every one of our mistakes. Blaming the problems on decentralization or on lower-level people not being disciplined or accountable doesn't pass muster. The decisions made by people throughout the organization would have been substantially the same if they had been made by me, Roger Sant, the executive office, or the board as a whole. Blaming the decentralized systems is nothing more than a convenient way to shift responsibility away from executives. It is vital to understand this because misdiagnosing the problem resulted in lower-level people losing the opportunity to offer advice, make decisions, and take responsibility. This undermined the progress we made in creating a joy-filled workplace.

Making work fulfilling and fun did not cause individuals to make business mistakes that injured the company. On the other hand, it did not prevent the company from making mistakes. But it helped us avoid some of the serious mistakes that plagued our industry. We did not, for example, get involved in any meaningful way in the "trading" aspect of the power business. We also had no major sales of AES stock by executives or board members prior to the stock decline.

We also did not order a substantial number of turbines in anticipation of building merchant plants that would sell thousands of megawatts of electricity at market prices, rather than under long-term contracts with set prices. This latter decision was helped greatly by not having centralized planning and purchasing groups that in all likelihood would have stressed the savings we could have realized from such a bulk purchase. These "savings" went out the window when energy prices plummeted. Finally, we were fortunate enough not to have any breaches of legal or ethical rules regarding the buying and selling of electricity or in the financial accounting of the company's activities. One large outside AES shareholder told me that AES would not have been able to refinance so soon after the stock collapse were it not for the enormous trust and respect the financial community had for the company's philosophy of service, integrity, and transparency. Our emphasis on shared values, including fun, helped AES weather the storm.

In addition, the mistakes we did make had little to do with

the precipitous fall in our stock price. When the AES stock price dropped to $12, I was asked by a board member what I thought the price would have been if we had not made the big mistakes I mentioned above. I estimated it would have been around $14 or $15. "Are you saying that the fall from $60 to $12 had almost nothing to do with our economic performance?" the board member asked incredulously. "Yes," I said. "I think the facts support my estimate." "This is unacceptable," the person replied. "You are not taking responsibility for the stock price crash." "I do take responsibility for the poor price. CEOs should always take responsibility for trouble, even if it's something that they can't control," I said. "I just don't think the performance of AES had much to do with its current stock price."

My argument started with the fact that the share price for an average company on the stock exchanges had dropped substantially without much regard to economic performance. In addition, every company in our industry, even those without significant businesses in England or South America, had experienced a stock price decline that was equal to or greater than ours. Could we all have made mistakes at the same time and with the same degree of gravity, or was something else going on?

What happened was a general recession with considerable fears about the future, compounded by the terrorist attacks of Sept. 11, 2001, the economic collapse of Argentina, and the California energy crisis. Even more problematic was the bankruptcy of Enron. Many outside investors and financial institutions worried that AES and others in the industry were going to experience the same fate. Some believed the whole industry was going to collapse. Differentiating among the various companies was almost impossible. Even companies like the venerable Duke Energy, with only minor parts of its business tied up in the independent electricity sector and with few liquidity worries, were treated almost as badly as those of us that were more typical of the industry.

The Senate Commerce Committee's hearing on Enron nearly

pushed AES into oblivion. It destroyed investor trust and blocked opportunities to refinance debt or sell equity. AES and other energy companies were punished severely by Wall Street. While the hearings focused on fraud and other wrongdoing by Enron, I believe the real reason they were held in the first place and stayed in the forefront of media attention for so long was because shareholders and employees lost money.

While it was appropriate to delve into Enron's malfeasance, I wish it had been done for the right reason, namely the ethical transgressions by Enron's top executives. This sort of malfeasance by senior people would have been next to impossible at AES because important decisions were discussed at every level of the company.

At age 10, I learned that when the river flooded at a 100-year level, it didn't matter how well our house was constructed. It didn't matter whether I did my homework or whether our family values were strong or whether my father was home or working in Alaska. It didn't matter whether I was smart or whether my little brother was a good athlete. If the house was anywhere near the river, it was going to be damaged by the rushing water. AES and every other energy company were hit by a series of events that were as powerful—and as unavoidable—as the flood that swallowed my boyhood home.

What should this teach us? Humility is the most important lesson. I was reading *The Washington Post* on my patio one beautiful late fall day in 2001. The article that caught my attention was a story about MicroStrategy and its visionary founder, Michael Saylor, a graduate of MIT. The company was in the database consulting business. It had become public at a stock price of a couple of dollars, had risen in a very few years to over $400 a share, and recently had fallen back to around $3 per share. At the stock's high, Saylor was reported to be the wealthiest person in the Washington area, with a net worth of more than $13 billion.

The night before, our family had seen the movie *A Beautiful Mind,* about a brilliant Princeton mathematician's struggle with schizophrenia. Reflecting on the movie that morning, I was reminded of the brilliant mathematicians, including Nobel laureates Myron Scholes and Robert Merton, who had founded Long-Term Capital Management, a hedge fund that for a time made financial trading seem like a sure bet. That firm also ran into major problems, and its collapse nearly caused a disaster in worldwide financial markets. At the time, Enron was in the middle of collapsing as well. Here were three seemingly invincible companies—MicroStrategy, Long-Term Capital Management, Enron—all going down like houses of cards.

What was the thread that ran through all three of these organizations? My first answer was "brilliance." All three companies were known for the intelligent, highly educated people at their senior levels. Could intelligence and education be a negative? I looked for another common thread that might be a better clue to what happened at these companies. I settled on hubris. Each of the firms seemed to believe they were masters of their domains. They were convinced that they had found the right and true way to be financially successful. They acted as if their brilliance put them beyond the risks and, in the case of Enron, even the laws that applied to mere mortals.

I silently congratulated myself that AES did not have a culture of arrogance. Then I remembered some of our conversations during the previous week about the company's economic problems. "If we just had better information, we wouldn't have made that mistake." "We need a better advice process." "We need smarter, better-trained people so we won't make bad decisions." "We need to get control."

Behind these seemingly logical statements was an arrogance that, if left unchecked, could easily cause the same kind of blindness that had destroyed so many of our "best" corporations. I was shaken by this insight into my own company and vowed to do what I could to warn my colleagues of the dangers of hubris.

There are many aspects of organizational life that you cannot control. No matter how many smart people you employ, no matter how many consultants and experts advise you, no matter how thorough your management information systems, many of the major actions that affect your organization's performance will be beyond your ability to control or even significantly influence.

The stock decline was devastating to many people. Six members of my extended family lost their entire retirement fund savings, which had been invested entirely in AES stock. Two family members were forced to sell their homes and rent apartments. Thousands of individual AES investors suffered painful economic losses. AES employees, especially those who had been with the company for 10 years or more, had their net worth reduced to a small fraction of what it had been before the price drop. I feel worse than I can say about the economic consequences to the people who trusted me and AES enough to invest their money in the company. The responsibility I feel for the economic plight of so many will stay with me as long as I live.

Congress, the executive branch, and watchdog organizations felt pressured by the Enron collapse and the misdeeds of the senior executives in other large companies to devise a host of new rules for governing corporations. They called for certification of financial information by senior executives. There was great pressure to separate the role of CEO and chairman of the board. Written charters were required for board committees. Reformers pushed for "independent" directors. (There will never be truly independent directors no matter what laws or rules are enacted. Remember, the Enron board met all the tests later required in the Sarbanes-Oxley Act.)

These new procedures and rules will not improve the quality of information provided to the public or reduce fraud. They will only bring lawyers and accountants into the center of corporate life and raise substantially the cost of products and services to all consumers. The reaction to the corporate governance crisis of 2002 was political, not practical.

On a Sunday evening shortly after the October 2001 stock price decline, I received an urgent phone call from an AES board member. I had known him for many years and considered him a loyal friend. "I need to see you right away," he said in a tone that I didn't recognize. An hour later he was at my home. "I think you should bring Roger [Sant] back into the company." "Why?" I asked. "He hasn't been involved on a day-to-day basis for six years." "We are in *big* trouble, and you need all the help you can get," he responded in an obviously troubled and uncomfortable manner. "I don't have any problem getting Roger's help if he is willing. Thanks for the suggestion." "That is not what I mean, Dennis. You *need* to give Roger a bigger role."

It finally dawned on me what he was really saying. He wanted me to step out of my CEO role, whether or not I gave up the actual title I had held for eight years. It was the first signal that my role at AES was in great jeopardy. A week or so later the board met in executive session without me. Spurred on by a strong minority, board members struggled to make changes that would be well received by the investment community without angering the large number of people at every level of the company who were loyal to me and to our approach to business.

They settled on a compromise that left me as CEO in name only, brought Roger back full time, and gave me a list of "instructions" to carry out in order to survive. I was angry and agreed to stay only after three days of soul-searching, numerous discussions with my senior staff, some adjustments in the specifics of the board's draft memo of understanding, and several long conversations with Roger.

Roger was placed in a very uncomfortable position. Out of respect and friendship, he did not want to do anything that was unfair or upsetting to me. On the other hand, he had told me at a lunch just a couple of months earlier that he was bored with not having a hands-on role in an organization like the one he had co-founded. The stock price crash and the complaints from several large shareholders also weighed heavily on him. Most of the board members had been with the company since its early days, when he was in charge. They felt comfortable with him. He was reluctant to come back, but most members of the board desperately wanted him to do so, and he was convinced that he could help the company get through this time of trouble.

The board's action started nine months of hell for me. I was neither fish nor fowl. It was almost as if the company had no CEO. Neither Roger nor I felt comfortable taking the leadership role that was needed at the time. Nearly every month, a minority group of board members met in private informal sessions to which I was not invited and suggested that I be replaced. I could never figure out exactly why they wanted me out of the company, and none would talk to me directly about their concerns. Did they think I caused the problems and should be held accountable? Did they lack confidence in my ability to lead the company out of its problems? Did they oppose my business philosophy and emphasis on values? Or did they think the company needed a human sacrifice before it could renew itself in the marketplace?

There was general agreement among the majority of the board that new members were needed to replace those who had been involved for 10 to 20 years. I worked diligently with the nominating committee in hopes that I could survive until a new group of directors could be elected. For months the stock price didn't budge, and fears about the company's ability to survive increased substantially, especially among some board members.

By late April and early May of 2002, several key board members seemed to be deserting me. Only one person said anything to me, but I could feel the shift. Board meetings were run as if I did not exist. It seemed as if my only role was to keep AES people around the world informed of the company's condition and to encourage them to keep performing at the highest level possible during this difficult time.

You can usually satisfy your superiors by turning in a strong economic performance, even if they do not agree with your methods. They will let you follow your own path on matters that are less important to them. Some of them may even support your ideas and beliefs during good economic times. Some of my board members were uncomfortable when I spoke of service, trust, and satisfying the needs of all of our stakeholders, but they tolerated it while the company stock price soared. When it plummeted, they changed the definition of AES's shared values. In closed meetings of the board, our purpose of "serving the world's need for electricity in an economically sustainable manner" became "add value for shareholders." Some suggested expunging fun from the values altogether, or making it synonymous with winning.

Roger and I disagreed on central philosophical issues, which made it difficult to work together. I believed that AES principles transcended time and circumstances; he believed our shared values, as they had been defined over the past eight to 10 years, could and should change over time. I believed these shared ideals were difficult to understand and to live consistently but were nonetheless immutable in our business, personal, and spiritual lives; he believed they were flexible and could be changed if they were not serving the company's goals, in this case the goal of economic success.

Late in May, I went to lunch as usual with six or seven members of my senior team. I told them of my tentative decision to retire in order to break the growing leadership impasse with Roger and the board. They were unanimous in urging me not to do so unless I thought the board would act unilaterally to strip me of my position. Several suggested that even if the board did decide to replace me as CEO, as the largest shareholder I could start a proxy fight. We all knew that with lots of support inside and outside the company, I would have a sporting chance of winning. But it would be messy and costly, and even if I were successful the company might be mortally wounded by the ordeal.

I left the lunch and that afternoon told Roger that I had decided to retire. I could tell he was surprised and very much relieved. He hated confrontations, and my decision avoided what promised to be the biggest one of his life. Two weeks later, in June 2002, the board accepted my retirement proposal, and I felt whole and at peace with myself for the first time in nine months. I wrote the retirement letter below and stepped away from the company I loved.

Dear Friends,

Today I asked my colleagues on the AES Board to allow me to retire from my role as Chief Executive Officer of AES. They have granted me that request and graciously given me the new title of Co-Founder and CEO Emeritus. This will greatly change my role, but it will not diminish my love for this company and the wonderful people who work here. I plan to stay on the AES Board and do whatever the new leadership team and other Board members want of me to help make the team and the company successful.

Since September of last year when we missed earnings and disappointed so many investors with our poor performance, the thought of stepping away after 20 plus years of service has been on my mind. It has taken almost nine months for me to get to a point where I felt comfortable taking the big step. Most of you know I am not a quitter and I did not want to abandon ship when the company was struggling as much as it was. Over the past few months we have strengthened our liquidity situation immensely and taken a number of other important actions toward recovery. With Paul Hanrahan, in whose selection I had a hand, leading the company it is now an acceptable time for me to leave.

An important part of my rationale for retiring now is that AES needs a different kind of leadership today than it did in the past. The world has changed, especially our industry, and AES needs to adjust to a new way of life. While I am proud enough to think I could have adapted, it would not have fit my strengths. I like to think of myself as a builder, a visionary (not always with 20/20 sight as you know), and a teacher. What will be needed for the foreseeable future will be leaders who are more inclined toward efficiency, discipline, accountability and control. Moreover, I tried to pour my life into AES people, especially its leaders, including Paul, for the last 10 to 18 years. I believe he and the rest of the leadership team can only reach their full potential if I step away. Roger Sant did that for me 8 ½ years ago and I am now following in his footsteps. In addition, by retiring from the CEO role at this time I want to model the kind of accountability to which leaders should be held. The economic performance of AES during the past year has been dreadful. As its leader, I take full responsibility and made this decision to leave accordingly.

While I have thought about this change for some time, I have not come to definite conclusions about what I will do in the future other than in my limited role as an AES director. Some ideas include:

- Search for another company or government organization that wants the kind of leadership I can bring.
- Definitely spend some extra time with my children and especially my wife, Eileen.
- Possibly write a book on principled leadership or organizational governance.
- Maybe some teaching and/or another corporate board.
- More time on our family foundation.
- Or, maybe even follow my lifelong whimsical desire to become a football coach.

There have, of course, been tensions among the AES family during these times. I am sure some of you have felt them as AES leaders and Board Members tried to deal with the major changes the company faced. Please believe the best about the people involved in these struggles and the decisions that resulted. We have all tried to discern what is best for AES, especially those of us on the AES Board. In times like this, the role of the Board is to ensure that the company is facing the realities of the marketplace and doing what is necessary to get the company on track for the future. Every AES Board member has gone the extra mile to guide the company effectively during this period.

I am so thankful for the last 21 years and for the incredible relationships formed. Most noteworthy, of course, is my partnership with Roger Sant. Because we hold very different worldviews, the kind of bond we have forged is something of a miracle and has outlasted many attempts to pull it apart. Likewise, I treasure the Senior leadership team, the Group managers, the Business leaders and the 35,000 AES people who made this journey so rewarding and fun.

Finally, I continue to be committed to the belief that every person wants to be part of a cause to serve the world and that ethically principled and economically robust companies are among the best ways to make the world a better place. I thank God for giving me the friends, courage, wisdom and stamina as I attempted to accomplish all of this at AES—with passion, with humility, and with love.

A couple of weeks later I was invited to a dinner celebration of my 21 years at AES. The 30 most senior leaders of the company were in attendance. Each person rose in the order in which they joined the company (they sorted out their start dates as they went along) to honor me with some of the most beautiful words I have had the privilege to hear. I will never forget the feelings of support and love that came from these dear friends and colleagues whom I had mentored over the years and who, in many ways, had encouraged and mentored me.

When it was my turn to speak, I thanked them for the fairy-tale journey they had made possible for me. I urged them to live the AES principles, including the creation and maintenance of the most fun place to work ever. I concluded by reading Rudyard Kipling's poem "If," which my son Peter had given me just days before as his tribute to me.

If

If you can keep your head when all about you
Are losing theirs and blaming it on you;
If you can trust yourself when all men doubt you,
But make allowance for their doubting too;

If you can wait and not be tired by waiting,
Or, being lied about, don't deal in lies,
Or, being hated, don't give way to hating,
And yet don't look too good, nor talk too wise:

If you can dream—and not make dreams your master;
If you can think—and not make thoughts your aim;
If you can meet with Triumph and Disaster
And treat those two imposters just the same;

If you can bear to hear the truth you've spoken
Twisted by knaves to make a trap for fools,
Or watch the things you gave your life to, broken,
And stoop and build 'em up with worn-out tools:

If you can make one heap of all your winnings
And risk it on one turn of pitch-and-toss,
And lose, and start again at your beginnings
And never breathe a word about your loss;

If you can force your heart and nerve and sinew
To serve your turn long after they are gone,
And so hold on when there is nothing in you
Except the Will which says to them: "Hold on!"

If you can talk with crowds and keep your virtue,
Or walk with kings—nor lose the common touch,

If neither foes nor loving friends can hurt you,
If all men count with you, but none too much;

If you can fill the unforgiving minute
With sixty seconds' worth of distance run—
Yours is the Earth and everything that's in it,
And—which is more—you'll be a Man, my son!

Retirement from AES gave me time to reflect and write *Joy at Work*. It did not quell my passion to pursue the real purpose of business and to continue my quest for the most fun workplace. My friend Bill Walton, chairman and CEO of Allied Capital, a large private-equity firm based in Washington, D.C., was the first to suggest that I consider a company to operate schools. He believed it would fit well with my understanding of the purpose of business. Effective schools require scores of people who are motivated by something other than high pay. Could a fun workplace that eliminated bureaucracy and decentralized decision making help?

Newspapers are replete with stories of urban schools failing academically, failing to inculcate positive, ethical character traits in students, and failing to operate in an economically sustainable manner. The challenges our schools present are immense. I was intrigued. When Eileen, a lifelong educator (she started her first school when she was 12 years old), agreed to join me in the venture, Imagine Schools was born.

Imagine Schools operates K–12 public charter schools. Forty states have enacted laws that give private organizations the opportunity to establish and operate schools "chartered" and funded by the government. The amount of funding received by a charter school depends on the number of students the school attracts. The advantage of a charter school is that it is locally controlled (like a private independent school). It can usually hire and fire its teachers and other employees, and it controls its own budget. However, it must meet all of the academic standards of the traditional public schools, and more. In most states, charter schools receive less money per student than traditional schools.

In June 2004, Imagine Schools acquired Chancellor Beacon Academies to form one of the largest charter-school companies in the United States. The company operates about 70 K–12 schools on 40 campuses in nine states and the District of Columbia, serving nearly 20,000 students.

The academic performance of Imagine Schools' for-profit predecessors and competitors has been quite good, especially considering the disproportionate share of low-income students they serve. However, economic performance has been abysmal. Most of the companies have lost significant amounts of their invested capital. Success as I have defined it in *Joy at Work* cannot be guaranteed. I do know that our leadership team will do everything reasonable to create a company environment that promotes academic achievement, character development, and economic sustainability—and will seek to operate according to the ethical principles embodied in integrity, justice, and a fun workplace.

*Leadership is about humility
and serving others.*

———————— ❊ ————————

EPILOGUE

THE STORY OF Aparecido Jose "Cas" Castellace was on my mind as the helicopter landed at AES's largest hydro power plant northeast of São Paulo, Brazil. It had been a thrilling day for me. At our first stop, the youth choir from a local church sang a passionate welcome. At subsequent stops, I could sense the enthusiasm that the people in these plants had for their work. They were grateful that I had come to honor their efforts. The progress they had made in adopting the AES philosophy of individual freedom, responsibility, and accountability was remarkable, especially because they had been with the company for less than two years. During one of the stops, I had the privilege of speaking with several of the people (none of them in official leadership positions) who had negotiated the compensation agreement with their own union leadership. But the highlight came on my final plant visit of the day. It was meeting Cas.

Not long after AES acquired eight hydro facilities in the state of São Paulo, I received a call from one of our leaders. He had just completed the process of offering a very generous severance program to the people who were working in the plants when we acquired them. Nearly 40 percent of the workforce voluntarily decided to take our offer. Just before the deadline for choosing the severance program, one of our plant managers noticed that Cas had not yet signed the agreement to take the money and leave the company. He called Cas into his office to make sure he didn't miss the deadline. Cas was one of the oldest people at the plant, and the severance package was heavily weighted in favor of people like him. "I don't plan to leave," Cas said. "I have been observing the new way AES people work, and I really like what I see." "That's great, Cas, but it is not for you," answered the manager. "You will lose money if you stay. It makes no sense. Please go home and talk it over with your wife, and come back here tomorrow and sign the papers." Cas came directly to the manager's office the next morning. "I have discussed it with my wife. She agrees with me that I have never loved working as much as I do today. I am good at what I do. I have significant responsibilities, and I have the freedom to make decisions. My health is good, and this is what I want to do. I have decided to stay." "That is impossible, Cas," the frustrated manager replied. "You must take the severance. The company can't allow you to make a decision that is totally counter to your own economic interest. Go home and talk with your wife. Let her talk some sense into you." Cas sought the plant manager out early the next morning. "You do what you must, but my decision is to stay."

Cas and I embraced that afternoon, and I told him that his decision had affirmed the AES way of doing business. Several days later I was in the town of Bariloche, a southern resort city in Argentina, to address over 200 AES people and their spouses who had traveled from plants in Argentina and Brazil for an orientation weekend. My keynote talk was built around a series of "love" stories. I told them about my mother, then 85 and the oldest employee of Safeway in the United States. I recounted how I had observed her light up the store with her warmth and enthusiasm as she bagged groceries and helped the "old folks" take them to their cars. Then I told the story of Cas. Earlier in the evening, someone had mentioned to me that he was part of a group that was attending the orientation from the hydro facilities in Brazil. As I finished his story, I glanced toward the table where he was seated. Tears of joy were streaming down the faces of both Cas and his wife. Spontaneously, the gathering of

AES people rose to their feet to give them a standing ovation. The love and respect he had for his work inspired everyone there to keep seeking the most fun workplace ever.

A year later, Eileen and I were scheduled to attend the annual Christmas party at our largest New York plant, located near Niagara Falls. We arrived two hours early so we could visit the plant before going to the hotel where the celebration was to be held. Our guide was a technician who had volunteered to escort us around before heading home to pick up his wife for the party. This large, 675-megawatt coal-fired power plant was being operated that night with a skeleton crew of five or six people. None were supervisors or plant leaders. In the central control room we had a spirited discussion with the two operators on shift. They had just returned from a conference held by the New York Independent System Operator, whose office schedules all electricity required by customers around the state.

They told us how intimidated they had been in the early sessions of the conference. The people from Enron and the other companies were all well versed in trading and dispatching electricity, and our people felt reluctant to enter the discussions. Soon, however, it became apparent that they were the only people there who knew anything about the daily operations of power plants. By the time the conference ended, they were at the center of almost all the important issues being discussed. They came back to work confident that they were on their way to learning what was necessary both to operate the facility and to market electricity effectively under the new rules. They were having a great time becoming full AES business people.

As we were leaving the plant, I mentioned Ed Kostecki, who I understood worked at the plant and had made a decision similar to the one made by Cas. He had decided to stay with AES after we purchased the plant even though it would have been more lucrative for him to leave under a voluntary severance program. He had initially decided to leave but changed his mind after seeing the kind of workplace that AES was trying to create. "He is in the plant tonight," our guide said. "Why would a maintenance technician, who typically works during daylight hours, be in the plant at night on the evening of the plant Christmas party?" I asked incredulously. "He took responsibility for some important work on the heat exchangers and has some contractors in tonight trying to finish repairs. The plant manager tried to get him to leave, but he insisted on staying with the project until it was complete." "Can I meet him?" I asked. A few minutes later, I climbed a ladder into one of the heat exchangers to find Ed busy welding. I thanked him for his dedication and for being the kind of person we hoped all AES people would aspire to be. "I love working in this place," he said. "After 40 years, I finally feel like I have responsibility and control over my work, including responsibility for contractors. Under the old system, I was never given the opportunity." I couldn't help mentioning this amazing example of an AES business person in my talk at the Christmas party a couple of hours later.

Abdul Qayyum works at AES's Lal Pir power plant in Pakistan. He wrote me a letter about the decision he made to stay at AES. The fact that it is written in his second language makes it especially touching.

> It was my second year in AES (1999) when I got a telephone call from my old friend (ex-boss) after 18 years (I was out of Pakistan for 16 years in Saudi Arabia). He was a Manager in one of the independent power plants and asked me to visit him. One day I visited that plant, he showed me every part of the plant and introduced me to almost every person at the plant. One week later he telephoned me and asked suddenly what was my opinion to join his plant. He offered me a salary which was nearly twice my then salary at AES. He also told me that a car would be provided (a car is a big thing in Pakistan). I was shocked, pleasantly, with that offer, and I was about to say to him that I am ready. But

I managed to tell him that I would reply to him after consulting my wife.

I was jubilant for the remaining part of that day and decided to give a surprise to my wife. So I contained my news until bed time when I revealed to her my friend's offer. We both were happy for some time. We were talking about a new plant and people. We realized that there will be extra money and a car, but we may lose things, also. She asked me if I would like to work with bosses, obeying orders, not asking questions and even begging permission for taking tea. It was something I had not considered earlier. We continued to talk on it along these lines. Jubilation disappeared. Our conclusion was that money cannot bring that much happiness, independence, and sense of being an adult human being as I was enjoying in AES. Next I informed my friend that I was very grateful for his nice offer and wished I could accept it, but I can't. He tried to asked me the reason, it was difficult for me to explain every reason. Finally he told me that I am crazy to believe in these Americans (AES). They will ruin me.

One of my favorite AES work stories was captured by reporter Alex Markels in a front-page *Wall Street Journal* article.

> MONTVILLE, Conn.—His hands still blackened from coal he has just unloaded from a barge, Jeff Hatch picks up the phone and calls his favorite broker.
>
> "What kind of rate can you give me for $10 million at 30 days?" he asks the agent, who handles Treasury bills. "Only 6.09? But I just got a 6.13 quote from Chase."
>
> In another room, Joe Oddo is working on J.P. Morgan & Co. "6.15 at 30 days?" confirms Mr. Oddo, a maintenance technician at AES Corp.'s power plant here. "I'll get right back to you."

Members of an ad hoc team that manages a $33 million plant investment fund, Messrs. Oddo and Hatch quickly confer with their associates, then close the deal. "It's like playing Monopoly," Mr. Oddo says as he heads off to fix a leaky valve in the boiler room. "Only the money's real."

It sounds like "empowerment" gone mad. Give workers more autonomy in their area of expertise? Sure. Open the books to employee purview? Perhaps. But what good could possibly come from handing corporate finance duties to workers whose collective borrowing experience totals a mortgage, two car loans and some paid-off credit-card debt?

Plenty of good, says AES, a maverick power producer that sells electricity to public utilities and steam to industry. "The more you increase individual responsibility, the better the chances for incremental improvements in operations," argues Dennis W. Bakke, the company's chief executive and one of its founders. He claims the team in Montville has matched, and once bettered, the returns of its corporate counterparts. "And more importantly," he says, "it makes work a lot more fun." ...

Is giving coal handlers investment responsibility risky? Mr. Bakke thinks not. He notes that the volunteer team in Montville does have a financial adviser, and they work within a narrow range of investment choices. They aren't exactly buying derivatives. What the CEO likes about the arrangement is that "they're changed people by this experience. They've learned so much about the total aspect of the business, they'll never be the same."

No person affirmed the principles of the workplace that I championed at AES better than Tommy Brooks. More than anything else, his example encouraged me to develop and articulate the ideas in this book. Tommy personified the kind of personal growth and pure enjoyment of work that occurs more often than not in large organizations that adopt the radical approach to management that I've described in this book.

Tommy was the sixth of seven children born to African-American parents in Hemphill, Texas. The family was poor but did not go hungry. When Tommy was in ninth grade, his father injured his back in an industrial accident and was never able to work again. His father's disability payments and his mother's earnings from being a nurse's aide and cleaning houses were all the money they had. Tommy and his siblings worked evenings after school, weekends, and summers to help keep the family off the welfare rolls.

His dream in high school was to attend Texas Southern University and become an engineer. However, his marriage at age 19 and his wife's pregnancy forced him to find work at the machine shop at Armco Steel instead.

Several years later, his younger brother died in an auto accident. Tommy was devastated. He sought solace in alcohol. At this low point in his life, he and his wife decided to attend a church service at the Fifth Ward Church of Christ in Houston. He listened carefully that day as the preacher suggested a new view of life that placed God at the center of everything. He left the church that day with a new faith, a new purpose, and a new perspective on his life.

Not long afterward, Tommy heard from his sister that the year-old AES Deepwater power plant located in Pasadena, Texas, was hiring. He joined the Deepwater plant and was assigned to the FGD (flue gas desulfurization, environmental cleanup) team as an operator. Over the next 18 months he moved to several other area teams within the plant. His enthusiasm for the work and his insatiable desire to learn prompted area supervisors to recruit him for their teams and motivated Tommy to move to other roles so he could learn as much as possible about the power plant in the shortest possible time.

The company's shared values of integrity, fairness, and social responsibility fit perfectly with Tommy's newfound faith. But it was the company's commitment to fun that affected him most. "At AES, I am somebody," Tommy said. "I am free to learn new things and to make decisions. I'm not a cog in the wheel. I'm not just a worker. I love my colleagues, supervisors, the values, and the entire approach to work."

By the time Dave McMillen visited the Deepwater plant looking for volunteers to help him start up the new AES power plant in Connecticut, Tommy was a prime recruit. He was already a member of the control room team, the job requiring the most knowledge of the entire plant operations. He was honored that he would be asked to help teach the AES way to all the new teams and assist in commissioning the new $200 million facility. He committed with enthusiasm for a six-to-nine-month assignment that was to begin when the plant neared completion in the next few months. During the months that followed, reality began to set in for Tommy. He didn't really want to leave Texas or his family, even for a short-term assignment. He decided to call Dave McMillen and tell him that he had decided against going to Connecticut. He was pretty sure that Dave would understand that his family needed him and that he was still learning his role at Deepwater.

It happened that I was visiting Deepwater at about this time. Tommy sought me out that evening. It was the first time I recall meeting him. He seemed so young, but I was most taken by his enthusiasm for work and learning. He seemed almost too driven to get ahead. Even though he was not in an official leadership position within the plant, he was already shaping the Honeycomb organizational structure and processes that had been adopted.

After an hour of lively discussion about the company and his personal situation, his mood changed. He had a question related to the shared values of integrity, fairness, social responsibility, and fun. He told me of his decision to rescind his commitment to Dave McMillen.

He explained why it didn't make sense for him to go to the East Coast at this point in his life. He also noted that there were others who had been with the company longer and were more capable of doing the job. "Are you or the company going to think badly of me because of this decision?" he asked. I responded with a question of my own. "Do you believe your decision is consistent with the company's shared value of integrity?"

As I recall, I asked him not to answer my question that evening. I told him that one of the purposes of our shared values was to help individuals discern right from wrong when confronted with difficult situations like the one he faced. A few weeks later, I heard that Tommy had called Dave McMillen to reconfirm his original commitment to be part of the start-up team.

Eventually, Tommy became part of the staff at the large new power station in Poteau, Oklahoma. He never sought or was chosen for a major leadership role in the company such as plant manager, vice president, or regional director. He was, however, chosen to lead one of the eight area work teams in the Oklahoma plant. He had about 15 employees reporting to him. In that role, he encouraged his subordinates to make decisions, including ones that had significant economic consequences. He refrained from making decisions for his people and fought every attempt by senior staff members and other line bosses to take decisions away from his team members. In his leadership role, he never forgot what made work fun for lower-level employees.

He was so articulate and passionate about the company's values that he was often invited to other plants around the world to help new employees understand the company approach. Even more remarkable was his interaction with Wall Street analysts and investors. On several occasions, Tommy played a starring role in describing life at AES to the company's biggest investors and analysts. No one was more effective in telling the company's story.

The excerpts below are from a letter he wrote me about working at AES and its effect on his life. It should not have been a surprise to me when I learned a few years ago that Tommy had left the company to become the minister of a church in Arkansas. In a recent conversation, Tommy told me he was following the model he had learned at AES and was giving away decision-making power on all nondoctrinal church matters to people in his congregation. "This is unusual in most churches, especially churches that are predominantly African-American," he noted. I asked how members of the church responded. "They love it. They absolutely love it!"

Dear Dennis,

When I hired on with AES in 1986, the doors were opened for me to accomplish my dreams and goals in this life. As I think back to my beginning year with the company, the organizational change from a traditional management style to the team concept was huge. The idea to make the workplace fun and enjoyable with few levels of management gave an extreme amount of decision-making power to all levels. This leadership style is what I believe really enhanced my opportunities to flourish and develop as an AES person.

The assumptions that people all over the world are unique, creative thinkers, fallible, capable of learning, trustworthy, capable of making decisions and willing to be held accountable really made sense to me. I now know that those [leaders] who believed these assumptions … [made it possible for me] to achieve my desire to be successful in life, and make a positive contribution to society.

These shared values of fairness, integrity, social responsibility, and fun all fit my basic beliefs. Of all the values, my favorite was fun in the workplace. [I was able to] accomplish [this] through empowerment, freedom to act, decision making, not having to be told what to do, but being trusted to make good decisions. I can say that I truly had fun during my years at AES. I enjoyed going to work and sharing with others my excitement.

Still today, I treat people with the same assumptions that I learned and believed [because of] your philosophy. I am confident that no other company would have hired me in an entry-level position and given me the same opportunities I had with AES.

Because of your ideas and radical approach to leadership, I was able to enjoy personal growth, unbelievable promotions, travel, and financial stability beyond my dreams. It truly [has] made a [major positive] difference in my life and that of my family.

Tommy Brooks

Few ministers are as prepared as he is to teach the congregation the real purpose of work and the essence of joy at work. Maybe he will even inspire some of them to start revolutions to change their own work settings.

My first question to one of the 15 or so people I met in our Pakistan plant—"How has your work life changed since you came to AES?"—resulted in a series of positive testimonials about how workplace freedom and responsibilities had helped them learn rapidly and feel like owners. Then I asked a question that I had never asked before anywhere in the company. "Has anything changed outside of work?" There was a long silence. Finally, one young man said, "Yes. There has been a change in my home. You know those assumptions about people that we make about AES employees—every person is assumed to be thoughtful, creative, trustworthy, and capable of making decisions. I started to realize that I needed to treat my wife that way also. I needed to let her make decisions." Another person followed with a smile, "Yes. At my house I hardly ever get to make decisions anymore."

Soon after our purchase of several power plants in New York state was announced to the public, employees of the plants began researching their new owners. One call mistakenly went to a large power plant in Monaca, Pennsylvania, near an AES plant with a similar name. "No, this isn't AES," said the plant technician who took the call. "I don't really know much about them," he continued, "but it must be quite a place. Half the people in this plant want to go to work there."

Over the years I spent helping to develop the ideas described in this book, dozens of people have told me stories about organizations where they worked that also were fun. They operated on principles similar to the ones I advocated at AES. "But they did not last" or "they didn't spread to the rest of the company." A question naturally arises: If the academic research is so positive about this approach, and the anecdotal evidence is so convincing, why aren't more companies trying to create fun workplaces? My experience suggests that there are nine main obstacles:

(1) Managers and bosses won't restrain themselves from making decisions. Leaders believe it is their right to do so. They are "in the best position" to make the call. By a large margin, their refusal to delegate responsibilities is the reason that so many people are bored and unhappy in their jobs.

(2) Leaders have the wrong motives. They may allow subordinates the freedom to make significant decisions, but they do so primarily because they believe it will lead to financial success or serve other objectives unrelated to a fun workplace. Working people aren't fooled.

(3) The organization's purpose is shallow or selfish. If employees can't adopt the mission of a company as their own, and if they can't see why it's worthwhile to society, the likelihood of joy at work diminishes dramatically.

(4) Mistakes are often attributed to systems rather than to human error or outside forces. When mistakes are made by lower-level employees in decentralized organizations, blame is often assigned to the practice of delegating decisions. The result: a return to the top-down, hierarchical structures of the past.

(5) Information is provided only to senior executives and board members. Sharing information, including financial data, with every employee is crucial to fun workplaces. It makes people feel trusted and important.

(6) Senior executives certify all information required by the government. Unless ways are found to circumvent this regulatory rigamarole—at AES, we would make plant people "officers" so they could perform certifications—lower-level employees are marginalized.

(7) Boards of directors require decisions to be made by themselves or by senior leaders. Board members work part time and typically get to know only a few top executives. Because directors are unfamiliar with people at lower levels, they tend not to seek their advice or rely on their expertise. When excluded from decisions, employees become estranged from the enterprise.

(8) Management and labor are adversaries. Hourly pay, overtime work, unions, perks, uniforms, and numerous other artificial and unnecessary distinctions create a class system in the workplace.

(9) Employees are treated like children. Paternalism and the desire for security prevent people from taking risks and responsibility.

During my visits to workplaces in the former Soviet Union, I noticed that government-owned businesses were run by managers in much the same way that large organizations are run in every other part of the world. Soviet managers told workers what to do and when to do it. In Western democracies, people are free almost everywhere except at work. They elect their political leaders, choose where to live, and decide what goods to buy. But the majority of

Western investors and corporate executives continue to believe that some people are ordained to lead and others to follow. The followers are replaceable parts in the economic machinery. When practiced this way, capitalism resembles a command economy. It lacks a moral dimension. Individual freedom and human dignity, which are the cornerstones of democracy, are eclipsed by the single-minded pursuit of economic goals.

After I retired from AES, one of my former colleagues confided that he had a new view of the recruiters who were calling and writing him about other positions. "Before," he said, "I never used to pay any attention to these letters or calls from recruiters. For the first time since I joined the company 15 years ago, however, these new employment possibilities are 'competition.' They are job opportunities. You see, Dennis, what I now have at the company is no longer something that is a unique calling. It's just a job." He had lost the passion that is both the cause and result of a wonderful workplace. Workplace passion comes from doing something that we believe is important. If only we could all be as passionate about our work as Michael Jordan was when he played basketball. Passion means that no one keeps track of time. No one says "it's just a job."

We can create these kinds of workplaces by linking the skills and aspirations of individuals to organizations dedicated to serving the needs of society in a manner that is economically strong and consistent with the highest ethical values and principles. To attain this goal we should allow every working person to be free to take actions and make decisions. This will make us more passionate about our work and ensure that organizations have the best chance to succeed economically.

Many have heard the story of the visitor to a job site where workers were busy in a variety of construction activities. "What are you doing?" the visitor asked one of the workmen. "I'm laying bricks," he responded. A few minutes later, the visitor repeated the question to another workman. "I'm building a wall," he said. The visitor then put the question to a third workman. "I'm helping to build a great cathedral," he replied, leaving no doubt about his passion for his work. It is my goal that people who work in organizations with which I am associated will answer the question with the purpose and enthusiasm of the third workman.

Living and working with humility is more difficult than being passionate about work. In my office is a sculpture by Esther Augsburger of Jesus washing the feet of His apostle Peter. I keep it to remind me (and I need a lot of reminding) that leadership is about humility and serving others. It reminds me not to be ashamed of my weaknesses, for it is in weakness that I can best help others to excel as human beings, rather than presuming I am strong enough to manage them as if they were resources or machines.

> *It is love that allows us to give up our power to control.*

With appropriate humility, we accept our inability to control the world, even the world of business. We quit searching for the secret to profits that rise quarter after quarter, to a stock price that ticks ever upward, to always winning. We accept that losing is part of life, as are making mistakes and falling on our faces. We do not fear adversity or suffering. We accept and even embrace problems. Out of them comes new learning, new growth, new hope, and new life. These principles apply not only to individuals but also to organizations of every sort. Where there is success, let there be humility.

I have hesitated to use the word "love" because of its romantic connotations, but as I come to the close of this book I feel compelled to use the word in one of its secondary meanings—the unselfish and benevolent concern for the good of others. This sort of love underlies everything we tried to do at AES. It is love that allows us to give up our power to control. It is love that allows us to treat each person in our organization with respect and dignity. Love sends people around the world to serve others. Love inspires people to work with greater purpose.

Love helps me understand why some colleagues, supervisors, board members, and subordinates did not subscribe to my theories or behave in a manner consistent with our highest principles and values. Love makes it possible for me to forgive those who derided my views and caused me so much pain. Because love is directed toward others, it allows for the possibility that my critics were right and I was wrong. And, if I was wrong, I would hope that love would enable my detractors to forgive the forceful way I pushed my philosophy.

I continue to believe that love is the final and crucial ingredient in a joy-filled workplace. It is a state of mind that requires no extra costs and no difficult trade-offs against competing organizational goals. It does not demand higher compensation or fancy offices or sophisticated information systems or more specialized staff people. Yet love is perfectly consistent with even the most aggressive economic goals.

In his poem "Two Tramps in Mud Time," Robert Frost tells the story of woodsmen who make a living felling trees and cutting wood. They happen upon a man on a weekend visit to his mountain cabin, chopping wood for his fireplace. These three selected verses explain my view of work and the kind of workplace that has been my quest:

> *Out of the mud two strangers came*
> *And caught me splitting wood in the yard.*
> *And one of them put me off my aim*
> *By hailing cheerily "Hit them hard!"*
>
> *I knew pretty well why he had dropped behind*
> *And let the other go on a way.*
> *I knew pretty well what he had in mind:*
> *He wanted to take my job for pay.*
> . . . .

Nothing on either side was said.
They knew they had but to stay their stay
And all their logic would fill my head:
As that I had no right to play

With what was another man's work for gain.
My right might be love but theirs was need.
And where the two exist in twain
Theirs was the better right—agreed.

But yield who will to their separation,
My object in living is to unite
My avocation and my vocation
As my two eyes make one in sight.

Only where love and need are one,
And the work is play for mortal stakes,
Is the deed ever really done
For Heaven and the future's sakes.

"Where do these ideas come from?" was a frequently asked question following my lectures at business schools and other forums on the subjects covered in this book. "Enter Into the Master's Joy" is my response. It is an attempt to describe the integration of my faith and the secular work to which I have been called. For clergy, this chapter is one person's view from the pew. –D. W. B.

POSTSCRIPT

Enter Into the Master's Joy

MISS MCINNES, a petite woman in her early 50s, was my math teacher from 8th to 11th grade. Polio had left her with a withered arm, but her brilliance and dedication were her most important features. During my senior year, I decided to stay at school before home football games, which were played on Friday nights, instead of spending an hour and a half riding the bus home and then turning right around to get back in time for the game. Miss McInnes invited me to have supper with her before those games, at the local cafe about a quarter of a mile from school. One evening she asked the question put to every high school senior. "What are you going to do with your life?" I gave her my usual answer: "I don't really have any idea, although I am hoping to go to college." I thought the college answer would bear out the faith she had shown in me. Fewer than 40 percent of my classmates planned to attend college. "I have some advice for you," she responded without hesitation. "Raymond and Lowell [my older and younger brothers, respectively, both of whom had scrupulously avoided taking math from her] have already committed to be pastors. Someone needs to support them."

To my knowledge, Miss McInnes was not a churchgoer or an amateur theologian. But her advice to me captured what I had been taught about the purpose of work and God's attitude toward it. The best occupation for a devout Christian, according to the teachings of my church, was to be a missionary, preferably in rural Africa. My cousin Gordon Bakke filled that role for over 20 years. Second best was to be a pastor or priest. My brothers were called to this kind of work. Third in the hierarchy was the "helping" professions: teachers, social workers, nurses, and others who served in similar ways, especially those who were not paid high salaries. People seemed to get more credit if they performed these kinds of jobs within a Christian-based organization, rather than working for the government, a public school, or a profit-making organization. Next in line was government work. Homemaking was a respected occupation as well. At the bottom were commercial and business jobs such as secretaries, technicians, factory workers, and executives. The primary path to redemption for these unfortunate souls was to make enough money to support those working in "full-time Christian ministry." They could also atone by volunteering their time to do something significant for the local church or another Christian activity when not at their jobs. Miss McInnes had advised me to use my talents to play the role dictated by my religious beliefs, at least to the extent that I understood them at the time.

When I left Harvard six years later, my ideas about work had not changed significantly. I accepted a position with the federal government in Washington partly because I had not served in the military. I felt a tug to do something useful for society. Somehow, spending time in government service seemed more consistent with my faith than jumping directly into business. After six more years working in the secretary's office at the Department of Health, Education, and Welfare and in the Executive Office of the President, my understanding of the interplay between my faith and my work remained the same.

A shift began several years after AES opened its doors for business. A small group of people from Washington Community Fellowship, the church that Eileen and I had helped start, began meeting to pray, study the Bible, and share our lives. For 15 years Eileen and I met weekly with this group. Over the years, members included Mim Mumaw (bookkeeper), Jerry and Jeannie Herbert (he was a professor, she a nurse), Rich and Kathy Gathro (college administrator, educator), John and Sue Seel (entrepreneur, writer; educator, counselor), Myron and Esther Augsburger (pastor, author; artist), Dan and Jennifer Van Horn (businessman, model), Bill and Ruth Brooks (U.S. Senate staffers), Ric and Lani Daniels (lawyers), and Bruce and Julia Overton (government lawyer, interior designer). My understanding of the relationship between work and faith was reshaped by our Bible studies, conversations, and prayers.

Every week I met with another group of friends, including Bill Brooks, Dan Van Horn, and Bob Muir, for breakfast in the cafeteria at the Supreme Court on Capitol Hill. Our discussions focused primarily on business and the role faith played in it. We called our group "The Business Square Table." In these conversations I tested some of the business ideas that came out of my understanding of Scripture. Soon I was putting them to use at AES, which was still struggling to get established.

One of my core beliefs, then and now, is that every entity incorporated by the state should serve the needs of society in an ethical and economically healthy manner. The same goal is appropriate for both profit-making and not-for-profit business organizations. My views on this point are based on biblical principles, starting with the Creation story in the Bible.

The Creation story begins with God working. He is creating the universe. He then creates mankind in His own image. He assigned humans to manage the Earth and all the animals, plants, and other resources it contained. God gave us the capability and authority to work. Through the act of Creation, He showed us how to undertake this responsibility. Genesis 2:6 says, "... and there was not a man to till the ground." This implies that one of the reasons mankind exists is to work.

Work itself was not the goal of life. We were not placed in the Garden purely to work. The Bible says that we were created to have a relationship with God and to honor Him. Work is one of the ways we honor or "glorify" God. Humankind's first important job description was to manage the Earth and all that comes from God's creation. I believe this includes the ideas, services, and products that come from the imaginations of people. We honor God by furthering His creation. Work should be an act of worship to God. God is pleased when people steward their talents and energy to achieve these ends.

The Bible does not appear to give priorities to the various kinds of stewardship or work. All kinds of production and management activities honor God. If the work is seen by the worker as something accomplished for God and meeting a need in society, it is pleasing to God. Some roles that modern society tends to see as less valuable and mundane—animal husbandry and tilling the soil, for instance—are specifically mentioned as worthy endeavors in the Garden. Isn't it logical that all work that results in food, clothing, shelter, rest or recreation, beauty, and a host of other worthy ends can be acts of worship to God and seen as valuable contributions to society? Are these not activities that can be as sacred as rearing children, teaching school, or even carrying out priestly duties?

When I was a teenager, a camp counselor introduced me to a Bible verse in Paul's letter to the church at Corinth. "Whether you eat or drink or whatever you do, do all to the glory of God" (1 Corinthians 10:31). This verse suggested that all my work and play was to be done for God. I tested the concept at home with what seemed to be the least creative and inspiring job I was assigned: washing dishes. I vowed to approach the twice-daily task as work done directly for God. Over time I realized that meant doing the work with a willing spirit, enthusiasm, and pride in the results. I continually worked on my dishwashing skills with a goal of being the best home dishwasher God ever employed. Forty years later, Eileen and my children will attest to my seriousness and special joy that is part of almost every dishwashing experience.

Though I often fail to live up to God's highest standards, I realize that my approach to the job is consistent with the expectation God places on all my daily work. God does not differentiate among types of work. Halfhearted efforts and sloppy work do not honor God. He expects me to use my best efforts, talents, and skills in every task I undertake, whatever its importance.

A survey of other biblical stories finds no evidence that God favors church or other religiously related work over other callings and vocations. The grocery store magnate Howard Butt points out that Bezaleel was the first person mentioned in the Bible who was "filled with the Spirit of God." Neither Moses or Joshua received that distinction. Was Bezaleel a priest? Was he God's chosen leader of the Israelites? No. Bezaleel was an artist, a designer, a master craftsman, and later a contracting executive. He was given the task of helping to design and build Israel's tabernacle in the wilderness.

Most of the heroes of the Bible are people called to secular vocations. Abraham developed real estate. Jacob was a rancher. Joseph was a high government official (in charge of agriculture, welfare, and interior lands and probably the equivalent of a modern-day prime minister) in a nation led by a Pharaoh who did not acknowledge the sovereignty of the Hebrew God. Esther won a beauty contest. Lydia manufactured cloth. Many heroes were military men. My favorite example is Daniel. He was an exiled refugee, an immigrant, who entered the King's University (Babylon's Harvard). Babylon was led by people who did not believe in the God whom Daniel served. There were no Jewish priests or synagogues in Babylon. Worship and prayer were conducted by lay people. In this setting, Daniel rose to the rank of prime minister and may have served as interim king when Nebuchadnezzar had to step down because of insanity. These biblical characters were not clerics or in the helping professions. Indeed, they served as leaders in organizations that stood in opposition to everything they believed about God and His role in the world. They worked for secular organizations.

There are some who argue that the New Testament paints a different picture in this regard. I do not read it that way. I have already mentioned Lydia, and I could list others with similar callings. Again I quote Howard Butt:

The idea that daily secular work is spiritually inferior comes to its ultimate destruction in the person of Jesus of Nazareth—the Carpenter. The word translated "carpenter" is also the word for "builder," someone in the construction trades (since there was little wood in the area, construction trades probably meant stone or masonry work). The Greek word is *tekton*, from which we get our word "technology."

Traditionally we have thought of Nazareth as a rural village and the carpenter's shop as a quiet, rustic place with a small number of employees. That may not be the real picture. In 1931, the University of Michigan began archaeological digs at the ancient city of Sepphoris, just 4 miles northwest of Nazareth. From that research we know today that Sepphoris was a burgeoning, upscale Greco-Roman metropolis of 30,000 or more people located on the powerful East-West trade routes. Sepphoris was a moneyed city full of Jews, but also Greeks, Arabs, and Romans. Following an uprising around the time of Jesus's birth, the Romans destroyed the city.

Sepphoris was being rebuilt during Jesus's lifetime—during his building-business lifetime. Herod Antipas made Sepphoris his capital for ruling Galilee. During Jesus's later public ministry He avoided Sepphoris, probably because of its Herodian politics and the fact that Herod had Jesus's friend and forerunner, John the Baptist, beheaded. During his years in the building business, I find it hard to believe that Jesus and his team didn't work in Sepphoris. In construction, it was the biggest thing going in his area and not far from home.

This is all speculation, of course, but it is likely that Jesus spent 75 to 85 percent of his working life in the building profession making money or its equivalent in order to support himself and his family. It is also likely that he sold his products and services to people who did not recognize or acknowledge His deity. Many of them may not even have been Jews. He did what most people in the Christian church today would call secular work.

Jesus ordains another type of work different from the stewardship approach described in this book. Introduced in Matthew's Gospel, this other type of work is commonly known as the Great Commission. "And Jesus came and spoke to them, saying, 'All authority has been given to Me in heaven and on Earth. Go therefore and make disciples of all the nations, baptizing them in the name of the Father and of the Son and of the Holy Spirit, teaching them to observe all things that I have commanded you; and lo, I am with you always, even to the end of the age'" (Matthew 28:18-20).

Thus, Christians have two callings, or job descriptions. First, they should use their talents and energy to steward the Earth's resources to meet their physical needs and those of others. Second, they should present the good news about Christ's redemption and all of its implications to people around the world. The Bible indicates that Christians are called to both these jobs, although our time commitment and effort toward each may not be equal. Family life is a good example where both job descriptions apply. Both of these assignments from God are part of our requirement to seek His holiness. Seeking holiness requires us to pray, study, reflect, and ask forgiveness for our transgressions. Our daily work is also an important element of the holy existence to which we are called. Our work and our faith come into alignment if we keep in mind these four lessons:

(1) As part of seeking holiness and honoring God, we are called both to steward resources to serve people's physical needs and also to spread the story of redemption and the other teachings of Jesus. While the evangelical wing of the modern Christian church often puts the emphasis on work related to the Great Commission, there is little evidence that God considers this a higher calling than the work of managing His creation.

(2) I realize that there is nothing more important than a person's coming into a relationship with God through Jesus Christ. Clergy and others who are set apart to lead us spiritually are obviously important in God's design for the world. However, their calling does not automatically rank higher than the work of farmers, executives, homemakers, administrative assistants, politicians, artists, teachers, factory workers, or investment bankers.

(3) Being called to work in a "secular" organization is no better or worse than being called to work in a church, a para-church organization (such as Habitat for Humanity and World Vision), or an institution run by Christians. God may call us to work for Him in any of these settings, regardless of our occupation and particular talents. Moreover, if I am called primarily to evangelism, working in a secular company or other institution might be a better fit than working in the friendly confines of a Christian setting.

(4) If I see my work as a mission for God, my attitude and behavior at work are likely to change in a markedly positive way.

The assistant pastor of a church I once attended counseled young people who were having trouble in a secular workplace to quit their jobs and seek positions in church work or employment in some other Christian organization. While there may be individual cases where this kind of advice is appropriate, I don't think it is a practical approach in a world where devout Christians are a minority. In the United States and Europe, there is a trend to make religion primarily a private matter. In other words, whatever a person does at home and church regarding God is acceptable, but don't bring faith into the public square. The movement to keep God out of the schools, government, and companies is contrary to the biblical mandate to steward all parts of the Creation, including the public institutions we call secular.

Some churches and other Christian organizations have abetted this separation of "sacred" from "secular" by operating their own nurseries, schools, social services, and charities. By doing so, they are inadvertently aiding those who would keep the church out of the public square. We should encourage the gifted people in church-related enterprises to at least consider switching to secular schools and companies where their faith may have a bigger impact. We need more Daniels to speak with words and deeds in all the important institutions of modern societies.

Members of my church developed an effective after-school learning center for children in the neighborhood. The program was expensive. It required over $100,000 of the church's $150,000 mission budget to provide part-time services for 30 to 40 children. A discussion among church members ensued regarding what changes should be made. I suggested shutting down the program (even though my wife had helped to start it 10 years earlier). In its place, I advocated a new approach. Why not provide $10,000-a-year supplements to entice up to 10 young Christian teachers to work in the public schools of the inner city around the church? The new teachers would be marked by the church as God's ambassadors to the children in the neighborhood schools. I suggested that this strategy might have a greater impact on neighborhood children than our little center at the church. Like a lot of my schemes, the idea did not fly with others in the congregation. It was, however, the kind of thinking that logically comes from understanding the concepts of work, callings, and mission as presented in the Bible.

I asked one of the volunteers at our church learning center where he was employed. "I am working part time serving tables at the local restaurant so I can have as much time as possible to work at the learning center," he said. Most church members saw his decision as laudable and consistent with his faith and with God's priorities. He believed the job at the learning center was much more significant in God's view than the role at the restaurant. I have already suggested that this isn't necessarily true, at least if I interpret Scripture correctly. With his attitude and philosophy about work, was he really doing justice to his job at the restaurant? Was he treating the role of waiter as one ordained by God? Was he performing his job as God's steward serving the dozens of people who sat in his area of the restaurant each night? Was he cutting corners? Did he have a godly attitude? If he didn't see his work as a sacred responsibility, would he do his best? Would his light shine brightly for God, or would he go through the motions to earn money and save his best efforts for the learning center? It is all too common for Christians to put their voluntary efforts in community service or at their church ahead of the work that pays their salary and occupies most of their time. Similarly, people often give a lower priority to their work at the factory or office than they do to their responsibilities at home. This is not biblical. I also am not convinced that the common admonition from pastors to put family life ahead of work outside the home is consistent with Scripture. Jesus, for example, appeared to put His work ahead of family. On the other hand, idolizing work, or always putting work ahead of family responsibilities, is not biblical, either.

A gracious, godly woman met me at the airport to take me to the Christian conference where I was to speak. On the drive to the hotel, she asked me what I was going to say during my workshop session the next day. I gave her a five-minute synopsis of what I believed to be the principal purpose of organizations and my passion to create joyful workplaces. "Are you part of the 'success to significance' movement?" she asked, indicating her approval if I was. "No," I said. "I think that idea is very dangerous and is based on an incorrect reading of Scripture." She almost drove off the road but recovered quickly enough to probe my thinking further.

The "success to significance" idea was popularized mostly among wealthy evangelical Christians through the inspirational book *Half Time*, written by my friend Bob Buford. Bob tells the story of owning and operating a very successful communications company. At the "halftime" of his life he decided that he had made enough money and that it was time to do something more significant. He chose to move into the nonprofit sector. Unfortunately, many people have taken Bob's personal story and made it a road map for their own lives. I see no evidence from the Bible or my Christian experience that working in a business is any more or less significant to God than becoming involved in the voluntary, church-related, or not-for-profit activities that many Christians now think are more worthy of their talents and time. My reading of Scripture indicates that nearly every kind of work is significant, if it is consistent with the person's calling and the person is working to glorify and worship God.

"Give something back" is another phrase thrown around by business leaders. It is a concept as flawed as "success to significance." Giving something back assumes that I took something I shouldn't have while working. Certainly this would not be the case if I saw my business as God intended it, a stewardship ministry to serve the needs of others and, in the process, my needs as well. Stewarding resources to meet needs of others is a legitimate "giving" activity. Few activities are more socially responsible or Christian than using one's talents to work at or manage a business. "Giving back" is relevant only if I have misappropriated and mismanaged the resources I have been given to steward.

John Pearson, the extraordinary CEO of the Christian Management Association, invited me to speak at his group's annual conference. Before the gathering, we discussed the disturbing implications of the "success to significance" philosophy. "You see those individuals standing over by the window?" he asked, pointing to three men who appeared to be in their 30s. "Each of them was very successful in a high-tech industry in Southern California. Each one made a large amount of money. All quit their jobs and began searching for something more significant to do. They have all become disillusioned. They have not found a more significant way to use their talents than the jobs they quit. Now, they play a lot of golf."

Christian Wright, a 22-year-old graduate student, was working for a Christian development organization trying to help poor people in rural Uganda who had no running water or electricity. He became aware of AES's efforts to build a power plant on the Nile River that would supply electricity to both Uganda and Kenya. He was later hired by AES leaders in London to assist the development team for the project in Kampala. For more than four years he applied integrity, creativity, enthusiasm, and business savvy to overcome economic, political, and environmental problems. He was able to bring the project near to the point where it could be funded and built. Chris is a devout follower of Jesus Christ. Like many others of faith at AES, Chris came to understand his role in the company as his calling from God, and his ministry, and his way of serving others. Few clergymen, missionaries, or social workers draw as heavily on their faith as Chris did while helping plan this project. If the Uganda power plant is eventually built, this profit-making venture will very likely do more good for the people of Uganda, especially the poor, than all the aid the government has received over the past 25 years from foreign nations, foundations, and church organizations. The projected price of the power from the plant is less than half that of the current fossil-fuel alternatives (and not nearly as damaging to the environment). It would triple the number of people who have access to electricity in that small country. Chris Wright and his colleagues at AES and in the Ugandan government were doing God's work.

I met Steve Hase at church on Capitol Hill in Washington several years after AES had opened its doors for business. He was a recent graduate of Duke, where he had played junior varsity basketball. I enticed him to join our young company as a bookkeeper and financial assistant in our central financial services office, which employed only three other people at the time. His 6-foot, 7-inch frame and basketball skills were prized when the AES Arlington office competed against the hotshots from the new power plants becoming part of the company. Within a few years Steve was recruited to help in the company's business-development efforts. His colleagues soon recognized his extraordinary skills as an ambassador, a bridge builder, negotiator, and problem solver when AES faced controversial issues that involved public citizens, government officials, and other interests.

After six years with the company, Steve volunteered to move with his wife and young children to Cumberland, Maryland, a small and economically struggling town in the mountains of western Maryland. AES had identified Cumberland as a possible site for a new coal-fired power plant. Steve was asked to lead the local development of the plant.

I recently spoke at a civic function in Cumberland. It had been over six years since Steve had left the city for another AES assignment. Even now, he is remembered for his gracious manner, integrity, and courage, his love of the people of the community, and his creativity and tenacity in solving problems. He left Cumberland to live in Manchester, New Hampshire. Again, he was able to solve problems and win the hearts of an entire community, allowing AES to build a power plant in a city where few thought it possible. He may be the best example of how a Christian should and can approach business. He lived his faith openly. It affected everything related to his work. He saw his work as a calling from God as well as a duty to AES. He used his talents to solve problems and serve the needs of the community. In all his work, he attempted to operate with the kind of humility, love, honesty, and persistence that Christ modeled for us. He did God's work as it is supposed to be done.

People of faith carry out their callings in a variety of settings and organizations. My sister, Marilyn Bakke Pearson, for example, has been a devoted mother, wife, and homemaker for most of her adult life. For many years she taught Bible each week to upwards of 500 women in Wilmette, Illinois, and in Devon, Pennsylvania. She also has a passion for making living spaces beautiful as well as functional. She manages to achieve that goal whether the budget is big or small. In her decorating business, she ministers to people by listening to the specifics of their lives and brings joy to others. Her decorating business honors God every bit as much as her roles teaching Bible or being a homemaker.

Genesis tells us that God paused at each step of the Creation process to pronounce His work "good." The joy He found in both the process and the extraordinary results is obvious. God enjoyed working. Jesus reminds us of God's enjoyment of work in the parable of the talents in Matthew 25:14-29:

> For the kingdom of heaven is like a man traveling to a far country, who called his own servants and delivered his goods to them. And to one he gave five talents, to another two, and to another one, to each according to his own ability; and immediately he went on a journey. Then he who had received the five talents went and traded with them, and made another five talents. And likewise he who had received two gained two more also. But he who had received one went and dug in the ground, and hid his lord's money. After a long time the lord of these servants came and settled accounts with them.
>
> So he who had received five talents came and brought five other talents, saying, "Lord, you delivered to me five talents; look, I have gained five more talents besides them." His lord said to him, "Well done, good and faithful servant; you were faithful over a few things, I will make you ruler over many things. Enter into the master's joy." He also who had received two talents came and said, "Lord, you delivered to me two talents; look, I have gained two more talents besides them." His lord said to him, "Well done, good and faithful servant; you have been faithful over a few things, I will make you ruler over many things. Enter into the master's joy."
>
> Then he who had received the one talent came and said, "Lord, I knew you to be a hard man, reaping where you have not sown, and gathering where you have not scattered seed. And I was afraid, and went and hid your talent in the ground. Look, there you have what is yours."
>
> But his lord answered and said to him, "You wicked and

lazy servant, you knew that I reap where I have not sown, and gather where I have not scattered seed. So you ought to have deposited my money with the bankers, and at my coming I would have received back my own with interest. So take the talent from him and give it to him who has 10 talents.

"For to everyone who had, more will be given, and he will have abundance; but from him who does not have, even what he has will be taken away. And cast the unprofitable servant into the outer darkness. There will be weeping and gnashing of teeth."

Most teachings on this passage focus on using our talents in a manner that will result in some useful product or service for the world. The parable also reinforces my interpretation of the purpose of work. It helps support my conclusion that the purpose of business and of other man-made institutions is to steward resources with a goal of creating products and services beneficial to people. It reminds me that stewardship is more about the eight to 10 hours a day I work at the office than it is about the two hours a week I volunteer at the church or at another not-for-profit organization. The parable also supports my emphasis on accountability in the workplace.

My primary reason for focusing on this passage, however, is the phrase "enter into the master's joy." I have never heard a sermon, read a book, or seen a study that concentrated on the meaning and importance of these words. Notice that each time the lord or master reviews the work of the servants who took risks in managing the resources entrusted to them, the master congratulates the servant for a job well done and then adds the words—"enter into the master's joy." I conclude from this parable that God enjoys our stewardship work just as He enjoys His own work. By implication, we ought to enjoy our work. Note also the absence of decision making by the Master. God is not a typical boss. All the stewardship decisions were delegated to the servants. The linkage between joy and decision making is very much evident in this passage of Scripture. Joy at work is possible if we invest our talents as God intended. In that way we honor God and can experience His joy. The Olympic runner Eric Liddell expressed it well in the movie *Chariots of Fire* when he said, "When I run, I feel His pleasure."

Until Adam and Eve sinned and were driven from the Garden, the working environment there was described as a paradise. Work was a central element of this paradise. Not only was work an act of worship, but it also was fulfilling and rewarding. Of course, after Adam and Eve broke their relationship with God, all of life, including work, became more difficult and troublesome. For some, that is where the story ends. Mundane daily work is seen as an obligation, a burden, or even pure drudgery, rather than the joyous experience it was meant to be.

Fortunately, that is not the end of the story. For Christians there is more. There is redemption. Christ came so we could re-establish our relationship with God. That fact has many implications, but for the purpose of this book it means that our work can be redeemed as well. While we cannot re-create the perfect work environment of the Garden, we can do everything possible to make our work environments as close to the Garden's standards as possible. We can approach our work as God designed from the beginning by helping create the workplaces that God intended. Despite sin, joy at work is still possible. We get more clues in Genesis and the rest of the Bible as to how to make work joyful. Above all, we must be humble. We are not God. We were created as limited, fallible human beings. Those characteristics apply to all people, including those of us who are leaders. Recognition of this truth, especially by leaders, is the first step to creating a workplace filled with joy.

Joy will be difficult to experience. It requires that we understand that the major purpose of work is to use the resources of the created world to serve our needs and the needs of others. Work is likely to be experienced as a difficult and meaningless endeavor if we stray from God's original purpose.

We may also find work less enjoyable if bosses make most of the important decisions. The Creation story does not assign people, even leaders, the responsibility of "managing" other people. The Bible says that people are to have dominion over the animals and plants. It encourages humans to act as stewards for the world we live in. It does not, however, encourage us to dominate other people. It never classifies people as "resources." The Bible does endorse leadership. What is the difference? Biblical leadership requires those in authority to *serve* the people they lead. Leaders do whatever it takes to allow followers to use their talents effectively. Thus, good leaders delegate decisions and create an environment in which others can manage God's world. Notice that God delegated the decision of naming the animals to Adam. Even more important in the Creation story is that God allowed humankind to make the ultimate decision of life. He gave us the choice to acknowledge and follow God or to reject Him. We were created in God's likeness as moral beings with the ability to reason, make decisions, and be held responsible for the consequences. Living in relationship to God in a manner that is consistent with God's plan for His creation is the best recipe for a joyous and productive life.

> *Biblical leadership requires those in authority to serve the people they lead.*

The question of leadership authority and its effect on organizational decisions remains difficult to understand. In my chapter on leadership, I discussed the dilemma of a leader who, on one hand, is given authority over the entire organization and, on the other, is supposed to refrain from making decisions that others in the organization can make. My research and experience suggest that leaders do have the authority to make all decisions and direct all actions. Leaders are responsible for all that goes on within the organization. There is, however, no requirement that leaders make all or even most of the decisions for which they have authority. God certainly had the authority to name the animals, but he did not use that authority. In the Parable of the Talents, the master gave his resources to his servants and entrusted them with decisions about their use. God could certainly control His creation through micromanagement, but He chose to delegate most decisions to us. Where God tends to take action is on matters of morality and questions of right and wrong. Shouldn't we follow His lead when we decide which decisions to make and which to delegate? God created humans in His image. We are to be creators like Him. We should follow His path. As the Parable of the Talents shows, I do not believe He meant that most important decisions should be left to Himself or to human leaders acting on His behalf. God wants us to enjoy our work just as He did.

Bear with me while I retell the story of Joseph's life in Egypt with a contemporary slant in order to make a contemporary point. When Joseph, son of Jacob, went to Canaan Temple of Yahweh on the Nile, he joined a small and struggling group of believers. There were servants and slaves who, like Joseph, had been sold into bondage and taken by force to Cairo. Other members were young people who had fled their homes in Canaan to seek their fortune in the exciting urban life of Egypt. Still others were merchants and travelers who had come to the great city to ply their trade.

Early on, Joseph distinguished himself as one of God's special people. He had moved rapidly from household slave to head steward at the home of a high government official. After being framed by the official's wife and sent to jail, Joseph received advice from the elders and priests of the temple to leave domestic management and join the temple staff. His ability to interpret dreams and understand prophecy would be especially useful at the temple.

The Hebrew priests became more aggressive in recruiting him for temple work after his prediction that a seven-year famine would hit the entire Middle East. Certainly those in the temple who were of Canaanitic descent understood the dire consequences that a famine would have on family and friends back home. They strongly encouraged Joseph to lead a new Center for Canaan Refugee Relief (CCRR), operated out of the temple. The CCRR would begin immediately to store food and other necessities for members of the temple and relatives in Canaan and elsewhere. The center would collect money and food from congregation members and other supporters. They would send requests to family and friends for similar support. With the money collected they would pay Joseph's salary in his important role as director of the center. They might also buy a little food with the extra money they received. Temple members would be encouraged to donate whatever food they could for the cause. Volunteers would be asked to drop by the Center after they finished their 16 hours toiling as domestic workers in Egyptian homes. They could help package and store the food.

Enter Pharaoh. He offered Joseph the job of chief operating officer of the country. The priests and elders of the temple tried to dissuade Joseph from accepting the job. "It is a godless government. It discriminates against our people," they argued. Joseph would be selling out to the worst kind of secular organization possible. One frustrated temple leader predicted the job would cause him to lose his faith in Yahweh or at least dilute righteousness. His once bright future in the ministry would be lost. He would be trading a chance of doing something significant for God for worldly wealth, fame, and power.

Joseph took the job with Pharaoh, of course, and served his God and society from the new position. He still worshiped weekly at Canaan Temple. His friends and temple leaders were friendly, but they made little connection between his new role in the government and the programs and ministries of the temple. The temple leaders scrambled to find a new leader for CCRR in order to continue their program to prepare for the upcoming famine.

This apocryphal story of Joseph is presented to show how many modern Christian churches, especially those with a bent toward social service, might react to people like Joseph in their congregations. Joseph is an Old Testament portrait of Christ. He is betrayed and falsely accused of wrongdoing. He is restored to a lofty position so he can help save the world. He forgives his brothers for betraying him. All too frequently, leaders in Christian churches do not understand the implications of the Joseph story for members of their congregation and the church's theology of work and mission.

One of the primary purposes of the local church is to encourage, prepare, and hold people responsible for their life missions, ministries, and callings. I suspect that the percentage of churches that do a good job of fulfilling this purpose is quite low. Few churches put the same emphasis on both the Great Commission in Matthew and the stewardship mission of Genesis. While churches generally do a good job helping people with religious matters, they often overlook the secular roles we fulfill at God's behest. Some jobs are wrongly considered more pleasing to God than others. The result is an institutional church that misses the opportunity to adequately prepare the majority of its members for the important roles they should play in the world.

The work set forth in the Great Commission of Matthew is almost always called "evangelism." But the church has had a hard time agreeing on a name for the responsibility God gave us to manage creation. Would our understanding and zeal increase if the Christian church could agree on a common way to identify this important work?

Presbyterians and a few others call it the "cultural mandate." Because of John Calvin's theological insights in the 16th century, Presbyterian doctrine concerning the redeeming qualities of working in secular organizations is quite similar to my own. While the theology of the "cultural mandate" might be alive in the Presbyterian church, it is my impression that the average layman neither understands the term "cultural mandate" nor uses it to describe his daily work for the Lord. "Cultural" has taken on different meanings in modern society and may no longer be an effective way to communicate the essence of this type of work.

My brother Ray identifies this kind of work as our public ministry. Unfortunately, "public" is today usually associated with secular or government institutions. Christians probably would not identify their work in business or other private institutions as public ministry.

Tent-making ministry, so named because the Apostle Paul made tents to fund his missionary work, is sometimes suggested as an alternative. However, this name suffers from the connotation that work is valuable only because it enables people to evangelize. The stewardship work I am referring to is not just an activity that supports evangelism. It is important and necessary work in and of itself—for the products and services it provides to society, as an act of worship to the Lord of Creation, and because it places Christians in positions of helping restore the world as God intended it to be. This kind of work puts more emphasis on the quality and quantity of tents than on the money it generates for evangelism.

The term "marketplace ministry" has become popular among para-church organizations and some churches as well. I like the word "marketplace," but it is not being used in a way consistent with my view on work. The marketplace movement appears to encourage people to use their workplaces to evangelize either by word or deed. This marketplace mission is certainly consistent with the Great Commission, but it does not sufficiently serve the important goal of stewarding God's resources to meet societal needs.

The phrase "lifestyle evangelism" also falls short. It is primarily a method of letting our behavior at home and at work reflect the character of Christ so that others might know the truth about who He is. This is certainly the way Christians should live and work, but it fails to recognize the importance of our creative efforts and the need to reform our workplaces.

Stewardship ministry reflects the essence of the role that God gave Adam and Eve in the Garden. They were managing resources to meet physical needs. Unfortunately, "stewardship" is a word that the church usually associates with charitable giving and tithing. It has come to refer to the small amount of money people give away, rather than the money they make and the talents they use to celebrate God in their daily lives.

Opus Dei (God's Work) is an increasingly important Catholic movement that advocates holiness in all that we do. It elevates the sacredness of our daily work. Even so, I don't believe it celebrates, to the extent God intended, the work we accomplish and the places where we work.

Someone suggested that I name the kind of work I am discussing "The Net Minders' Ministry." Jesus called his disciples away from the fishing nets so they could spend most of their time in evangelism. Today, many of us are called to tend the nets so that others can eat and meet other material needs. We could also name this kind of mission effort after Daniel, Joseph, Esther, or any of the hundreds of biblical characters who made this kind of ministry famous. Their example is a powerful reminder that God intends our daily work to be a substantial part of our service to Him.

The way Christians identify the type of work they do often reveals their attitudes toward work. When devout Christians say someone is working "in full-time Christian service" or "in ministry," it usually means that the person works for a church or a para-church organization. It does not cover Christians employed by governments, businesses, or public schools. Does this imply that people are not doing God's work "full time" if they work in secular organizations, especially profit-making enterprises? There appears to be a misguided notion in many Christian circles that someone working for *The Washington Post*, General Motors, Harvard University, the Department of Energy, Walt Disney, Goldman Sachs, or the local barbershop is doing something less significant for God than people who work at the First Baptist Church, Young Life, or the Presbyterian Mission Hospital in Pakistan.

If Joseph had been a member of a modern Christian church, he might have quit his job in the Egyptian government and headed back to his family in Israel. By today's logic, it would have been time for him to give up his power and wealth so he could give something back to his people at home. This idea that "Christian work" is somehow superior to the practical work of commerce most likely came from the Greek philosophers Plato and Aristotle. They influenced early Christian theologians such as Augustine and Thomas Aquinas. Plato's dualism divided the world into a higher level of great ideas and rational thought and a lower level of less worthy activity, such as work. In *Your Work Matters to God,* Doug Sherman and William Hendricks argue that this dualistic thinking led Christians to believe that their daily work has no intrinsic value. Christian churches and theologians have perpetuated these ideas by elevating the clergy and spirituality above the laity and the practical work that most people undertake. This is not at all consistent with Judeo-Christian Scriptures.

In addition, the powerful 20th-century movement to make faith private by pushing religious thought and opinion from the public square has contributed to the idea that religious beliefs should not be part of our public life, which for many of us is our work. This approach encourages people to freely exercise their faith at home and at church, but not at their workplace. Some churches have unwittingly abetted the movement to remove God from our schools, businesses, and governments by isolating themselves from the secular world. Churches have created their own schools, social services, and enterprises in an effort to help disadvantaged people. This separation of the "spiritual" from the "worldly" has contributed to the confusion among people of faith regarding the sacred nature of their daily work.

In *Joy at Work,* I suggest how faith fits into businesses and other secular organizations. What about the local church? If church leaders believe what I have written, what changes should they consider in prayer, missions, sermons, pastoral visits, church programs, and the empowerment of church members?

I have put significant emphasis on accountability to God and to our business supervisors for the work we undertake. As discussed earlier, accountability is a necessary ingredient of the enjoyment of the work we do. The local church ought to be a primary vehicle for holding Christian people responsible for their vocational work.

Most Christian churches require people classified as "missionaries" to report periodically to the congregation on their work. Pastors and staff members also report on their efforts to serve, as do volunteers and participants in church-sponsored programs. People who work outside the realm of the institutional church are rarely asked by the church to account for their work. There are no reports from homemakers. Government employees don't talk about their work. Lawyers, accountants, nurses, and teachers are not required to tell their fellow congregants about their efforts to serve God through their work. People in business are not asked to provide a record of their stewardship.

Years ago, I asked the elders of my church if I could submit AES's annual report as part of my accountability to the church and its members. I received no response. For the next few years, I placed a few dozen of the company reports in a conspicuous location within the church as both a partial report on my "ministry" and as a way of saying that the church should hold me accountable for all of my work, not just the 5 percent of my time I spent in worship and other church-sponsored activities. In addition, I added the annual report of the Mustard Seed Foundation, our family foundation, so that church members could better hold Eileen and me responsible for our work in that part of our lives. Few other individuals or families followed my lead. Leaders of the church seldom discussed the need for accountability for the way we served God through our secular work.

I noticed that most people who were paid a stipend or salary by the local church were expected to report on a regular basis on their activities. Missionaries and pastors who were financially supported by the church were held accountable for their work. I asked to be part of the church budget. "Put me in for $1," I suggested. No leaders took seriously my request to be part of the church budget so that I would be held accountable for my daily vocation. Why should someone with an income in excess of $1 million a year be included in the church budget? Why should a business person report on his activities to other church members?

Each of us is accountable to God and our fellow man for the stewardship of our talents and skills, no matter what financial remuneration we receive for our work. Every organization should hold its members and employees responsible for their work. The local church should develop methods to do this for all its members. The Catholic tradition of regular confession is one way to get at this, although confession focuses mainly on one's failures. It misses the opportunity for fellow congregants to celebrate the contributions and accomplishments of another member's work. There is little doubt that the relevance and vibrancy of the local church would increase if it were more engaged with its members. Similarly, asking members to report regularly to the church community on their jobs, social and recreational activities, and home life would encourage and expand their faith and their appreciation of God's work in the world.

Most churches hold important ceremonies to commission people for jobs or tasks they are planning to undertake. The ceremony celebrates the commitment the person has made to the job, asks the Lord's blessing on the work, and "marks" or sets the person apart for the special role he or she will undertake. Commissioning is both a solemn and an affirming act.

Unfortunately, commissioning is almost always limited to pastors, missionaries, church staff, and volunteers. We are missing the opportunity to honor people who are called to other work, including parents and homemakers, through the uplifting process of commissioning. I have several times requested from my church leaders that I receive such a commission, but it has never been given. Some suggested mass commissionings—all the lawyers in one group, all the homemakers in another, and all the business people in another. I do not favor a group approach. I believe commissioning should be administered in a manner similar to baptism. Commissioning should be reserved for those who are mature in their faith and are fully committed to carry out their calling in a manner that is consistent with God's word. Refusing to commission people for secular contributions runs contrary to God's view of work.

Several years ago, my brother Lowell invited Eileen and me to speak on the fourth and final weekend of a missions conference at his church. It was the first missions conference I had ever attended that included business and other daily work by its members as missions of the church. As a prelude to the conference, a person from the church had taken dozens of pictures of individual church members doing their daily work: a man pumping gas, my mother pushing a grocery cart at Safeway, a young mother caring for her children. The sign above the pictures read "Our Missionaries." During the conference, over 50 church members who were teachers in the local public schools were honored. What a powerful and beautiful way to help people understand their mission role.

Mission conferences, especially in the evangelical wing of the church, tend to concentrate on the important mission of the Great Commission. Some mission conferences also include the work of Christian-run organizations. Mainline denomination churches often emphasize their social outreach programs, such as tutoring, drug counseling, and operating senior centers. However, few incorporate the work of those called to use their talents to provide products or services to society. These missionaries deserve a place in the missions conference. God is holding them accountable for their ministry. Shouldn't His church do likewise? These ministers are painters, government bureaucrats, football players, students, homemakers, waiters, taxicab drivers, bankers, and car salesmen. In most congregations, 80 to 90 percent of the members fit this missionary category. These people need encouragement in their mission. Mission conferences would be structured in a very different way if church leaders understood and supported the stewardship roles that these people play in God's kingdom.

Would churches assign staff members to focus on the work missions of all its members, not just those who are listed in the church's mission budget?

For one full year, Rich Gathro led our church prayers each Sunday morning. During the week he contacted three individuals in the congregation and asked how they wished to be prayed for on the following Sunday. He did not follow the usual custom of many Protestant churches of praying only for church leaders or traditional missionaries or volunteer workers in the church or members who were sick. He lifted before God and the congregation the daily work of individuals. His prayers reminded us that all callings can be sacred and that people are accountable to God for all their work. This was a simple but powerful tool to remind church members of God's presence as they went about their daily work.

I recall only two or three visits to my place of work by one of my pastors in the past 30 years. I doubt that I am an exception. If our daily work is a sacred calling from God, pastors and priests should come to the workplace often. For people like me, a pastoral visit affirms the importance to God of my daily tasks and reinforces the idea that my work has been ordained by God. It inspires me to do my best. I am reminded that I am God's representative at my place of work and that I am accountable to Him for my behavior and actions on the job and especially for the service or product I help provide to society.

For pastors, these visits help celebrate the variety and importance of each calling and vocation that God ordains. They lead to a fuller understanding of the challenges and temptations church members face. Sermons and teachings can be better targeted to the needs of the congregation. As the Catholic scholar Michael Novak notes, "Few preachers seem to take pains to understand, reinforce, and encourage business as a Christian calling. Preachers seem more comfortable in the pre-modern economy with pre-modern images and therefore give very little guidance regarding the unique opportunities, restraints, and temptations of a business person's realm. A preacher who is able to use business metaphors would touch a lot of hearts." In *Your Work Matters to God*, Sherman and Hendricks estimate that more than 90 percent of Christians have never heard a sermon that drew a connection between their religious beliefs and their work life.

In visiting workplaces, pastors are going where their congregation ministers. My brother Ray was visiting one of his parishioners at her factory job. "This is my minister," she shouted to her colleagues over the workplace noise. "No, she is *your* minister. I am *her* pastor," he corrected. The local church ministers to the community primarily in the places where church members work. There is no better place for pastors to connect with church members and the larger community than in the workplace.

The local church is mainly concerned with drawing people into worship, helping them establish a relationship with Christ, and nurturing and preparing them for service to others. Within the Christian church worldwide there is considerable disagreement about the definition and priority of each of these goals. My own bias is that the church should concentrate its pastoral and administrative resources on evangelism, worship, and nurturing and equipping members for service. I suggest that churches operate service programs (schools, companies, feeding programs, social service organizations, housing complexes, and other businesses) only in the rarest instances.

The church should encourage governments, private social service agencies, and companies to perform these services rather than diverting scarce economic and leadership resources away from its primary mission. There are exceptions, of course. The church may participate in one of these undertakings because it offers an opportunity to evangelize. Or it may operate one of these services because no other organization is willing or capable of doing so. Even in these cases, I think it would be better if churches enlisted their members to own and operate programs rather than relying on church staff. This is the Joseph model that I have long advocated.

Some church leaders argue that this approach makes it impossible for the church to control the faith component of the program. They fear it would become just another social service. I believe this problem can be overcome by requiring that the president or the majority of the private organization's board be members of the sponsoring church or be required to make a faith statement consistent with the church's doctrine. This would empower gifted individual leaders within the local church and leave the church staff free to carry out its other responsibilities.

One of the reasons that churches hesitate to pull out of social programs is their desire for public credit and acclaim. I have been involved in several late-night meetings with church leaders to discuss who should operate a proposed new program. Inevitably, someone will say, "The church won't get credit if we don't run the program." This is true. A church that initiates and manages a service program is often honored for being progressive and responding to the needs of the community. However, most churches are not good administrators or owners of organizations that make products or deliver services. Typically, neither the church's primary mission nor its governance structure fits the management needs of this type of organization.

I believe the pressure to run such organizations would decline greatly if churches used different criteria to judge their effectiveness. I think local churches should show their love for the community and evaluate the effectiveness of their service in a very different way. A church's service to the community should be measured by the sum of the work carried out by its members. This would include both voluntary and paid work at home, in businesses, at church, and in other not-for-profit organizations. Thus, the services of the church might include the efforts of 15 public-school teachers and two principals, the owner of a local florist shop, three police officers, the county councilwomen, a metal lathe worker at a local factory, a CFO of a large international oil company, the headmaster of a Christian school, a retail clerk at the local hardware store, an instructor at Gold's Gym, a local leader of Young Life, 42 mothers with small children at home, six members of the military, and a volunteer youth football coach. As members of the church, all these people would bring credit to the local church and, more important, to God. This approach is far more consistent with the idea that all work should be equally useful to the Kingdom of God. The combined efforts of individual church members would probably exceed the impact of even the largest and most sophisticated local church operation.

One of the most important roles of the local church is helping people discover the work that God has planned for them and then empowering them to perform that work. As parents, we are urged to raise our children in a way that's consistent with their natural gifts so that they can use their talents in the way God intended. The church is expected to help parents in this task. Many churches do an excellent job of encouraging and empowering children for vocations that are considered Christian in nature. Church leaders write recommendations for young people to Christian colleges. Sometimes churches even provide scholarships for those headed to Bible schools or seminaries. But most churches are less helpful and encouraging when it comes to areas of service in secular organizations. This is another hangover caused by the dualism in the church. It is better to be a pastor than an actor and better to teach homiletics at a seminary than mathematics at MIT.

At the Mustard Seed Foundation (MSF), we are trying to counter this bias with a radical scholarship plan. Our Harvey Fellows program provides funds to graduate students who are headed for careers where Christians are underrepresented in such fields as the arts, media, finance, academia, and technology. For example, the MSF might award a stipend to a devout Christian who wants to study journalism, as long as that person plans to attend one of the nation's top five graduate programs in journalism. This program is the foundation's way of empowering and marking those Christians who will be the "missionaries" in these fields later in life. It is an example of a strategy the church could use to increase its involvement in all of society.

Recently, I joined my brothers Ray and Lowell and my sister, Marilyn Bakke Pearson, to develop a university that will give doctorate ministry degrees and a master's in business administration. The school, not so modestly named Bakke Graduate University, will seek to celebrate the study and practice of both the stewardship command of Genesis and the Great Commission of Matthew's Gospel.

In the Parable of the Talents, Jesus referred to the full range of gifts that people have been given to carry out their life's work. The Master did not consider one type of work more worthy than another. His only injunction was that people should be willing to risk failure by using their gifts so that the results for the Master might multiply.

Business and other secular work is both a mission (to help people in practical ways) and a mission field. The good news of the Bible is that God plans to redeem us and that we were made in His image so that we could continue His work of creation. We glorify God through our enthusiastic and creative stewardship of the resources he has given us to serve others and provide for ourselves.

When I was a child, we sang a song in Sunday school called "Dare to Be a Daniel." Back then, interpretation of the song focused on Daniel's courage when he faced the lions, standing firm against his enemies and refusing to recant his faith in God. Today, the song takes on additional meaning. I am called to be like Daniel and serve God by working effectively in a world that is hostile, or at least indifferent, to His existence and to His message. Like Daniel, I am called to steward the resources entrusted to me, both to meet my own needs and the needs of the world around me. In all of this work, I am charged with using my talents and skills to glorify God. Dare to be a Daniel and enter into the Master's joy!

APPENDIX A

Case Study of AES

"THE TWO PEOPLE who started Applied Energy Services (AES) in 1982 launched their venture with a modest-sounding goal. They weren't out to make millions, or to change the world with a new product, or to see their names in the headlines. They simply wanted to build an enterprise they could be proud of. They were clear about that even before they knew exactly what the company would do. The founders wanted a company that valued people and acted responsibly, that was fair and honest in its approach not only to customers, suppliers, and employees, but to the greater society in which we live. If they happened to make good profits, so much the better. But that wasn't their goal—they cared more about the kind of company they could build than its bottom line. To the mild surprise of some and the amazement of many, they have been able to achieve both."[1]

Early 1970s	The founders of AES (Roger Sant and Dennis Bakke) meet in the Federal Energy Administration, where they are leading the government's conservation programs during the energy crisis of the early 1970s.
1977 to 1981	Sant and Bakke come up with the idea for the company while writing a study for the Mellon Institute at Carnegie Mellon University. The study results in a book, *Creating Abundance: The Least Cost*

[1] Waterman, Jr., Robert H., The Frontiers of Excellence, 1994. London: Nicholas Brealey

Energy Strategy. The study argues for the separation of electricity generation from the distribution of electricity. The authors believe that if the generation of electricity was not owned or regulated by the government, the competition between private owners would lower prices to consumers and improve efficiencies and service.

Sept. 1980   Sant and Bakke plan the new company during a car ride from Annapolis to Washington, D.C.

Jan. 1982   AES is formed with a $60,000 bank loan guaranteed by the principals. Soon afterward they attract $1 million from other investors, including a few family members.

March 1983   The first "shared values" statement is unveiled and defended at a corporate retreat.

Dec. 1983   The company's first power plant is financed. It is a $181 million facility in Houston, Texas. Fuel for the plant is made from petroleum coke, a waste product from a nearby oil refinery.

1986   A special task force recommends against developing a large corporate personnel staff; instead, human resources becomes a part of each line job in the plants.

1987   The Honeycomb system of self-management teams is introduced. This radically different workplace emphasizes openness. It is flat, not hierarchical. Decision making is decentralized, and managers do not give orders or make decisions on their own.

Employees are paid salaries, not hourly wages. Everyone is considered a business person.

By 1990   The company owns and operates new and refurbished independent power-producing facilities in California, Connecticut, Hawaii, Oklahoma, Pennsylvania, and Texas.

1991   AES goes public with a statement that shared values are more important than profits. The initial public offering price is $19.25 per share ($2.78 when adjusted for several splits). Its stock trades first on Nasdaq and later on the New York Stock Exchange.

1992   A well-organized citizens group forces AES to sell a plant under construction in Florida to a competitor. At the Shady Point plant in Oklahoma, AES technicians falsify environmental reports to the Environmental Protection Agency. The stock price drops 57 percent, to $17.

1992   AES starts construction on a natural-gas-fired power plant in England and purchases several power plants in Northern Ireland. These are the company's first businesses outside the United States.

1992   Sant and Bakke are jointly named Entrepreneur of the Year for Social Responsibility in Washington, D.C.

Early 1990s   AES begins business operations in Argentina, Australia, Bangladesh, Brazil, Cameroon, Canada, Chile, China, Colombia, the Czech Republic, the Dominican Republic, El Salvador, Georgia, Hungary, India,

Italy, Kazakhstan, Mexico, the Netherlands, Nigeria, Oman, Pakistan, Panama, Qatar, South Africa, Sri Lanka, Tanzania, Uganda, and Ukraine.

1994	Bakke becomes CEO.
1995	The "advice process" replaces conventional approvals for most major decisions in the corporation.
1995	AES joins several other companies in the purchase of the utility serving Rio de Janeiro in Brazil and later the utility and many of the hydroelectric facilities serving São Paulo.
1996	The company decides to overcome self-doubt about its size and questions about its image by adding "The Global Power Company" to its name.
By 2000	AES produces more than 50,000 megawatts of electricity capacity. Only a few utilities in the world have more generating capacity. The company operates in 31 countries, has more than 40,000 employees, $33.7 billion in assets, and serves the electricity needs of more than 100 million people. AES also owns or oversees 17 electric distribution companies worldwide.
Sept. 2000	Bakke is named CEO of the Year by ING Barings for Worldwide Emerging Markets.
Oct. 2000	AES stock hits an all-time high of $70.62 per share.
2001	The company purchases the utility serving Peoria, Illinois, and its surrounding counties and, not long afterward, the utility serving Indianapolis, Indiana.

2001   Electricity companies are hit hard by poor market conditions. Enron and other competitors collapse. AES reports poor economic results. Its stock price drops more than $50 a share.

2002   In February, the AES stock price dips below $5 per share.

June 2002   Bakke retires from AES; Paul Hanrahan becomes CEO.

The Joy at Work Approach

A Conventional Approach	The Joy at Work Approach
Treatment of Employees	
More than 95% of important decisions are made by official leaders of the organization, officers, and board members.	Some 99% of all important decisions are made by nonleaders.
Decisions are made or "approved" by leaders at the highest practicable organizational level.	Decisions are made by nonleaders at the lowest practicable organizational level.
Employees have an established expenditure limit, above which they must obtain prior approval from supervisors.	No approval by supervisors and higher-ups is required for spending company money; only obtaining advice is mandatory.
Organizational charts are published and job descriptions determined for everyone by managers and/or the human resources department. Organizational charts use first initial and last names of employees.	No official organization charts; no job descriptions except those that say "Do whatever it takes" or ones written by the employee.
Job positions, slots, and titles remain basically the same over time. Only the names with the boxes change.	No company-wide job descriptions. Every person is considered unique and must build a job around his or her unique skills and passions.

A Conventional Approach	The Joy at Work Approach

Treatment of Employees

Management and labor are treated and paid differently. Problems between management and labor will often arise.	There is only one category of employee within the organization. There are no separate management people.
Under "control" philosophy, the job of supervisors is to make decisions, hold people accountable, assign responsibility, and perform a host of other tasks, making it impossible to have more than a few people reporting to any one leader. A large organization may require eight to 12 layers of management.	Minimum number of supervisory layers (no more than three to five between the CEO and an entry-level person) to minimize the number of bosses and hierarchy. Each person is responsible for managing himself or herself.
Separate organizations for operations, business development, and financial control. A central controller, along with numerous regional controllers, reports directly to the CFO.	New business development and financial management are linked as closely as possible to day-to-day operations. Most of these functions exist within same team or same co-organizational unit.
Many separate staff groups oversee operations. Most members of these groups have similar skills and educational backgrounds.	A minimal number of specialist staff groups (strategy, financial analysis, planning, purchasing, human resources, etc.). These functions are assigned to local operating teams.
Central office has substantial number of executives and staff-support organizations.	Few people in the central office.

A Conventional Approach	The Joy at Work Approach
	Treatment of Employees
Financial management and risk assessment are set apart from general operations. New business development also requires a separate office.	Financial management and risk assessment are important elements of each person's job.
Most "central" functions are carried out by permanent central staff employees.	Functions requiring heavy central coordination (auditing, corporate capital allocation and balance-sheet management, global sourcing) are performed by volunteer task forces.
Promotes specialization and organizes employees in groups composed of people with the same specialties.	Encourages people to be generalists. Assigns a limited number of specialists to groups of generalists so they can teach their skills throughout the organization.
Minimal use of task forces.	Substantial use of temporary task forces at all levels of the company to deal with issues that cross organizational lines.
Low level of "volunteerism." Employees are characterized by a high degree of passivity.	High degree of "volunteerism" for special assignments and task forces. People at all levels of the organization are actively engaged in its operations.

A Conventional Approach	The Joy at Work Approach
Purpose, Mission, Goal	
The principal purpose of the company is "creating shareholder value," although other purposes or goals may be mentioned.	The principal goal or purpose of the company is stewarding its resources to serve society in an economically strong manner.
Important differences exist between public and internal communications regarding the company's purposes and goals.	Company communications to all stakeholders contain the same corporate ideas of purpose, mission, and goals.
Messages outside the company are controlled by a public-relations firm and the director of investor relations. Only designated senior people are allowed to speak for the company in public.	Every employee is allowed to make statements to the public about the company, including to shareholders.
The primary evaluation criterion is economic performance related to creating shareholder value.	Evaluation of company and individual performance linked to the company's mission and purposes of serving, economic sustainability, and shared values.
Shared values are mentioned in public primarily to promote the competitive advantage they give the company in creating value for shareholders and as a recruiting tool.	When the mission is discussed inside and outside the company, it will often include references to shared values and principles.
Shared values are promoted as a technique to improve chances to achieve economic goals.	Shared values are goals to which the company aspires in and of themselves, not merely as a means to financial ends.

A Conventional Approach	The Joy at Work Approach

Annual Reports

CEO's annual letter is addressed to shareholders.	CEO's annual letter is addressed to all stakeholders, including employees, governments, communities, customers, shareholders, and suppliers.
Focuses primarily on issues and economics related to shareholders. Will not contain assessment of company performance regarding shared principles and values.	Includes reports on the company's purpose, the economics relevant to each group of stakeholders, and shared values and principles.
May acknowledge regular employees as the company's best "assets," but photographs and text focus on senior leaders and board members.	Contains the names of ordinary employees to emphasize that the company respects and values each employee.

Leaders and Managers

Leaders see their role as managing people and resources.	Leaders see their role as serving other employees.
Leaders see themselves as initiators, creators of vision, developers of action plans, accountability officers, and those who have an ability "to get things done."	Leaders are mentors, coaches, teachers, helpers, and cheerleaders.
Adopt "participative management" techniques, in which bosses ask subordinates for advice but make final decisions themselves.	Allow subordinates to manage resources and make decisions. Oversee rigorous advice process and fire people who do not use it appropriately.

A Conventional Approach	The Joy at Work Approach

Leaders and Managers

Managers are responsible for closely monitoring employees and holding them accountable for performance.	Leaders advocate self-accountability, self-initiative, self-control, and individual responsibility among employees.

Compensation

About 75 to 95 percent based on economic performance.	Based as much on an individual's performance on values and principles as on economics.
Different pay programs for leaders than for workers.	Everyone is paid according to the same criteria. No special program for senior leaders or "management."
Huge emphasis on "incentive pay," "performance units," and other quantitative, predetermined formulas for calculating compensation, especially for senior managers.	Few predetermined formulas or quantitative measures for calculating individual compensation.
Pay is widely used to modify future behavior rather than to reward past performance.	Individual initiative and willingness to take responsibility and be held accountable considered positively in compensation decisions.
Most attention will be on the leaders (fewer than 10% of the people), because they are the major decision makers of the organization and the ones expected	Team and company performance are more important than individual performance in determining compensation. Many organizational units give same bonus to every

A Conventional Approach	The Joy at Work Approach

Compensation

to "control" and motivate the other employees.	person or divide the bonus and long-term compensation using a percentage of base salary for all employees, including managers.
Hourly pay and overtime pay for the majority of employees.	Most employees receive salary and no overtime pay.
Strict adherence to a policy of written performance assessments of each individual, written by supervisor after an annual review of each subordinate.	Annual performance evaluation is based on self-review combined with advice from colleagues and leaders.
Pay set by bosses.	Ongoing experiments allowing individuals to set their own compensation, after getting advice from colleagues and supervisors.
Turnover of employees is higher.	The number of people leaving voluntarily is extremely low.

Education, Training, and Information

Assume people learn best through formal training (i.e., classroom) programs and by watching others make decisions.	Assume people learn primarily through informal mentoring, getting advice on problems and issues for which they are responsible. Assume the most effective education comes from taking actions, making decisions, and being accountable for results.

A Conventional Approach	The Joy at Work Approach

Education, Training, and Information

Management information system designed to provide information primarily to managers (leaders). Financial and other "sensitive" information shared only with leaders. Other information given to people on a "need to know" basis.	"Management" information is shared with everyone in the company, not just senior leaders. Most decisions made by people other than leaders.
SEC-designated "insiders," who have access to all financial data, include fewer than two dozen individuals.	Almost everyone in the company is an "insider" as defined by the Securities and Exchange Commission.
Business reviews limited to relatively small number of senior people to assure "quality" discussions. Being invited is considered a major perk. Seen as a way to educate senior managers about the issues facing the company. Presentations made by the most sophisticated senior leaders with experience using PowerPoint and other visual techniques.	Business reviews are open to a large group of company leaders and others. Seen as a way to inform and educate about values and economic issues facing the company. Presentations given by those closest to the issues, despite lack of experience in making such presentations. Because teachers learn more than students, learning will be maximized for the very people who need it most.
Concentrate on hiring great people because the company leadership assumes that only a few people with wide experience and special skills have what it takes to make the company successful.	Most adults (80-95%) are assumed to thrive in a joy-filled workplace; will do what it takes to help the company fulfill its purpose in an economically sustainable manner. The company does what it can to assist employees to reach their potential, but their development is primarily an individual responsibility.

A Conventional Approach	The Joy at Work Approach

Auditing

A Conventional Approach	The Joy at Work Approach
Audits are conducted by full-time experts from central office or professional auditors.	Audit teams consist of people from varied backgrounds who volunteer to work part time on the audits, advised by outside experts.
Auditing is seen primarily as a compliance function and is limited primarily to the financial functions of the company.	Auditing is seen both as an educational tool for those auditing and a help to those being audited. Afterward, the "auditors" are expected to return to their workplaces and lead change and the pursuit of excellence.
There are no values surveys that "audit" compliance with the organization's purpose and principles.	Performance is audited on values/principles, mission/purpose, safety, and environment. Values surveys and other audits are reviewed by each local business unit.

Board of Directors

A Conventional Approach	The Joy at Work Approach
Sees primary role as representing the interests of shareholders.	Sees role as representing the interests of all stakeholders (employees, suppliers, shareholders, customers).
Hires, fires and compensates CEO, and approves compensation for all senior officers.	Hires, fires and compensates CEO; nominates new board members.
Votes on all major financial matters, development of new business, organizational changes, and strategy decisions, even if these are primarily rubber-stamp actions.	Primarily advisers to CEO and other senior leaders, with occasional ratification of employee decisions.

Sample AES Corporate Values and Principles Survey Questions

1999 survey

How well do you believe that you communicate in words and actions the AES principles/values? Please explain your answer.

In your opinion, how well do your colleagues live and communicate the AES principles/values?

In your opinion, how well do AES leaders live and communicate the AES principles and values? Why?

What is the biggest problem you experience with the AES shared values/principles? Why?

1997 survey

If you had it to do it over again, would you apply for a job at AES? Why or why not?

How would you rate your level of confidence in AES leaders? Why?

1996 survey

How comfortable would you feel expressing your opinion within AES if you disagreed with a company decision? Why?

In some situations, doing what is right and making a profit are not the same. In such situations, from what you have heard and observed, how good a job do you believe AES people do in choosing what is consistent with AES's principles over making a profit? Why?

Several of AES's plants have opted to change from an hourly pay with overtime approach to a system in which everyone in the plant is paid on an all-salary/no-overtime basis. What is your opinion of this type of compensation system?

How well is AES doing on its mission to steward resources and nurture relationships to help meet the world's need for safe, clean, reliable, cost-effective electricity?

1995 survey

How would you rate AES as a company to work for compared with other companies for which you have worked or heard about?

How much information do you believe AES people receive regarding developments in the company?

Based on what you have observed at AES, how often do you believe the interests of *all* stakeholders (i.e., AES people, customers, suppliers, shareholders, governments, communities) are taken into consideration when decisions are made?

How well do you believe AES people company-wide are doing in relation to the four principles listed below? (Fun, fairness, integrity, and social responsibility)

How satisfied were you with AES's actions and/or response to the concerns expressed in last year's survey?

ACKNOWLEDGMENTS

I am grateful to Stephen Smith for his remarkable editing job. He had the good sense and skill to convert my written draft into a book that captures the way I speak and conveys the meaning I intended.

My family helped shape the major themes of the book with their lives, words, encouragement, and editing. Without the advice and support of Eileen, this book could not have been completed. My daughter, Margaret, and sons, Brett, Scott, Dennis Jr., and Peter, greatly influenced my ideas and figured in the stories that illustrate them. My brothers, Ray and Lowell, and sister, Marilyn Bakke Pearson, gave me immeasurable assistance. Eileen's parents, Helen and Brantley Harvey, adopted me into their family. My mom, Ruth Hawkinson Bakke, guided me into organizational life as a child. My late father, Tollef Bakke, who grounded me in faith and taught me contentment, significantly influenced my life's work as well. My assistant, Susie Paek, worked with me on every step of the book's development. Sally Sears Belcher was the first "outsider" to read my draft manuscript and add her suggestions and encouragement. Susan Gaynor, Sara Casey, Jen Keister, Quinn Paek, copy editor James Bock, and publisher Mark Pearson all had a hand in putting the book together.

Joel Fleishman hounded me for years to write this book. I owe him much for his persuasion. Others in academia who made a mark on my thinking include Wally Scott at Kellogg, Lynn Sharp Paine at Harvard, and Jeff Pfeffer at Stanford.

Peter Block is the author who has had the greatest impact on me. As the bibliography shows, many other writers were important as well. Foremost among them was Bob Waterman, who tested me on organizational issues for more than 20 years with his books and conversation.

Max De Pree, Dennis Autry, Jim Collins, Randy Spitzer, and Rob Lebow did much to shape my thinking, even though I never had the opportunity to meet them personally. Peter Woicke at the International Finance Corporation of the World Bank influenced my views as well.

At AES, Roger Sant gave me the great gift of freedom to institute workplace reforms. For 21 years, he supported most of the ideas in this book, even when he had personal doubts. The philosophy expressed in this book could not have been developed, let alone put between hard covers, if it were not for my senior AES colleagues. My debt to them for their ideas, encouragement, and loyalty can never be repaid. Roger Naill, Barry Sharp, Stu Ryan, Tom Tribone, Bob Hemphill, the late Dave McMillen, Bill Arnold, Mark Fitzpatrick, John Ruggirello, Bill Luraschi, Ken Woodcock, and Paul Hanrahan lead the list, backed up by Lenny Lee, Ann Murtlow, Damian Obiglio, Shahzad Qasim, Dan Rothrupt, Sarah Slusser, and Paul Stinson. Both Paul and Dan made telephone calls to me in 1992 while I was on vacation that helped me decide to stay with the company and pursue my vision. Many others helped push me in the right direction: Mark Adams, Michael Armstrong, Peter Bajc, Leon Ballard, Chip Bergeson, Leslie Biddle, Ed Blackford, Joe Brandt, Tommy Brooks, Jason Bryant, Rich Bulger, Larry Cantrell, Tony Chavez, Steven Clancy, Pete Convey, Rebecca Cranna, Steve Dahm, Glen Davis, Randy DeWulf, Al Dyer, Charles Falter, Stewart Ferguson, James Ferrar, Harold Franson, Susan Gaynor, Andres Gluski, Terry Gould, Mark Green, John Grier, Joan Halbert (my assistant for 11 years), Ned Hall, Trey Hall, Bill Harshbarger, Steve Hase, Doyle Hibler, Sharon Hillman, Chris Hollingshead, Randy Holloway, Andrew Horrocks, Karl Huber, Dwane Ingalls, Naveed Ismail, Haresh Jaisinghani and Flora Zhao (the couple for whose marriage Flora asked both my permission and blessing), Bob Johnson, Rod Jorgenson, David Kehres, Jerry Kelm, Shahid Zulfiqar Khan, Lundy Kiger, Csaba Kiss, Tom Kunde, Jerry Kurek, Ricky Lam,

Jennifer Lehmann, Gary Levesley, Harry Lovrak, James Luckey, Sonny Lulla, Shane Lynch, Leith Mann, Rod Martin, Tim McCullough, John McLaren, Mark Miller, Rob Morgan, Patrick Murphy, Peter Norgeot, Bill O'Reilly, Clem Palevich, Derek Paton, Dale Perry, Kevin Pierce, Bob Price, Jim Price, Bill Rady, Bob Reece, Brian Reeves, Matt Riel, Patty Rollin, Bill Ruccius, Greg Russell, Mike Scholey, Hamsa Shadaksharappa, Surrender Singh, Dale Sinkler, Ruben Soroeta, Jeff Stafford, Dave Sundstrom, Jeff Swain, C.J. Thompson, Mark Tracey, David Travesso, Kerry Varkonda, David Warden, Billy White, Mark Woodruff, Chris Wright, and Kerry Yeager.

Members of the AES board were remarkable for their loyalty, dedication, and guidance. Many spent 15 to 20 years serving a company that one auditor, early in the company's history, called the "puppy with large paws." Those who served the longest and had the greatest impact were Roger Sant, Alice "Tish" Emerson, Bob Hemphill, Frank Jungers, Phil Lader, Henry Linden, John MacArthur, Hazel O'Leary, Art Rolander, Russell Train, Tom Unterberg, and Bob Waterman. I am thankful for the opportunity they gave me to help steward the resources we had been given to serve the world's need for safe, clean, reliable electricity.

There is no doubt that the group of people Eileen and I met with weekly during the 1980s and '90s for study, sharing, and recreation were influential in developing the ideas for the book. They included Myron and Esther Augsburger, Bill and Ruth Brooks, Ric and Lani Daniels, Rich and Kathy Gathro, Jerry and Jeannie Herbert, Mim Mumaw, Bruce and Julia Overton, John and Sue Seel, and Dan and Jennifer Van Horn.

Lee and Carlie Dixon and Ken and Meredith Brown have played a similar role in more recent times. During the past 20 years, two of my pastors, Myron Augsburger and Steve King, have had a strong effect on how I viewed my work and the world around me. Even before that, Linda Brown Rahman, Nancy Benson Krook, Roy Nelson, Bill and Louise Sygitowicz, Dan Seelye, Johanna Lund Bakke, Booth Gardner (former director of the University of Puget Sound Business School),

Paul Grimsrud, and Fred Molinari befriended and supported me.

I owe an immense debt to my friend Fred Malek, who brought me to Washington, D.C.; Jonathan Moore, who has been a mentor to me since my early days in government; the late John Sawhill, who gave me my first government executive role; Tom Firth, for his financial counsel; and President Bill Clinton and Sen. Hillary Rodham Clinton for their longtime friendship.

For a dozen years, my friends in my Saturday morning old men's basketball group pushed me to write an op-ed piece about some of the ideas in *Joy at Work*. It was not published, so they urged me to get started on the book instead. The group includes Brett Bernhardt, Erik Byker, Phil Brasher, Mike Cavanaugh, Guy Chetta, Mike Cromartie, Cliff Dean, Dennis Freemyer, William Haseltine, Steve Larson, Byron List, Steve McFarland, Patrick Mellan, John Potthast, John Sado, Phil Sechler, Curt Thompson, and Joe White.

The men that I meet with monthly for Bible study nourished and encouraged me during the entire book-writing process. We are led by Jerry Leachman, and others include Charles Balch, Fred Barnes, David Bradley, Bob Giaimo, Robert Haft, Morton Kondracke, Jeff Martin, Ken Starr, and John Yates.

Thanks to Brad Smith for putting these ideas at the center of a new school he leads, Bakke Graduate University in Seattle, Washington, which plans to offer courses of study leading to both a master's in business administration and a doctorate in ministry. Similarly, my gratitude goes to Paul Devlin, who captured much of my philosophy in his award-winning documentary, *Power Trip*, which cataloged AES's efforts to supply electricity to the people of Tbilisi, Georgia.

BIBLIOGRAPHY

Autry, James A. 1991. *Love and Profit: The Art of Caring Leadership*. New York: Avon Books.

Beckett, John D. 1998. *Loving Monday: Succeeding in Business Without Selling Your Soul*. Downers Grove, IL: InterVarsity Press.

Behr, Peter. "Power Surge: Global Market to Test AES's Risk-Based Style." *The Washington Post*. Dec. 18, 2000, E1.

Berman, Phyllis. "Throwing Away the Book." *Forbes*. Nov. 2, 1998, 174–181.

Bhide, Amar V., and Howard H. Stevenson. "Why Be Honest if Honesty Doesn't Pay?" *Harvard Business Review*. September 1990, 121–129.

Blair, Margaret M. 1999. *Ownership and Control: Rethinking Corporate Governance for the Twenty-First Century*. Washington, D.C.: The Brookings Institution.

Blanchard, Kenneth, and Norman Vincent Peale. 1988. *The Power of Ethical Management*. New York: William Morrow and Company, Inc.

Block, Peter. 2002. *The Answer to How Is Yes: Acting on What Matters*. San Francisco: Berrett-Koehler Publishers.

———. 1993. *Stewardship: Choosing Service over Self-Interest*. San Francisco: Berrett-Koehler Publishers.

Briner, Bob, and Ray Pritchard. 1998. *More Leadership Lessons of Jesus: A Timeless Model for Today's Leaders*. Nashville: Broadman & Holman Publishers.

———. 1997. *The Leadership Lessons of Jesus: A Timeless Model for Today's Leaders*. Nashville: Broadman & Holman Publishers.

Buford, Bob. 1994. *Half Time: Changing Your Game Plan From Success to Significance.* Grand Rapids: Zondervan.

Burr, Michael T. "Executive of the Year, Dennis Bakke, AES." *Independent Energy.* November 1998, 20–28.

Case, John. "When Salaries Aren't Secret." *Harvard Business Review.* May 2001, 37–49.

———. 1995. *Open-Book Management: The Coming Business Revolution.* New York: HarperBusiness.

Chappell, Tom. 1993. *The Soul of a Business: Managing for Profit and the Common Good.* New York: Bantam Books.

Collins, Jim. 2001. *Good to Great: Why Some Companies Make the Leap . . . and Others Don't.* New York: HarperBusiness.

Conroy, Pat. 2002. *My Losing Season.* New York: Nan A. Talese/ Doubleday.

Covey, Stephen R. 1990. *The Seven Habits of Highly Effective People: Powerful Lessons in Personal Change.* New York: Simon & Schuster.

Crane, Christopher A., and Mike Hamel. 2003. *Executive Influence: Impacting Your Workplace for Christ.* Colorado Springs: NavPress.

Cruver, Brian. 2002. *Anatomy of Greed: The Unshredded Truth From an Enron Insider.* New York: Carroll & Graf Publishers.

De Pree, Max. 1997. *Leading Without Power: Finding Hope in Serving Community.* San Francisco: Jossey Bass.

———. 1992. *Leadership Jazz.* New York: Currency/Doubleday.

Drucker, Peter F. 1993. *Post-Capitalist Society.* New York: HarperBusiness.

Druckerman, Pamela. "How to Project Power Around the World." *The Wall Street Journal.* Nov. 13, 2000, A23.

Eastland, Terry. "This Is Not Ours: Good Stewards Hold All Things Lightly." *The Washingtonian.* July 1991, 31–34.

Griffiths, Lord Brian of Fforestfach. 1996. "The Business of Values." Hansen-Wessner Memorial Lecture, Peter F. Drucker Graduate School of Management, Claremont, CA.

Grimsley, Kirstin Downey. "The Power of a Team." *The Washington Post*. Feb. 12, 1996, Washington Business section, 12–14.

Guinness, Oz. 1998. *The Call: Finding Purpose and Fulfilling the Central Purpose of Your Life*. Nashville: World Publishing.

Hamilton, Martha M. "The Principles Behind Its Power." *The Washington Post*. Nov. 2, 1998, F12.

Hunter, James C. 1998. *The Servant: A Simple Story About the True Essence of Leadership*. Roseville, CA: Prima Publishing.

Hurst, James Willard. 1970. *The Legitimacy of the Business Corporation in the Law of the United States, 1780–1970*. Charlottesville: The University Press of Virginia.

Jacobs, Jane. 1985. *Cities and the Wealth of Nations: Principles of Economic Life*. New York: Vintage Books.

Jennings, Ken, and John Stahl-Wert. 2003. *The Serving Leader: 5 Powerful Actions That Will Transform Your Team, Your Business and Your Community*. San Francisco: Berrett-Koehler Publishers.

Kepner-Tregoe Business Issues Research Group. *Decision Making in the Digital Age: Challenges and Responses*. Executive Summary, December 2000.

Kroeker, Wally. 1998. *God's Week Has 7 Days: Monday Musings for Marketplace Christians*. Waterloo, Ontario, Canada: Herald Press.

Lebow, Rob, and Randy Spitzer. 2002. *Accountability: Freedom and Responsibility Without Control*. San Francisco: Berrett-Koehler Publishers.

Mahedy, The Rev. William, and Dr. Christopher Carstens. 1987. *Starting on Monday: Christian Living in the Workplace*. New York: Ballentine/Epiphany, Ballentine Books.

Manz, Charles C., and Henry P. Sims, Jr. 1995. *Company of Heroes: Unleashing the Power of Self-Leadership*. New York: John Wiley & Sons.

————. 1993. *Business Without Bosses: How Self-Managing Teams Are Building High-Performing Companies*. New York: John Wiley & Sons.

Markels, Alex. "Power to the People." *Fast Company*. February/March 1998, 155–165.

Melrose, Ken. 1995. *Making the Grass Greener on Your Side: A CEO's Journey to Leading by Serving*. San Francisco: Berrett-Koehler Publishers.

Miller, Calvin. 1995. *The Empowered Leader: 10 Keys to Servant Leadership*. Nashville: Broadman & Holman Publishers.

Monks, Robert A. G., and Nell Minow. 1995. *Corporate Governance*. Cambridge: Blackwell Business.

Naisbitt, John. 1988. *Megatrends: Ten New Directions Transforming Our Lives*. New York: Warner Books.

Novak, Michael. 1996. *Business as a Calling: Work and the Examined Life*. New York: Free Press, a division of Simon & Schuster.

Oster, Merrill J., and Mike Hamel. 2003. *Giving Back: Using Your Influence to Create Social Change*. Colorado Springs: NavPress.

Paine, Lynn Sharp. 2003. *Value Shift: Why Companies Must Merge Social and Financial Imperatives to Achieve Superior Performance*. New York: McGraw-Hill.

Paine, Lynn Sharp, and Sarah Mavrinac. 1995. "AES Honeycomb (A)." No. 9-395-132. Harvard Business School, Harvard University, Cambridge, MA.

Percy, The Rev. Anthony G. 2001. "The Meaning of Entrepreneurial Work and the Modern Corporation as a Communion of Persons: A Case Study of the AES Corporation in Light of the Principles in *Laborem Exercens* and *Centesimus Annus*." Diss., Pontifical John Paul II Institute for Studies on Marriage and Family.

Peters, Thomas J., and Robert H. Waterman, Jr. 1982. *In Search of Excellence: Lessons from America's Best-Run Companies*. New York: Warner Books.

Pfeffer, Jeffrey, and Robert I. Sutton. 2000. *The Knowing-Doing Gap: How*

Smart Companies Turn Knowledge Into Action. Boston: Harvard Business School Press.

Pfeffer, Jeffrey. 1998. *The Human Equation: Building Profits by Putting People First*. Boston: Harvard Business School Press.

———. 1997. "Human Resources at the AES Corporation: The Case of the Missing Department." Graduate School of Business, Stanford University, Stanford, CA.

Pfeffer, Jeffrey. 1994. *Competitive Advantage Through People: Unleashing the Power of the Work Force*. Boston: Harvard Business School Press.

———. 1992. *Managing With Power: Politics and Influence in Organizations*. Boston: Harvard Business School Press.

Pollard, C. William. 1996. *The Soul of the Firm*. Grand Rapids: HarperBusiness and Zondervan Publishing House.

Powell, Susan. 1998. "The Master's Joy: Dennis and Eileen Bakke's Unusual Wealth." *Regeneration Quarterly* 4:4.

Power Trip. Produced and directed by Paul Devlin. 86 minutes. Paul Devlin, Films Transit, Alpha CineLabs, Artistic License Films, 2003. VHS and DVD.

Robinson, William P. 2002. *Leading People From the Middle: The Universal Mission of Heart and Mind*. Provo, Utah: Executive Excellence Publishing.

Rush, Myron. 1987. *Management: A Biblical Approach*. Wheaton, IL: Victor Books, a division of Scripture Press Publications.

Ryser, Jeff. "Camelot Revisited." *Global Energy Business*. January/February 2000.

Schumacher, Christian. 1987. *To Live & Work: A Theological Interpretation*. Bromley, Kent, U.K.: MARC Europe.

Sherman, Doug, and William Hendricks. 1987. *Your Work Matters to God*. Colorado Springs: NavPress.

Spitzer, Robert J. 2000. *The Spirit of Leadership: Optimizing Creativity and Change in Organizations*. Provo, Utah: Executive Excellence Publishing.

Sproul, R. C. 1980. *Stronger Than Steel: The Wayne Alderson Story*. New York: Harper & Row.

Sutherland, Daniel. "AES Corp. Has the Money, So Pakistan Gets the Power: Arlington Firm's Plants to Serve 10 Million." *The Washington Post*. May 17, 1995, F1.

Terry, Roger. 1995. *Economic Insanity: How Growth-Driven Capitalism Is Devouring the American Dream*. San Francisco: Berrett-Koehler Publishers.

Waterman, Robert H., Jr. 1998. *What America Does Right: Learning From Companies That Put People First*. New York: W. W. Norton & Company.

———. 1996. *Adhocracy: The Power to Change*. New York: W. W. Norton & Company.

———. 1994. *The Frontiers of Excellence: Learning From Companies That Put People First*. London: Nicholas Brealey Publishing.

———. 1987. *The Renewal Factor: How the Best Get and Keep the Competitive Edge*. New York: Bantam Books.

Weber, Bruce. "The Myth Maker: The Creative Mind of Novelist E. L. Doctorow." *New York Times Magazine*. Oct. 20, 1985, 42.

Wetlaufer, Suzy, and Patricia Lloyd Williams. "Organizing for Empowerment: An Interview with AES's Roger Sant and Dennis Bakke." *Harvard Business Review*, January/February 1999.

INDEX

JOY AT WORK
RESOURCES

Discover how you can bring Joy at Work to your
business, non-profit, government or church
by using the following resources:

Audio Book

Listen to Dennis Bakke share his inspiring tale in his own voice.

Unabridged; 9 hours 28 minutes

CD: $30.00/$40.00 Can.
8 compact discs; 0-9762686-2-0

Cassette: $26.00/$36.00 Can.
6 cassettes; 0-9762686-1-2

Academic Resources

Power Trip

Emmy award-winner Paul Devlin captures the principles of Joy at Work in his internationally acclaimed documentary, Power Trip. It's the amazing story of how AES tries to transform the dysfunctional electricity-distribution system in Tbilisi, capital of the former Soviet Republic of Georgia.

Struggling against corruption, assassination, and street rioting, AES manager Piers Lewis must persuade the Georgians to pay for, rather than steal, electricity. This "compelling and passionate tale of a country rebuilding itself" (Hollywood Reporter) has "suspense, comedy, and some colorful characters" (Variety) and develops into an "increasingly absurdist standoff between Communist-inspired cynicism and tenacious capitalist zeal" (New York Daily News).

Available on DVD and VHS. Running time 85 minutes.

Harvard Business School Case Studies

- Human Resources at the AES Corp.: The Case of the Missing Department; Jeffery Pfeffer; Feb 1, 1997; 28p

AES develops and operates electric power plants all over the world, and, by late 1996, has approximately 20,000 employees. But the corporation has no human-resources staff, neither at corporate headquarters in Arlington, VA, nor in any of its operating facilities. In fact, the company has very little centralized staff at all—almost no strategic planning, no environmental department, and almost no legal staff. The question is: Should the company continue to operate in this same way as it continues to expand and geographically diversify? And how had the organization been so successful without specialized expertise?

Visit www.DennisBakke.com to order

- AES Global Values; Lynn Sharp Paine; May 18, 1999; 19p

Members of the development team for the AES Corp.'s power-plant project in India must decide which technology to specify in their application for techno-economic clearance from the Indian government's Central Electric Authority. Their choice is between expensive technology that would meet more-demanding U.S. environmental standards and less-costly technology that would meet local environmental standards and free up funds to contribute to the other needs of the communities surrounding the new plant.

- AES Honeycomb; Lynn Sharp Paine and Sarah Mavrinac; Dec 9, 1994; 29p

Senior managers of the AES Corp. must decide whether to drop the company's emphasis on corporate values and revamp organizational controls, as advised by investment analysts and outside counsel. The company is recovering from an incident of environmental fraud at one of its plants where an innovative decentralized "honeycomb" structure has been put in place. Some believe the structure is too decentralized and that lack of controls contributed to the incident. This case study illustrates an aspirations-driven approach to organizational integrity and shows the interdependence of values and organizational structure. It invites discussion about the relationship of values, organizational performance, and shareholder gain.

- AES: Hungarian Project (A); Lynn Sharp Paine and Ann Leamon; March 15, 2000; 25p

The AES Corp. has put out a request for bids to build a new power plant in Hungary. Just after the closing date for submitting bids, one of the contractors calls to request an opportunity to "improve" its bid. Although AES has not yet completed its analysis, this contractor appears to be the low bidder. What should the coordinator do? The decision is one of several faced by AES as it attempts to do business in post-socialist Hungary. This case study explores how AES implements its values and ethical standards in a post-Communist context, including its distinctive approach to downsizing the workforce at the power plants it purchases.

Visit www.DennisBakke.com to order

Harvard Business Review Interview

Organizing for Empowerment: An Interview with AES's Roger Sant and Dennis Bakke; Jan 1, 1999; 14p

In this interview with HBR Senior Editor Suzy Wetlaufer, AES Chairman Roger Sant and CEO Dennis Bakke reflect on their trials and triumphs in creating an exceptional company. When they founded AES in 1981, Sant and Bakke set out to create an employee-run company where people could have engaging experiences on a daily basis—a company that embodied the principles of fairness, integrity, social responsibility, and fun.

Leadership Resources

DVD Seminar

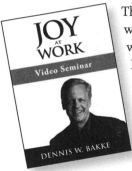

The *Joy at Work* DVD Seminar is a must for any leader who wants to bring principles, purpose, and fun to the workplace. In four inspiring lectures, you'll experience Dennis Bakke's passion for transforming organizations, where every person—from custodian to CEO—has the power to use his or her talents free of needless bureaucracy. Filmed before a live audience, the following lectures will challenge everything you thought you knew about business.

- Purpose Matters
- Assumptions About People
- The Advice Process
- The New Role of Leadership

Running time 3 hours; includes bonus footage.

The DVD is an excellent training resource for any business or non-profit. Available exclusively at DennisBakke.com.

Visit www.DennisBakke.com to order

Church Resources

Bible Study

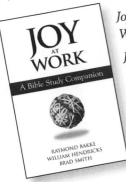

Joy at Work: A Bible Study Companion; Dr. Raymond Bakke, William D. Hendricks, and Brad Smith.

Joy at Work: A Bible Study Companion provides the biblical map that Dennis Bakke used as he charted and led his journey as co-founder and CEO of AES. Using the examples of Dennis Bakke and AES, this eight-week Bible study sets out to examine what the Bible says about the purpose of business and fun on the job. Starting with the Genesis story of creation and moving through Revelation, this Bible study supplements *Joy at Work* with:

- Biblical readings that unveil the principles behind each chapter in the AES story
- Synthesis of theological principles
- Reflective questions to prepare readers for small group discussion
- Questions for small group discussion
- Guidelines for immediate and long-term application for business leaders at all levels of corporations

Printable version available on the web at: www.DennisBakke.com

Bible Study DVD

The Joy at Work Bible Study DVD is designed to be used with *Joy at Work: A Bible Study Companion*. Dennis Bakke, along with Christian business leaders and ministers, discuss the biblical principles underpinning *Joy at Work*. These insightful conversations take your Bible study into the lives of leaders who have integrated their faith and work. Bible Study Guide authors Raymond Bakke, William Hendricks, and Brad Smith host these video segments that will enrich your study experience.

80 minutes (divided into 8 sessions), plus bonus material.
Preview available at DennisBakke.com